1994

MIDDLE LEVEL CURRICULUM

CURRICULUM

in Action

MIDDLE LEVEL CURRICULUM

in Action

Rosemary G. Messick

San Jose State University

Karen E. Reynolds

San Jose State University

Longman

New York & London

Middle Level Curriculum in Action

Longman, 95 Church Street, White Plains, N.Y. 10601

Associated companies:
Longman Group Ltd., London
Longman Cheshire Pty., Melbourne
Longman Paul Pty., Auckland
Copp Clark Pitman, Toronto

Executive editor: Raymond T. O'Connell
Development editor: Virginia K. Blanford
Production editors: Kathryn Dix and The Book Studio, Inc.
Cover design: Anne M. Pompeo
Text art: Pompeo Designs; cartoon art by Karen E. Reynolds
Production supervisor: Anne P. Armeny

Library of Congress Cataloging-in-Publication Data

Messick, Rosemary G.
    Middle level curriculum in action / Rosemary G. Messick, Karen E.
  Reynolds.
      p.   cm.
  Includes bibliographical references (p.) and index.
  ISBN 0-8013-0540-3
  1. Middle schools—Curricula. I. Reynolds, Karen E. II. Title.
LB1623.M38 1991
373.19—dc20   91-7624
                                                CIP

1 2 3 4 5 6 7 8 9 10-MA-9594939291

Contents

Contents

150, 273

CHAPTER 6 BASICS OF EXPLORATORY CURRICULUM   **111**

CHAPTER 7 THE AFFECTIVE CURRICULUM   **133**

CHAPTER 8 CORE CURRICULUM IMPLEMENTATION   **161**

Acknowledgments

This book was written with the assistance and support of many individuals. We thank June Chapin for her helpful comments on an early draft of the manuscript and Karen Hart for her suggestions on selected chapters. During the refining stages, the contributions of our reviewers and facilitating editors were essential to the project. We particularly appreciate the middle level teachers we have worked with, whose insights and fine practices continue to inspire us. We also recognize our preservice students at San Jose State University. They always challenge our assumptions and conclusions with their energy, creativity, and care for young adolescents.

CHAPTER 1

Introduction to the Middle Level

You are invited to join the ranks of talented and dedicated educators with patience, special interpersonal skills, and respect for early adolescents, and to accept the challenge of becoming an excellent teacher at the middle level. Plan to engage your self-discipline, self-confidence, and love of learning. Bring your flexibility and sense of humor.

Students at the middle level, in fifth through eighth grades, are ready to (1) apply earlier learning in higher level contexts, (2) explore a variety of subject areas to broaden their knowledge of possibilities in which to develop individual talents, and (3) acquire a sense of self in relation to the larger society. These students need teachers who like early adolescents and are sensitive to their needs. In addition, these teachers must be well versed in general education but should have in-depth preparation in two or more basic or exploratory subject areas. They need to be team players and reflective practitioners as they plan instruction and implement middle level curriculum. This book, *Middle Level Curriculum in Action*, is designed to assist you in constructing your own professional platform for excellence as a middle level teacher.

In this chapter, we:

- Present an overview of the content and organization of the book,
- Compare middle level schooling to other levels in the K–12 spectrum, and
- Invite you to assess your own thinking about early adolescents, teaching, your personal talents and career plans.

MEETING THE CHALLENGE

There are many areas to investigate as you prepare for middle level teaching. We have designed this book to address major concerns of teaching at this level and help you build a structure of knowledge that will be useful as you extend your experience and pursue special interests in greater depth. This book is about middle level curriculum, about what makes up a program of instruction for grades 5–8, and how that program is implemented. The middle level curriculum, in action, involves people, places, and practices, all of which must relate to needs of the early adolescent.

The first three chapters provide a background and foundation for teaching at this level. Main features, content strands, and suggestions for using the book in ways other than sequential reading are presented in this chapter. Warm-up activities allow you to explore attitudes about early adolescents, as well as some of your thinking about teaching and learning. Chapter 2 presents a historical perspective of the middle level movement. Chapter 3 reviews characteristics of early adolescents and establishes a student-centered focus for developing curriculum and planning for instruction and organization at the middle level.

The next four chapters develop the structure and content of the middle level curriculum. Chapter 4 looks at a variety of concepts used in curriculum design and development. Chapter 5 surveys the content and skills of the basic subjects and discusses current trends in each. Chapter 6 considers the exploratory curriculum and examines issues of integration. Chapter 7 describes the affective side of curriculum, contrasting various approaches to school guidance programs.

Chapter 8 compares several approaches for structuring and implementing the core curriculum and outlines strategies for teaming. Chapters 9 and 10 look at instruction and evaluation, respectively, with attention to ensuring student success.

In order to facilitate exploration and discussion, we addressed elements of curriculum design and implementation separately. To review: chapters 2–4 provide the foundations while chapters 5–7 focus on the content, and chapters 8–10 on the practical and procedural aspects of curriculum development. We recognize that the ideas presented in this book are, in practice, implemented in concert. Chapter 11 brings the main ideas together by embedding them in a series of instructional units.

Following the Thematic Strands in This Book

This book is organized to develop main ideas about middle level curriculum and progresses from (1) historical background and nature of the students to be served, to (2) description of curriculum elements and their interrelationships, to (3) implementation in instruction and assessment, to (4) synthesis in planning for thematic instruction. However, if you want to read for special purposes, you can do so by using chapter headings or themes that interest you. If your interest is in exploratory or core programs, you may want to start with the chapters devoted to those topics. If you are new to middle level education, we suggest reading from the beginning. If you have special concerns, such as at-risk students or cooperative learning or technology, you should let the index guide your reading sequences. For example, an inspection of the index of this book indicates that topics related to technology include teacher-centered uses for productivity, research, instruction, and assessment; student-centered uses for productivity, investigations, and independent work; integration of different kinds of technologies such as computers, videocameras, and videodiscs in the program; and effects on achievement and affective curriculum objectives. You can plot your own route through the book according to your familiarity with middle level education and your specific interests.

Middle Level Schooling in the K–12 Spectrum

The middle level school is a transitional phase between the self-contained elementary classroom and the departmentalized high school. At the elementary level, students learn nearly all subjects through one teacher in the same room and with the same classmates. In the abruptly contrasting secondary school, students pursue their own programs of study consisting of distinct subjects taught by different teachers. At the secondary level each class is composed of students who move from room to room following individual schedules. The middle level school provides the stability of intact classes, the enrichment of in-depth expertise provided by a team of teachers and an intermediate level of individualized scheduling.

Middle level curriculum is constructed around a framework of knowledge about the (1) student, (2) subject area content, and (3) skills and attitudes taken from the academic disciplines, as well as around the mandates formulated by our cultural tradition and our citizens about how this level of education should be defined. Currently the specific middle level curriculum agenda, in addition to the distinction between this level and those above and below it, is coming together to form a different kind of educational institution. Elements defining this new way of looking at middle level education and how they are contrasted to other levels are organized in Table 1.1.

The intent of *Middle School Curriculum in Action* is to explore the distinctions highlighted in Table 1.1 so that you will gain a broad, yet solid, view of the elements that must be considered as schools attempt to develop programs more appropriate for young adolescents.

ASSESSING YOUR THINKING

The content and activities that make up this book are designed to assist you in developing understanding about early adolescents, middle level curriculum, and

TABLE 1.1. COMPARISON OF THREE LEVELS OF SCHOOLING

Schooling Variable	Elementary	Middle Level	Secondary
Class composition	Intact class	Intact class	Varies with individual student schedules
Student grouping	Chronological	Multi-stage developmental	Subject dependent
Guidance	Diagnostic development	Teacher helper	Career-vocational
Teacher-student relationship	Parental	Advisor, facilitator	Instructor
Teacher organization	Self-contained, often grade level cooperation	Interdisciplinary team, often with grade level coordination	Department areas Often course coordination
Curricular emphasis	Skills	Exploration	Depth
Subjects	Specific set for all students, some special pull outs	Required core, required explorations, and some electives	General courses required, electives based on life plans
Psychomotor development	Skills and games	Skills and intramural	Skills and interscholastic
Schedule	Self-contained, flexible	Block, with some flexibility within each year	Periods, flexible within range of several years
Utilization of media and resource centers	Classroom groups	Balance of classroom groups and individuals	Individual study
Focus of building plan	Classroom areas	Team areas	Department areas
Teacher preparation	Child-oriented generalist	Flexible resource Core subjects expert	Subject-oriented specialist
Teacher to student contact ratio	1 to 25–30	1 to 50–60	1 to 125–160

effective facilitation of learning. Before you begin, we suggest doing some warm-up activities in order to get a sense of your current thinking and to establish a baseline for comparison after you expand your knowledge of middle level curriculum and its implementation. Try responding to the following three self-assessment activities. Then discuss your responses with a colleague.

Activity 1.1: Attitudes about Early Adolescents

Teachers who choose to teach at the middle level are revered by many citizens as a special group of educators, endowed with an extra measure of patience, bravery, and insanity. Early adolescents, as a group, do not enjoy a consistent reputation. The following list of characteristics were identified with this age group by a sample of parents, teachers, and other adults. With which descriptions, or to what extent, do you agree? Circle your position.

Agree			Disagree		Early adolescents:
1	2	3	4	5	A. Are honest and sincere.
1	2	3	4	5	B. Have needs very much like young high school students.
1	2	3	4	5	C. Know a lot about sex and sexually transmitted diseases.
1	2	3	4	5	D. Want to improve the world around them.
1	2	3	4	5	E. Have self-centered interests and egocentric perceptions.
1	2	3	4	5	F. Are always restless because of hormone imbalances.
1	2	3	4	5	G. Like to carry out independent projects.
1	2	3	4	5	H. Cannot live without hair dryers, chewing gum, or radios.
1	2	3	4	5	I. Are socially shy because of physical awkwardness.
1	2	3	4	5	J. Rebel against adult authority.
1	2	3	4	5	K. Need to repeat basic skills to be prepared for high school.
1	2	3	4	5	L. Want to be like their friends.
1	2	3	4	5	M. Are thinking about jobs, careers, college, and future adult life.
1	2	3	4	5	N. Have here-and-now attitudes.
1	2	3	4	5	O. Consider school irrelevant.
1	2	3	4	5	P. Do not like to talk about their problems.
1	2	3	4	5	Q. Have good health and a lot of energy.
1	2	3	4	5	R. Are the products of their parents. There is little schools can do.

Review the descriptions listed and your reactions to them. Which characteristics do you consider to be positive? Negative? Neither positive nor negative?
Which of your reactions would you consider negative? Positive? Neutral? To be
successful as a middle level teacher, you must like early adolescents and be able
to accept them without judgment. Can you explain why you have chosen to
teach in the grade 5–9 range? After you have learned more about this age
group, you might want to look over this list again and change or expand on
your responses.

Activity 1.2: Thinking about Teaching and Learning

Below are three statements, each with four possible responses.[1] On a scale of 1
to 10, with 10 being *most important,* rate each of the four possibilities to
indicate your predominant way of thinking for each of the three statements. Try
to identify examples that would illustrate those you rate *most important.*

A. The goal of instruction is for students to attain

_____ **1.** A large store of facts and procedures.

_____ **2.** Skills that are essential for attaining and using facts and procedures.

_____ **3.** Correct understandings of the concepts that underlie the facts, procedures, and skills in a given subject.

_____ **4.** Conceptual understandings of a sort that are better than before and
may improve still further.

B. In order to attain these learning objectives, students must

_____ **1.** Be able and receptive.

_____ **2.** Practice the new skills in questions, having first acquired whatever
prerequisites are needed.

_____ **3.** Explore and manipulate relevant aspects of the real world, having
reached the stage of development at which the concepts in question
can be correctly understood.

_____ **4.** Be actively engaged in using their most advanced ways of thinking to
construct understandings of the concepts in question at their present
level of development.

C. Teachers teach by

_____ **1.** Telling and showing students what they need to know, in ways that are
appealing.

_____ **2.** Giving students a lot of directed practice, with corrective feedback and
positive reinforcement as needed.

_____ 3. Giving students opportunities to explore and manipulate developmentally appropriate materials.

_____ 4. Engaging students in thought-provoking activities and guiding their thinking toward better understanding.

Becoming an effective teacher does not happen instantly and without effort. The development of excellence, however, can be accelerated by professional preparation and in-service programs that are sensitive to your needs and allow you to construct, for yourself, an understanding of effective practice. What you do in your classroom and how you interact with your students changes from year to year. How you think about teaching and learning also changes over time. There seems to be a consistency of stages one must pass through as one develops ways of thinking about learning and teaching. The responses to the three statements above correlate with the stages, listed in order, through which most teachers pass as they change their thinking about learning and teaching. Each of the stages represents a valid view, and later stages subsume earlier stages. With teaching experience and an increase in awareness of learning processes, the focus of teachers' thinking, or the response receiving the highest rating in each set, shifts toward more complex understanding and applications. You might want to rate the items above again at a later time.

Activity 1.3: Teaching Practices

What do you think about teaching practices? Have you identified some that you want to adopt as your own? The following list represents activities and approaches used in the seventh grade by several teachers during their first two years of teaching. Which are exemplary? Innovative? Outmoded? Which have potential for helping the teachers improve their own effectiveness? Write down strengths and weaknesses or debate with colleagues the value of the methods used.

1. On the first day of class, students were presented with three class rules and allowed to add two more of their own. The set of rules was signed by each student and posted in the classroom.
2. Twice each week, students were grouped in fours, two girls and two boys, for science activities.
3. On most mornings, a "mystery object" was placed at the front of the room. The object was brought in by the teacher or by a student and was usually related to a lesson carried out during the week.
4. Each week, three students were assigned to update the current events bulletin board. Often only one or two students brought news articles, so the teacher provided a copy of the daily newspaper.
5. A modem was connected to one of the two classroom computers. Students worked in teams communicating with other local schools and

with student teachers at a nearby university. Each student had the opportunity to serve as message transmitter and receiver.

6. Worksheets were used to reinforce knowledge and skills in math and social studies about three times per week, and always when there was a substitute teacher.

7. Once or twice each day the teacher lectured for periods of only five to ten minutes, at which time an outline was provided on the overhead projector to help students take notes.

8. Twice during the year, students gave social studies reports accompanied by visual presentations that they had designed using videotapes and interactive videodiscs.

9. The students were asked to draw a "typical" scientist working in a lab. The teacher then facilitated a discussion on common characteristics and stereotypes.

10. During one month, five students who consistently talked in class were kept after class three times and required to copy spelling words. Two of them were kept for this kind of detention on three other days.

11. All students in the class were required to carry out a science fair project. They could review each other's work and progress, but each had responsibility for completing his or her own project. Only one student did not finish something to put on display.

12. On Tuesdays and Thursdays, students had sustained silent reading for fifteen minutes immediately after lunch. They could read anything they chose, even comic books.

13. One computer in the classroom was dedicated as a word-processing station for any student, or group of students, who wanted to use it. Students could sign up for reserved time.

14. During oral math, the teacher led the class in a round of applause for correct answers.

15. Students regularly had a multiple-choice and essay test on Fridays at the end of a week-long unit in either science or social studies.

16. The teacher provided a variety of materials on a table at the front of the class for student teams to use in experiments on heat conduction and insulation. None of the students finished the activity during the lab period. For another lab, on electrical conductors and insulators, the teacher sorted materials into individual boxes and assigned one box to each student team.

17. On one day the teacher came to school dressed as an Iroquois Indian and spent the entire morning teaching about eighteenth century North America from an Iroquois Indian's point of view.

18. In one classroom, calculators and radios were forbidden. Students were allowed to use calculators in the classroom next door, and the teacher had a radio that was turned on occasionally during independent work periods.

These examples are related to many of the issues that are addressed in subsequent chapters. It would be interesting to use this list as a pre- and posttest by comparing your present perceptions of them with your views and insights after you have completed the book or after you have gained additional experience in the classroom.

ASSESSING PERSONAL TALENTS

Most of us have more talents and skills than we realize. As you explore the middle level curriculum and consider your role in its implementation, you might like to think about what you bring to middle level teaching and make plans to extend your preparation in areas you perceive as necessary. To begin this process, fill in the checklists and conduct the discussions suggested in Activity 1.4.

Activity 1.4: Assessing Teaching Talents and Readiness

I. Assessing Skills and Experiences

This open-ended checklist asks you to explore the relationship between your interests, hobbies, and skills and your teaching. After completing this form you should ask a colleague to suggest additional ways to expand your middle school teaching potential.

School Activities and Service

Possible Transfer to Role as a Middle School Teacher

_____   _____

_____   _____

_____   _____

_____   _____

_____   _____

_____   _____

_____   _____

_____   _____

Hobbies, Activities, Interests

_____   _____

_____   _____

_____   _____

Activity 1.4 (continued)

_____   _____

_____   _____

_____   _____

_____   _____

_____   _____

_____   _____

Experiences Leading Groups

_____   _____

_____   _____

_____   _____

_____   _____

_____   _____

_____   _____

_____   _____

_____   _____

II. Planning for Instruction

Respond to each item on this list with a 1 for *no knowledge,* 2 for *some knowledge,* or 3 for *ready.* After assessing your readiness, you need to share your results with a colleague. Explore your 1's with each other. Make a list of questions about how and/or where to obtain information on these topics.

_____ 1. Materials for organizing instruction in principal subject area.

_____ 2. Objectives for principal subject.

_____ 3. Evaluation plan for principal subject.

_____ 4. Materials for organizing instruction in second subject area.

_____ 5. Objectives for second subject.

_____ 6. Evaluation plan for second subject.

_____ 7. Ideas for teaming projects within grade level and/or across subjects.

_____ 8. Ideas for working with aides and support staff to enrich instruction.

Activity 1.4 (continued)

_____ 9. Ideas for diversifying instruction by integrating computers, media, varying group size, and composition.

_____ 10. Strategies for assisting at-risk, limited English, and special need students.

_____ 11. Plans for setting up records of student progress.

_____ 12. Strategy for setting up classroom management.

III. Career Plans

Picture what you want to be doing five years from now. What will it take to acquire this image? Set your five-year professional goal. Are you willing to discuss it with a colleague?

Five years from now I want to _____

_____

_____

Steps I plan to take to accomplish this goal are:

Year 1: _____

_____

Year 2: _____

_____

Year 3: _____

_____

Year 4: _____

_____

Year 5: _____

_____

CONCLUSIONS

Becoming a middle level teacher is a complex and multifaceted endeavor. It is challenging, exciting, and rewarding. It involves patience, hard work, and dedication. It requires sensible use of personal energy and the establishment of professional perspectives and priorities. We look forward to helping you develop your potential through the discussions and experiences provided by the remaining chapters.

EXTENSIONS

Here are some suggestions for taking advantage of opportunities to improve your own professional knowledge and skills.

1. Keep a professional log. Categorize your entries into sections that are related to (a) students, (b) instruction, (c) management or organization, (d) community, and (e) personal professional growth. Be sure you analyze after you describe. Journals are for pondering, questioning, making "to do" and "find out" lists.

2. Establish and maintain a resource file. Use it to organize materials useful to you in teaching, including lesson ideas, posters, field trip locations, resource people, sample worksheets, testing examples, pictures, bulletin board plans, bibliographies, location of manipulatives, and other information.

3. Read professional literature, attend professional conferences, and engage in other scholarly activities. Maintain a computer-based data base of interesting journals, articles you have read, special lectures, educational TV programs, and academic topics you would like to bring to your teaching.

4. Establish a collegial support group of peers and mentor teachers. Plan to interact with the group on a regular basis by personal conferencing, phone, fax, telecommunications, exchange of videotapes, and other means.

NOTES AND REFERENCES

1. Adapted from A. Black and P. Ammon, "Developmental Teacher Education," *The Educator,* 4 (1), Spring 1990, p. 8.

CHAPTER 2

Evolution of Middle Level Schooling

Societies use schools to promote their own success and ensure their survival by instructing young people in ideas and skills considered important. This generalization is easier to demonstrate in countries that have a national system of education than in the United States. In France and Japan, for example, the social agenda of the country is more evident in the classroom due to the uniformity of what is taught in schools and how schools are organized nationwide. Using the school system as a reflection of the country's values in the United States, however, is like being in an old-fashioned carnival hall of curved mirrors that reveal images of our twelve years of basic schooling in a variety of shapes and bulges. The middle years of the American system are characterized by different names, age arrangements, and curricula. Middle level educational institutions, sometimes called junior high schools and sometimes middle schools, appear to vary in their goals for students and in educational programs. These differences indicate various interpretations of what middle level schooling should accomplish for students. To appreciate how this apparent lack of consensus came about, we need to trace the development of middle level education, in both historical and contemporary contexts.

In this chapter we:

- Review the evolution of middle level schooling in this country,
- Address the impact of the educational reform movement of the eighties on middle level schooling, and
- Discuss the challenges of balancing the goals for middle level schooling with conflicting social demands.

13

AMERICAN BEGINNINGS OF MIDDLE SCHOOLING

Since the U.S. Constitution did not mention the subject of education, the financing and organizing of public schooling was assumed to be a state right, developing as each state and township or community within the states saw fit. Local governments raised funds through property taxes to provide for the building, staffing, and maintaining of public schools. As populations grew and business and industry became more complex, local taxpayers and private groups built secondary schools and academies and lengthened the typical period of primary or elementary schooling to seven or eight years.

The general concept was that the first years of schooling were to be the "common trunk" that provided all young people with the tools of literacy to become self-sufficient, contributing members of society. High school education was organized as a classic preparation for the brightest students, less than 10 percent of the school-aged population, who would attend college and become members of a liberal profession. Vocational schools for students wishing to become bookkeepers or nurses or mechanics or elementary teachers opened their doors. Some were public and some private.

Social Changes

The late 1800s was a time when the population was growing rapidly. Millions of immigrants flocked to the United States. In the early part of the twentieth century, one in three people was either foreign born or had parents who were. Urbanization and industrialization prompted increasing demands from employers for better educated and nationally assimilated workers. A group of studies documented the rate of school finishing in the United States. Their findings raised concern about the limited role schools played in Americanizing the new immigrants and educating workers. Only one-third of the children entering public schools reached the ninth grade, and only one in ten finished high school. Grade failure was common, with one of every six children repeating at all grade levels. Educators concluded that the kind of schooling provided was contributing to the drop-out and failure rates.[1]

Educational decision makers began a series of meetings and investigations that led them toward a consensus about the role that education should play in preparing people to live in those changing times. Their deliberations formed the first national agenda for high schools. Published in 1918, the set of recommendations known as the *Cardinal Principles of Secondary Education*[2] set the direction for thousands of local school districts for the next thirty-some years. The high school was to serve a broad social purpose by preparing all students to become effective citizens. Dividing the high school period into two sections—junior and senior—was recommended.

In fact, over 200 school districts had already begun to establish junior high schools that included grades seven to eight or grades seven to nine. The reasons for their establishment varied. Some were started as a way to house the rapidly growing numbers of young people. Others were started as a way to speed college prep of able youth. Still others were started in response to the findings made by several psychologists about early adolescence. Examining these last two motivations can help us comprehend the cross-pressures that influenced educational change just after the turn of the century.

Activity 2.1: Build a Chart

To recall and analyze the historical permutations of American middle level education, draw up a chart with these headings and fill it in as you read this chapter.

Course of Middle Level Education in the United States

Group/Individual Proposing	Change Proposed	Date	Reasons

Interpretations of the 1918 Recommendations

The set of recommendations provided in 1918 by the *Cardinal Principles of Secondary Education* was supported for a variety of reasons, particularly with regard to the establishment of a separate institution for early adolescents.

The cardinal principles included a recommendation that elementary school include the first six years of education for students from six to twelve years of age, and that secondary education take students from twelve to eighteen years of age and be "divided into two periods which may be designated as the junior and senior periods." The idea of starting college preparation at an earlier age began with the concern of the president of Harvard College who influenced the commission that wrote the cardinal principles. President Charles W. Eliot, addressing a meeting of school superintendents in 1888, wondered if the preparation for college could begin earlier: "Can school programmes [*sic*] be shortened and enriched?" The argument was that if college prep courses could be started earlier, the students would come better prepared and perhaps more quickly to college. We do not know if leaders of secondary schools on this commission disagreed with the college perspective of the mission of secondary education.

A second line of thinking that also inspired educators to favor a different sort of school for early adolescents involved new knowledge about human growth and development. Edward L. Thorndike and James M. Cattell published studies that quantified how uneven an individual's ability in different areas can be, and what extreme differences existed among individuals. As part of the new science of psychology, these new studies pointed out not only obvious rates of physical difference but also the variance in social, emotional, and intellectual abilities and skills. A girl of ten might be capable of reading adult material, yet unable to handle the reasoning required to solve a math word problem. How could the needs of the fully mature girl of thirteen and the four-foot, eight-inch boy be met in the typical self-contained elementary classroom? The argument of the day was that the drop-out rate would decline if schooling for the crucial years between 10 and 14 could be organized to meet varied rates of development.

A third influence on the formulation of a separate school for early adolescents was provided by the psychologist G. Stanley Hall who theorized that an individual went through the same stages of growth as civilizations. For Hall, a young child's egocentrism reflected the way humans of early civilizations were. With time, the child learned to share and follow authority as in a feudal society. Hall argued that early adolescents needed "a distinct change in matter and method of education" as they were undergoing a new birth which would bring them to a higher level of human traits much like those found in a republic. Today, with the advantage of three generations of studies in human growth and development, Hall's ideas appear to us as merely quaint. But during the early 1900s Hall's culture-epoch or recapitulation theory appealed to many educators in search of better rationales for educating a population they knew to have special needs.[3]

MIDDLE LEVEL SCHOOLING COMES OF AGE WITHOUT AGREEMENT ON GOALS

Following one or more of these rationales, new schools baptized as junior high schools appeared throughout the country. They typically included grades 7 and 8 and, less often, grades 7 through 9. Educational leaders participating in the development of this new institution were eager to have the purposes of middle schooling widely understood, and several attempts at consensus building were made. The following list sets out the most enduring results, although this list was never published as one complete consensus. Rather, it is a compilation of various views held in the 1920s.

Educators' Views in the 1920s of the Purposes
for Middle Level Schooling

1. Meeting individual differences of pupils—enabling pupils to follow the lines of their interest and ability.
2. Prevocational training and exploration resulting in wise choice of later school courses and life work.
3. Counseling or guidance—bringing pupils into contact with influences that should give direction and purpose to their lives.
4. Meeting the needs of the early adolescent group.

5. Bridging the gap between elementary and secondary schools—proper coordination between lower and higher schools.
6. Development of qualities of good citizenship—preparation of pupils to play a larger part in the life of the community.
7. Providing opportunities for profitable self-activity—early development of leadership, individuality, and initiative.
8. Retention of pupils beyond compulsory school age.
9. Continuation of common education or regular scholastic or academic training.
10. Rounding out a complete unit of training beyond the elementary grades for those who must leave school early.
11. Introduction of new subjects into the curriculum.
12. Effecting economy of time in education.
13. Stimulation of educational advancement.
14. Beginning of definite occupational training.
15. Giving opportunity for earlier preparation for college.[4]

Careful study of this list reveals the existence of a broad range of reasons and a lack of focus for having a separate junior high school. Although most educational leaders of the time agreed that the institution should meet individual needs, they differed about how meeting them should be accomplished. Some felt that introducing earlier college preparation would do it, while others saw the new school as a place for initiating occupational training.

Continuing Change in Middle Schooling

Even without a clear agreement about the purposes they were to serve, most school districts incorporated some version of schooling known as junior high school. Changes occurred in the institution as it grew. During the decades of the thirties, forties, and fifties, the original pressure to begin college preparation earlier received less and less attention. Instead many schools experimented with curricula and scheduling in attempts to meet the needs of early adolescents more effectively. Homeroom classes were instituted in an attempt to put every student in closer contact with one teacher and to facilitate a period of time when issues of getting along personally and academically were discussed. Core classes combining disciplines such as language arts and social studies emerged. Block-time scheduling to accommodate experiential learning caught on in many schools. Most pervasive of all the junior high innovations was the establishment of exploratory and elective classes. Intended as vehicles for becoming acquainted with careers and living in families, the idea was most commonly implemented as classes in industrial arts and home economics.

Starting in the late forties, results of new work on the stages of human development began to appear. Robert Havighurst and Erik Erickson's writings supported attempts to make the learner the starting point of educational planning. The focus on developmental characteristics and tasks along the life span, further augmented by Jean Piaget's mapping of cognitive development, held great appeal for educators.

Using these insights about early adolescent learners to build a schooling experience that was responsive to their needs, however, proved to be an arduous and elusive task. Forces external and internal to the schools worked against making significant shifts from practices already established.

Schooling to Meet National Needs

A major external influence arose from concern about American national security. National response to the Russian launching of Sputnik in 1957 made an impact on junior high school programs. As one facet of a national effort to win the new cold war in outer space, study teams led by college educators looked at what students were taught at all levels of schooling. In his report on high schools, James B. Conant, president of Harvard University, recommended grouping students by ability in individual subjects to allow academically talented high school students to pursue four years of science and three years of mathematics and four years of foreign language.[5] Conant was not alone in his criticism. Jerome Bruner concluded that "the top quarter of public school students, from which we must draw intellectual leadership in the next generation, is perhaps the group most neglected by our schools in the recent past."[6]

Writing a special set of recommendations about junior high schools, Conant supported the emphasis he found to exist on helping students make a transition between elementary and high school.[7] He criticized as anti-intellectual junior high schools that imitated the social ambiance of high schools with football teams and cheer leaders. In addition, and consistent with his high school recommendations, he urged junior high school leaders to begin algebra earlier for talented students and use ability grouping as a way to meet individual differences.

National pressures to compete in the race to control space influenced the studies of students at all levels. Government-funded curriculum projects aimed at updating and adding greater intellectual vigor to academic subjects brought new focus to junior high programs. New versions of biology and physics were introduced to high schools. New mathematics programs that incorporated pre-algebra and geometry as well as a conceptual approach to problem solving were adopted by all levels of schooling. University scholars from the social sciences vied to incorporate their techniques of inquiry into the earlier levels of schooling. The effect of the curriculum projects on middle level schooling was to reinforce further the separate subject approach to instruction as well as to form groups of talented students who could operate at the levels of sophistication that many of the projects required.

Resistance to Change

There also existed internal obstacles to the formulation of programs responsive to the developmental needs of early adolescents. Teachers in many junior high schools had been educated to be high school teachers. They were specialized in math or English or history or biology. Their socialization as professionals usually took place in high schools or with middle level educators trained and/or experienced in high school teaching. Their perception of school was that it consisted of a series of instructional segments of 55 minutes, Carnegie units for graduation, in an environment that was competitive in both academics and athletics. Often these teachers accepted positions in junior high school as a second best option to teaching in a high school. Typically, their professional education did not prepare them to deal with the developmental issues involved in teaching early adolescents. In many districts successful teachers at the junior high level were "rewarded" with transfers to high school positions.

Probably the highest hurdle the new schools confronted in formulating a program for early adolescents was tradition. Reverence and admiration for high school traditions made emulation of those traditions attractive to administrators and teachers working in a school whose very name declared that it was the offspring of a senior institution. By the mid-sixties there were over 7,000 junior high schools. Some included grades 7, 8, and 9. Others included only seventh and eighth grades. Still others included the sixth grade as part of the intermediate schooling experience. Regardless of the grade level arrangements, junior high schools increasingly incorporated the social and organizational aspects of high schools. Many sponsored dances and interscholastic sports programs. Subjects were taught separately, and teachers were organized by subjects into departments.

Movement toward Consensus

Reacting to the conflicting professional views and public pressures of the late fifties and early sixties about the purposes of intermediate schooling and the ages it should serve, several professional educators started a new movement. Prominent spokespersons included William Alexander, Donald Eichhorn, Paul George, John Lounsbury, and Gordon Vars. They were dissatisfied with the typical junior high schools that replicated the organization and social milieu of a high school. New studies on the earlier maturation of children seemed to support the calls for rethinking what happens to young adolescents in schools and in what age constellations they were grouped. Ninth graders were seen as more appropriately placed in a high school setting, while sixth graders now seemed to fit with seventh and eighth graders. Also, the teachers of early adolescents were concerned that the needs of most students could not be addressed by the ways schools were responding to society's pressures to place greater emphasis on academic excellence. Through their writings and organizational efforts a new wave of innovation was launched, a movement based on the characteristics and developmental tasks of the early adolescent.

Efforts to influence the reform of intermediate schooling coalesced in 1973 with the founding of the National Middle School Association (NMSA). Insisting that the school for early adolescents should have a distinctive program, the organization promoted the use of the title *Middle School* to differentiate it from the notion of a miniature senior high school. The innovators maintained that development of an educational program must start by considering the needs and characteristics of youth, then build administrative arrangements and group grade levels in response to these needs. Within professional educational circles the goals of the Middle School Association held strong appeal. The new group began publishing a periodical and holding national conventions. Several states organized middle school leagues. Older professional organizations acknowledged the movement by devoting special conferences and publications to the middle schools.[8] By 1977 the NMSA published a set of middle school goals (presented below) in an attempt to guide local schools as they rethought intermediate schooling.

National Middle School Association View of Goals
for Middle Level Schooling

1. Every student should be well known as a person by at least one adult in the school who accepts responsibility for his/her guidance.
2. Every student should be helped to achieve optimum mastery of the skills of continued learning together with a commitment to their use and improvement.
3. Every student should have ample experiences designed to develop decision-making and problem-solving skills.
4. Every student should acquire a functional body of fundamental knowledge.
5. Every student should have opportunities to explore and develop interests in esthetic, leisure, career, and other aspects of life.[9]

The NMSA goals are firmly grounded in the characteristics of the learner. Emphasis on organizational aspects of teacher closeness to students and the exploratory nature of the curriculum help to put the learner-based orientation into practice. For the first time since the advent of middle level schooling, there appeared an internally consistent agenda about what this level of schooling should accomplish.

Beyond the student-centered agenda, however, there were economic and social pressures that stimulated the reorganization of middle level schooling. Reshuffling grade levels allowed districts to solve problems of enrollment increases caused by the baby boom of the late 1950s and early 1960s. Economy of scale indicated that a few larger buildings would be less expensive than more units that were smaller. The solution to accommodating growing numbers was to move children at an earlier age, in fifth and sixth grades, into larger, centralized locations. Urban districts saw larger middle level schools that incorporated the earlier grades as a way to manage more children. Metropolitan districts were under pressure from the federal courts to provide equality of educational opportunity by ending de facto segregation, which was largely an artifact of the neighborhood elementary schools. Middle level schools that started with fifth or sixth graders facilitated the orchestration of racial integration at earlier ages.

IMPACT OF THE 1970s AND 1980s REFORM MOVEMENT

The growing agreement among educators about the purposes for middle education had little time to gain momentum before it was overtaken by a new tide of public concern about the quality of schools. This concern grew out of the recognition that the international status of the United States was in flux. No longer was America the dominant world power. Japan and Western Europe emerged as economic competitors. Nations such as Japan, West Germany, Taiwan, and South Korea produced cheaper and often more reliable goods than domestic firms did. Americans imported more than they sold, creating a growing debt. Concurrent with the growing unfavorable balance in U.S. trade was the restructuring of American business and industry. Advances in technology brought the world ever closer to a global system of information and trade. Making the economic decline sharper was the American investment in defense spending. Government priorities funneled multibillion-dollar budgets on sophisticated weapons into the 40-year-old arms race with the Soviet Union.

As in the previous national wave of concern about the world status of the United States, attention was directed to the schools. On the one hand, the policy-makers' habit of looking to the schools as the hope for leading the country to a better future was flattering. On the other hand, it represented a source of further support for replacing the learner-centered focus of the seventies with a national security focus for schools.

Back to Basics

This new pressure for reform joined forces with proponents of fewer "frills" and more hard work on basic subjects in schools. Even before America's international leadership in technology and trade became doubtful, a shift back to the basics of schooling had already begun to influence all levels of instruction. The back-to-the-basics movement started as a backlash to the trend toward more humanistic, student-centered education.

To see what the "basics" supporters were opposing, let us review recent social history. Proponents of humanistic education, for their part, often questioned the relevance of traditional schooling as well as what they perceived as the overly academic curriculum projects resulting from the round of Sputnik-inspired educational reform. Growing awareness of the inequities in society and in the schools for minorities and women, and the dissension and unrest in reaction to the war in Vietnam, prompted many parents and educators alike to explore new topics and strategies in schools. Black English was officially acknowledged in some schools that had predominantly black enrollments. The history and literature of non-Western societies, minority groups, and women entered the curriculum. Exercises in values exploration led students into investigations of personal issues and social problems in the classroom. Against the backdrop of this intellectual ferment, as well, was the controversial movement toward racial integration and ability integration in schools. Mandated vehicles for attaining greater equality of access to educational opportunity—busing and mainstreaming and bilingual education—kept urban schools in a constant state of turmoil as they met federal requirements and answered to unhappy parents.

While all these social pressures competed to make changes in the schools, the demographics and economics of schooling were also forcing districts to change. The bulge created by baby boomers in school enrollments passed through the system and left many districts with more schools and teachers than could be supported. Budget cuts resulting from a series of circumstances—enrollment-driven state payments to districts, taxpayer revolts, higher proportions of school budgets devoted to salary maintenance, inflation, increased cost of energy—all combined with demographic changes and social pressures to rearrange the grade organization of many school districts. Many districts put together a newer constellation of grades, from fifth through eighth, and labeled them middle schools.

For many school personnel and members of the general public, all the changes in education served to erode the traditional order and undermine the quality of knowledge and skills students acquired in public schools. Indeed, declining results of standardized test scores, the traditional gauge used to evaluate how schools were doing, seemed to confirm that schools were not as good as they once had been. State legislatures, responding to this shift in public concern, passed laws requiring minimum competency testing. The effect was to force schools to concentrate on basic skills. By 1980 the mood of the country turned away from social experimentation. President Ronald Reagan seemed to ratify this mood. During the eight years of his presidency (1981–1988), the new wave of reform took shape.

A Nation at Risk—And Other Dire Warnings

The publication of several national reports galvanized public attention. The reports were similar in several ways. First, nearly all were based on the assumption that results of standardized test scores were the best indicators of the quality of education in American schools. Second, they were organized and written by researchers representing a university-level perspective. Third, they saw the educational system as the primary means of fulfilling national interests. In order to reflect on the impact these reports have for middle level education, let us briefly review the recommendations and tone of these reports, a sample of which are listed in Table 2.1.

The National Science Foundation (NSF) report on educating Americans for the next century echoed its earlier concerns.[10] The tone of the report suggested that inadequate performance by students in mathematics and science was a threat to national interests. Achievement test scores showed Japanese and European students outperforming American students. Just as with Sputnik, the NSF proposed to lead in promoting curriculum evaluation and development.[11] The National Commission on Excellence in Education, however, captured everyone's attention with its report entitled *A Nation at Risk*. The report linked the steady decline in American industrial productivity to the schools in this famous sentence: "If an unfriendly foreign power had attempted to impose on America the mediocre educational performance that exists today, we might well have viewed it as an act of war."[12] The tone was dire. Some educators reasoned that such an

TABLE 2.1. A SAMPLING OF NATIONAL REPORTS ON SCHOOLING IN THE 1980s

Title	Date	Author	Data Base
High School: A Report on Secondary Education in America	1983	Ernest L. Boyer	Field studies in 15 high schools, secondary analysis of Goodlad study data and Coleman study (*High School and Beyond*) test scores
A Place Called School: Study of Secondary Education in America	1983	John I. Goodlad	38 schools in 7 states—structured observations, interviews, study of curricula, materials
100 Good Schools	1984	Kappa Delta Pi	106 good schools at all levels: visits, interviews, background information, test scores
A Nation at Risk: The Imperative for Educational Reform	1983	National Commission on Excellence in Education	Commissioned papers, testimony, panel discussions, test scores
Action for Excellence: A Comprehensive Plan to Improve Our Nation's Schools	1983	Education Commission	Task force sessions, deliberations, test of the states' scores
Turning Points: Preparing American Youth for the 21st Century	1989	Carnegie Council on Adolescent Development	17-member task force commissioned papers

approach might be the only way to secure educational spending programs from Congress. Other reports reinforced the message. Japanese education was held up as the paragon of productivity, with student scores in mathematics and science far ahead of American students. Comparison of the two systems revealed that Japanese students spent more time in school per day and during the year than did American students. They were exposed to more science and mathematics than American students and held to higher standards of achievement as well.

The agenda flowing from the various national commission reports of the early eighties seemed clear. More academic rigor was the order of the day. Accountability became the educational watchword. The public wanted tangible results for their investment in education. Increasingly, the public came to look at test score trends as a measure of educational productivity. Politicians pointed to statistics that showed that increased funding of education did not translate into improved test scores. The financial support that educators felt was necessary to implement the reform agenda did not follow. Rather than spend more monies generally for education, a trend began whereby state legislatures tied increased funding to reform plans competitively submitted by school districts.

School-Based Studies Promote Reform

While most of the national reports based their recommendations for reform on the results of standardized test scores, the study conducted by Goodlad's team, *A Study of Schooling,* took an in-depth look. Data from 18,000 students, 1,350 teachers, 1,016 classrooms, and 8,600 parents were analyzed. Kenneth Tye analyzed the Goodlad data that were pertinent to middle level schooling[13] and found that the same ills afflicting high school and elementary school were evident at the middle level: isolation of teachers, the mindless nature of much of the curriculum, the lack of administrative and financial support for the act of learning.

As a result of his analysis, Tye suggested recommendations (summarized below) for improving middle level education.

Tye's Recommendations for Middle Level Schooling
Based on Data from A Study of Schooling

1. Development of a common curriculum for all students including increased attention to science and foreign language, a reduction in the time devoted to mathematics accompanied by improved instruction, opportunity for all students to participate in at least one performing art, coeducational practical arts experiences, and a course for all students in computer science.
2. Elimination of ability grouping and the conscious formation of heterogeneous classes at the school.
3. Organization of large junior high schools into smaller subunits known as learning communities.

4. Utilization of core or block-time scheduling wherever possible, particularly with English and social studies.

5. Use of more active teaching strategies in all classrooms, with emphasis upon group problem solving.

6. Globalization of all curricula to help overcome the extensive ethnocentrism that permeates our schools and society.

7. Improvement of student guidance through the establishment of a teacher-advisor program.[14]

Note that some of Tye's recommendations are similar to those proposed in the 1940s and again by the spokespersons in the Middle School Association of the 1970s, while some reflect the national concerns about academic rigor reminiscent of the fifties. Indeed, this intertwining of recommendations for reforms, including issues of student-centered and academic rigor, marks the later public policy reports that focused on middle level schooling.

At the state level, one of the most comprehensive sets of recommendations came from California. The report, *Caught in the Middle: Educational Reform for Young Adolescents for California Public Schools,*[15] represented an attempt to adhere to the middle school philosophy while, at the same time, responding to public demands for improved test results by pushing for greater academic excellence. For example, the report cites educators, such as Diane Ravich[16] and E.D. Hirsch,[17] who are known as proponents of returning to the classics in curriculum, to agree that every student should have access to the same common core of studies while incorporating the concerns for physical and emotional development expressed by middle school advocates such as Paul George[18] and Joan Lipsitz.[19]

Almost every state initiated middle level schooling reform efforts during the late 1980s. Task force statements vary in their rationales for curriculum reform at this level. In contrast to the California statement, Maryland's *What Matters in the Middle Grades*[20] affirms a set of recommendations more consistent with the goals of the National Middle School Association and straightforwardly values "the diversity of cultures and ethnic groups in modern American and global society."[21] Some states, such as New York, are concentrating efforts on improving delivery of state mandated curriculum. New York's Board of Regents and State Department of Education are sponsoring extra funding for schools undertaking change in the direction of reorganization that continues to strive toward an outcomes-based approach to the 10 Regents Goals for grades K–12 and various state syllabi.

At the national level, the 1989 *Turning Points* report of the Carnegie Foundation's Commission on Adolescence finally gave middle level education its moment in the national policy spotlight. Charging that "a volatile mismatch exists between the organization and curriculum of middle grade schools and the intellectual, emotional and interpersonal needs of young adolescents," the report recommends reforms that echo those of the seventies' middle school advocates.

Urging that students be taught to learn well and test well, the report focuses on ways to provide stable, positive human interactions within the school while upgrading the curriculum by integrating subjects and incorporating critical thinking. Attention to middle level schooling increased.

The widely read professional periodical *Phi Delta Kappan* devoted its February 1990 issue to reporting results of a national survey of middle level schooling practices. The policies of school administrators continue to reflect an interplay between traditional measures of academic progress and educational practices that are more responsive to early adolescent needs, between a curriculum that is organized by specialized subjects and a yearning to provide skills and knowledge that connect students to themselves and their world.[22]

CHALLENGES OF BALANCING SOCIAL DEMANDS WITH MIDDLE LEVEL GOALS

What can we learn from this tour of the development of middle level education that can help us as teachers? Many teachers argue that there is little to learn from a survey of the past. After all, they say, why should we have to know about all these long-ago and faraway events? We just want to help young people become the best they can be. These teachers want to get on with the business of teaching. We are not certain that Hegel was right in saying that those who do not know history are condemned to repeat the errors of the past. However, we believe that awareness of the historical development of middle level schooling can make us politically wiser and professionally more insightful, thus providing us a broader perspective as we get on with teaching.

The recital of historical events and trends in middle level education may not conclude for us which professional ideas are best, or which will stand the test of time. Even so, analysis of the evolution of middle level schooling should alert us to some ideas that we will continue to hear in the current recommendations about middle level schooling. Some of these ideas, such as acceleration for bright students and heterogeneous grouping, are antagonistic, yet may appear on the same listing of policy guidelines. As professionals we need to become sensitive to the significance of guidelines and policies made for schools to follow. We need to question their internal consistency. We need to question how applicable they are for the students we have in our schools.

Most of the topics of this chapter are about trends, not individual schools. To become astute consumers of such studies we need to read them critically. Usually they start with the conclusions that were reached from the data collected. Instead of stopping there, we need to question further. We must train ourselves to examine the way the data are collected and analyzed. We might discover that the data gathered do not apply to our situation, or that the very questions asked are inappropriate to the mission of our individual school.

Professional wisdom, now being observed by researchers and practitioners as well as funding agencies active in the movement toward excellence, tells us that middle level schools are each significantly different from the other. We need to keep this in mind when reading reports of test score trends. Our challenge is to use such results to help us think critically about the work we do within each school for educational coherence and improvement.

Current NMSA publications are valuable in keeping the goals of middle level education clear. The association's publication on excellence honors the primary concern of developing excellence within each school and lists the characteristics (presented below) of an excellent middle school.

National Middle School Association: Characteristics of Excellence

1. Features a program that responds to the physical, intellectual, social-emotional, and moral needs of early adolescents.
2. Has a set of documents to guide all aspects of the program.
3. Possesses a definite curriculum plan that includes organized knowledge, skills, and personal development activities.
4. Has a clearly established program of studies based upon the concept of exploration and provides opportunities for student growth.
5. Builds on the strengths of elementary education and prepares students for success in high school.
6. Employs teachers who focus on the learning needs of pupils by using appropriate teaching strategies.
7. Creates teaching teams using blocks of time to best deliver the instructional program.
8. Emphasizes the guidance and counseling function of staff members by providing for a home-base program, stressing the importance of self-concept and providing a positive climate.
9. Promotes flexibility in implementing the daily, weekly, and monthly schedule to meet the varying needs of students.
10. Actively involves parents in various aspects of the school experience.
11. Evaluates the program on a regular basis and makes changes that enhance the learning.[23]

If we were to compare the NMSA list with earlier lists, we would find that since the 1940s a consensus persists about the goals of middle level schooling. Appropriateness of developmental approaches expressed in terms of exploratory activities, home bases for students, flexibility in scheduling, and teachers performing guidance functions continue to be basic items. That they continue is an important professional perspective from which to analyze what we do as teachers.

CONCLUSIONS

Changes and development in American middle level schools, whether middle schools or junior high schools, have occurred for more than a century. Excellence at the middle level has supported emphases on vocations, academic basics, tracking, and other strategies, as well as student-centered curricular programs. Local community and home characteristics are among additional environmental factors that affect student success in school. Educators must have the general welfare of the larger society in mind as a guiding principle for their work, but they must also analyze data and recommendations from the perspectives of their specific school, or even classroom, when selecting and promoting practices that will be most beneficial to their students.

EXTENSIONS

1. Carry out a study of the local history of a middle level school near you. When was it formed? Has it changed titles over the years? Has it changed in the grade range included at this level? How has its program evolved?

2. Interview a middle level teacher about the goals of his or her school. How have these goals changed over the years?

3. What kind of license or certificate is required to become a middle level educator in your state? Have the requirements changed lately? How do the changes fit the reform trends surveyed in this chapter?

NOTES AND REFERENCES

1. E. L. Thorndike, *The Elimination of Pupils from School* Bulletin 1907, No. 4. Washington, DC: U.S. Department of the Interior, Bureau of Education, 1907; Leonard P. Ayers, *Laggards in Our Schools*. New York: Russell Sage Foundation, Survey Associates, Inc., 1909; George D. Strayer, *Age and Grade Census of Schools and Colleges*, Bulletin 1911, No. 5. Washington, DC: U.S. Department of Interior, Bureau of Education, 1911.

2. Commission on the Reorganization of Secondary Education, *Cardinal Principles of Secondary Education*, Bulletin 1918, No. 35. Washington, DC: U.S. Department of the Interior, Bureau of Education, 1918.

3. R. A. Mackie, *Education During Adolescence*. New York: E.P. Dutton & Co., 1920.

4. Adapted from Department of Superintendence, *The Junior High School Curriculum*, Fifth Yearbook. Washington, DC: National Education Association, Department of Superintendence, 1927, p. 20.

5. James B. Conant, *The American High School Today*. New York: McGraw-Hill, 1959.

6. J. S. Bruner. *The Process of Education*. Cambridge, MA: Harvard University Press, 1960, pp. 1, 10.

7. James B. Conant, *A Memorandum to School Boards: Recommendations for Education in the Junior High School Years*. Princeton, N.J.: Educational Testing Service, 1960.
8. See Robert R. Leeper, ed., *Middle School in the Making*. Washington, DC: National Association for Supervision and Curriculum Development, 1974; Mauritz Johnson, ed., *Toward Adolescence: The Middle School Years*. Chicago: University of Chicago Press, 1980; note National Association for Secondary School Principals change in Bulletin title to include middle school now subtitled *NASSP Bulletin: The Journal for Middle Level and High School Administrators*.
9. Report of the NMSA Committee on Future Goals and Directions. *Middle School Journal* 8 (November) 1977, 16.
10. National Science Foundation. *Educating Americans for the 21st Century*. Washington, DC: NSF, 1989.
11. National Science Foundation, *Educating Americans for the 21st Century*. Washington, DC: National Science Foundation, 1989.
12. National Commission on Excellence in Education, *A Nation at Risk*. Washington, DC: U.S. Department of Education, 1988.
13. Kenneth A. Tye, *The Junior High: School in Search of a Mission*. Lanham, MD: University Press of America, 1985.
14. Adapted from Tye, *The Junior High: School in Search of a Mission*, pp. 35–51.
15. Middle Grade Task Force, *Caught in the Middle*. Sacramento, CA: California State Department of Education, 1987.
16. Diane Ravich, "All Children Need the Power of Knowledge." *ASCD Update* (May 1986).
17. E. D. Hirsch, Jr., "Cultural Literacy." *The American Scholar* 52 (Spring 1983): 159–169.
18. Paul S. George and Lynn L. Oldaker, "A National Survey of Middle School Effectiveness." *Educational Leadership* 42 (Dec.-Jan., 1985-86): 79–85.
19. Joan Lipsitz, *Successful Schools for Young Adolescents*. New Brunswick, NJ: Transaction, 1984.
20. Maryland Task Force on the Middle Learning Years, *What Matters in the Middle Grades*. Baltimore, 1989.
21. *Op. cit.*, p. 12.
22. Joyce L. Epstein and James M. McPartland, *Education in the Middle Grades: A National Survey of Practices and Trends—Survey and Telephone Interview Forms*. Baltimore: Johns Hopkins University Center for Research on Elementary and Middle Schools, 1988.
23. Elliot Y. Merenbloom, *Developing Effective Middle Schools Through Faculty Participation*. Columbus, OH: National Middle School Association, 1988, pp. 5–8.

FOR FURTHER READING

Cawelti, G. Middle Schools a Better Match with Early Adolescent Needs, ASCD Survey Finds. *ASCD Curriculum Update* (November 1988), entire issue.
Hornbeck, D. *Turning Point: Preparing American Youth for the 21st Century*. New York: Carnegie Council on Adolescent Development, 1989.

Phi Delta Kappan special series on middle schools:

Becker, H. J. Curriculum and Instruction in Middle-Grade Schools. *Phi Delta Kappan* 71(6) (1990): 450–457.

Braddock, J. H. Tracking the Middle Grades: National Patterns of Grouping for Instruction. *Phi Delta Kappan* 71(6) (1990): 445–449.

Epstein, J. L. What Matters in the Middle Grades—Grade Span or Practices? *Phi Delta Kappan* 71(6) (1990): 438–444.

MacIver, D. J. Meeting the Needs of Young Adolescents: Advisory Groups, Interdisciplinary Teaching Teams, and School Transition Programs. *Phi Delta Kappan* 71(6) (1990): 458–464.

McPartland, J. M. Staffing Decisions in the Middle Grades: Balancing Quality Instruction and Teacher/Student Relations. *Phi Delta Kappan* 71(6) (1990): 465–469.

Education in The Middle Grades: A National Survey of Practices and Trends. *Phi Delta Kappan* 71(6) (1990): 436–437.

CHAPTER 3

The Middle Level Student

Really? She wasn't at all like that last year!

Is anyone else having trouble with *the new fad*? I confiscated six this morning.

Hey! Great display in the library! That social studies in art unit really worked! And the kids are very proud of their work. What'll we do next?

. . . and then, when I thought she'd lost it, she turned around and apologized. I was really proud of her.

Last year I nearly had a riot when I chose the lead based on the audition instead of picking Mr. Beautiful. This year I had a panel of students do the judging, and they picked talent over popularity, too. And everyone thought they did the right thing. I learn.

I'm sure glad we don't have tests on Fridays! I remember what a downer that was for me in school. Besides, I need some of my weekends for me.

Gumpy George broke another one; that's three since vacation.

That one's going to be in juvey [juvenile court] very soon if we don't get her hooked on some other way to go.

Then it dawned on me that density is a proportion, and they aren't there yet.

Why is your room so quiet? I can't seem to do that.

Anyone want to read *Lust in Lollyland?* It dropped out of a backpack. Someone's going to worry about who stole it, no doubt.

The above remarks about students were exchanged in the teachers' room of Elford Middle School. These comments by middle level teachers reflect concern for, and recognition of, the multifaceted nature of the early adolescents they teach. Do any seem familiar to you? What might *you* have said as a teacher in this middle school?

In general, this group of students, from 10 to 14 years of age, represents a broad range of characteristics and behaviors, so much so that at no other time in life does an individual have so many same-age peers that are so different from each other and from him- or herself. At the same time there are patterns and behaviors that, although not demonstrated by all middle level students, are normal for the transescent period. One thing is certain: the early adolescent is a special kind of student, and you must be a special kind of teacher to be a happy professional in a middle level school.

In this chapter we:

- Explore the cognitive, social, and physical characteristics of early adolescents,
- Consider the contributions of several theories toward understanding how the early adolescent functions in a learning environment, and
- Anticipate the impact of early adolescent characteristics on the decisions we make for middle level students and their education.

INTRODUCTION TO EARLY ADOLESCENTS

Much of what we think we understand about 10- through 14-year-olds is based on the memories of our own lives during that period—years that stand out as unique for most of us. However, we must be cautious about making judgments based on our own personal experiences. A wide range of behaviors is normal for this age group. Each of us has experienced only a portion of them. Students now at the middle level of schooling have grown up and are part of a substantially different society than the one that shaped our youths. Some children will experience life in ways that are similar to your own experience; others will not. What we must remember is that this period is a normal, multifaceted, transitional, and important time of life.

Theories of education and of learning present explanations. As is the nature of all theories, theories of education are subject to adjustment as new observations provide support, or reveal lack of support, for given lines of thought. Principles or general rules for teaching or for facilitating learning are derived from theory. They, too, are subject to adjustment as new evidence confirms, or fails to confirm, their effectiveness. No single explanation or theory seems to be

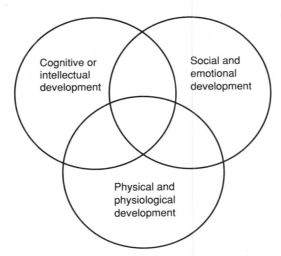

Figure 3.1. Characteristics of Early Adolescents: A Venn Diagram for Organizing Observations and Practices.

entirely satisfactory in helping us construct guidelines or formulae for making decisions in the classroom. All contribute, each related to a certain aspect of the big picture, to our understanding of how students learn. By combining explanations and refining our ability to benefit from them, we develop an expanded, personal knowledge base to make decisions that affect the learning environment for our own students. We also recognize that general rules apply to most students in a large population. We still need to check each individual student we teach to see how well the general rules fit.

In order to facilitate discussion let us consider the nature of the middle level student from three major perspectives: (1) cognitive or intellectual development, (2) social and emotional development, and (3) physical and physiological development. The Venn diagram in Figure 3.1 can help us to sort student characteristics and their relationships to middle school practices and curricular decisions. Using this model, we can consider different, isolated facets of the nature of the student and then move into the overlapping areas to look at ways that the needs of the "whole student" are addressed in practice.

COGNITIVE AND INTELLECTUAL DEVELOPMENT

Early adolescents are entering a new age of thinking, a time when propositional logic is possible, when they can think about thinking itself, when they can imagine and develop "what if" situations, and when they can enjoy and invent metaphors, similes, puns, and satire. A number of theories and approaches have been advanced in an effort to explain how students think and learn. Some are based on behavior patterns and some on neurological studies. Each one contributes ideas that are helpful in determining where students are in a growth continuum, why they are the way they are, and what is appropriate for them. We will survey a few of these theoretical ideas here and suggest implications for understanding the middle level student.

Piaget's Theory of Cognitive Development

Intellectual growth takes place from childhood to adulthood as individuals become more able to think in complex ways. This growth involves progressing from the ability to think only through reference to concrete objects and direct experience to the ability to think about indirect relationships, or to think about abstractions. In Piagetian terms, this involves moving from the *concrete stage* of

TABLE 3.1. CONCRETE AND FORMAL OPERATIONAL STAGES BASED ON PIAGET'S THEORY OF COGNITIVE DEVELOPMENT

Characteristics of Concrete Thought	Characteristics of Formal Thought
The individual:	The individual:
(a) Needs reference to familiar actions, objects, and observable properties in order to solve logical problems.	Can reason with concepts, indirect relationships and properties, axioms, and theories; recognizes necessary and sufficient conditions for a conclusion.
(b) Uses reasoning patterns that include classifying and serial ordering. Can mentally reverse actions and operations. Can understand that objects do not change in number, weight, or volume when they are spatially rearranged. Cannot identify and control variables, use proportional reasoning or propositional logic, or generate multiple possibilities without assistance. Cannot reason in the abstract.	Can interact in the hypothetical. Can formulate and test hypotheses by identifying and controlling variables. Can generate multiple possibilities. Can solve problems using proportional thought processes. Can incorporate reasoning characteristic of concrete thought.
(c) Needs step-by-step instructions in a lengthy procedure.	Plans a lengthy procedure given certain overall goals and resources.
(d) Is not aware of his or her own reasoning, inconsistencies among various statements, or contradictions with other known facts.	Is aware and critical of his or her own reasoning; actively seeks checks on the validity of conclusions by appealing to other known information.

Compiled from R. Karplus et al., Science Teaching and the Development of Reasoning, *University of California, Berkeley (Lawrence Hall of Science), 1977; and M. Padilla, Formal Operations and Middle/ Junior High School Science Education.* Science and the Early Adolescent, *edited by M. Padilla. Washington, DC: National Science Teachers Association, 1983.*

cognitive development and entering the *formal stage*. Piagetian theorists point out that exact timing cannot be made but suggest age ranges for each stage. Children in various global locations do not always match in age the observations Piaget made, but the order from concrete to formal stage appears to be the same worldwide. At the middle level in the United States, many students might operate predominantly at the concrete stage or in transition between concrete and formal stages. Some might be at the formal stage. It is typical that students exhibit growth in some subject areas at one time and in other subject areas at another time. A student in transition might function at the concrete stage in mathematics and demonstrate some abilities at the formal stage in social studies, or for a particular problem-solving task demonstrate reasoning that is characteristic of both concrete and formal stages. Table 3.1 outlines characteristics of concrete and formal thought based on Piaget's Theory of Cognitive Development. Into their explanations of cognitive growth, cognitive scientists have incorporated the acquisition of schemas, or mental representations of specific kinds of knowledge, and the capacity for simultaneously attending to an increasing number of different entities.

Brain Studies

Brain growth periodization studies by Epstein[1] indicate that a large percentage of 10- to 12-year-olds experience significant brain growth. This increase in neurologic capacity allows them to respond positively to efforts to raise the level of cognitive processes. A similarly large percentage at the 12- to 14-year-age range experiences a plateau in brain growth. Not all students adhere to this specific pattern. However, the fact that brain growth, which is necessary for an increase in cognitive ability, does not occur at a constant rate is significant in how it affects the expectations we have for thinking ability. It is apparent that learning expectations and evaluation standards are unfair if they require that all students arrive at a specific stage of cognitive development at the same time.

Human brains acquire their maximum complement of neurons, whole brain cells, shortly after birth and lose them gradually with age. Substance abuse and other environmental factors hasten the loss. However, as the brain develops, there is increase in dendrite branching and connections made between neurons. Studies with rats have demonstrated that dendrite growth increases in an enriched environment.[2] Of note is that surroundings that are too stimulating, such as changing toys too often, perhaps with no chance to assimilate or adjust to the experience, do not result in increased dendrite growth or advanced behaviors. Parallels noted from observation of humans are interesting to brain scientists and psychologists: (1) children, within limits, also benefit from enriched environments; and (2) neuron activity does not necessarily decrease in humans at the onset of "old age." The quality of the intellectual environment is important not only in early years but throughout life.

Mental Representations

The idea that knowledge involves mental representations or mental models has permeated cognitive science.[3] Mental representations can be described at the neurological level or expressed in terms of observed behaviors, including verbal reports. When students change their understandings of specific concepts, the mental representation has been changed. For example, the understanding of the concept of *vision* that is source-centered, or understood in terms of where light comes from, can shift to an understanding that centers around the eye as a receptor of light.[4] Once the shift has occurred, the mental representation is thought not to regress.

Kinds of Intelligence

It is apparent from individual behavior, productivity, and interests that not all students, or adults, are identical in talents or capacities for success. Society and the education system tend to favor those who are strong in verbal and analytic skills. Several descriptions provide us with frameworks for addressing the variety of orientations exhibited in our classrooms.

Right and Left Brain Comparisons. The two hemispheres of the human brain, although working together, are known to develop differentially for certain functions.[5] The left hemisphere verbalizes, analyzes, counts, plans procedures, keeps track of time, rationalizes. Its mode is objective and analytical. The right half, in contrast, has been attributed with our ability to visualize, see spatial relations, put parts together, communicate in gestures, understand metaphors, dream, invent, and imagine. In this way both sides of the brain are involved in thinking, reasoning, and communicating. Schooling, which tends to emphasize left brain modes, should utilize both left and right brain functions.

Gardner's Multiple Intelligences. Recognition that students exhibit different kinds of talents, or clusters of talents, has prompted the formation of Howard Gardner's Theory of Multiple Intelligences. Individual students tend to be oriented, when given the choice or when allowed to pursue natural interests, around several kinds of cognitive strengths or intelligences, including linguistic, logical/mathematical, spatial, musical, and bodily/kinesthetic. In addition, they might tend to be interpersonal or intrapersonal in their approach to problem-solving or learning new information. The characteristics of each are described in Table 3.2. Our educational system tends to reinforce students who succeed in studies that are linguistic and logical/mathematical in nature. In order to provide the opportunity for all to succeed in their natural arenas of excellence as well as their adopted-by-necessity areas, our curricula and instructional designs should address this variation within our student population.

TABLE 3.2. CHARACTERISTICS OF GARDNER'S MULTIPLE INTELLIGENCES

Intelligence	Likes To—	Is Good At—	Learns Best By—
Linguistic	Read Write Tell stories	Memorizing names, places, dates, and trivia	Saying, hearing, and seeing words
Logical/mathematical	Do experiments Figure things out Work with numbers Ask questions	Math Reasoning Logic Problem solving	Categorizing Classifying Working with abstract patterns/relationships
Spatial	Draw, build, design, and create things Daydream Look at pictures and slides, watch movies Play with machines	Imagining things Sensing changes Mazes/puzzles Reading maps, charts	Visualizing Dreaming Using the mind's eye Working with colors and pictures
Musical	Sing, hum tunes Listen to music Play an instrument Respond to music	Picking up sounds Remembering melodies Noticing pitches and rhythms Keeping time	Rhythm Melody Music
Bodily/kinesthetic	Move around Touch and talk Use body language	Physical activities (sports/dance/acting) Crafts	Touching Moving Interacting with space Processing knowledge through bodily sensations
Interpersonal	Have lots of friends Talk to people Join groups	Understanding people Leading others Organizing Communicating Manipulating Mediating conflicts	Sharing Comparing Relating Cooperating Interviewing
Intrapersonal	Work alone Pursue own interests	Understanding self Focusing inward on feelings and dreams Following instincts Pursuing interests and goals Being original	Working alone Doing individualized projects Having self-paced instruction Having own space

Based on Howard Gardner's Frames of Mind. *Table adapted from K. Faggella and J. Horowitz,* Different Child, Different Style. *Instructor (Sept. 1990): 49–54.*

Personality Types. Student behaviors, or preferences for certain patterns of behaviors, have been associated with the personality types identified by psychologist Carl Jung, described as *thinker, feeler, sensor*, and *intuitor*, as outlined in Table 3.3. These personality types can be connected to student cognitive strengths and suggest ways to modify instructional strategies and management.

Implications for Teaching

Additional intellectual characteristics of early adolescents are manifested in their reactions to life at school, home, and in the community. The middle level

TABLE 3.3. CHARACTERISTICS OF JUNGIAN-BASED LEARNING STYLES

Personality Type	Learning and Thinking Pocesses	Difficulties Arise When Student Is—
Thinker	Uses analysis, logical breakdown of problems into parts. Needs facts, rules, and definitions. Likes lectures, written materials, and instructions Needs structure and guidelines in order to concentrate.	Expected to know the why of a concept before knowing the rules and vocabulary. Expected to concentrate in a disorderly environment.
Intuitor	Evaluates, builds, examines and modifies images in head. Is helped by pictures, charts, graphs, analogies, and metaphors. Processes randomly to find patterns and relationships. Might have right answers without explanations.	Pressed for a response before an idea feels comfortable. Not given time to internalize before working with others.
Feeler	Is emotionally expressive and perceptive. Reacts sensitively to feelings of others. Learns to verbalize, ask questions, and listen. Needs interaction with others and thrives using curriculum with a human element.	Not allowed to talk. Exposed to a theoretical approach that seems nonpersonal and unresponsive to human sensitivities.
Sensor	Is physically active, competitive, action-oriented. Likes to be in charge and work in groups. Benefits from concrete materials, simulations, and contests. Likes instant results. Learns through movement, touch, and manipulation.	Spending too much time on rote memorization or listening beyond a shortened attention span.

Derived from V. R. Johnson, Learning Styles and Instructional Strategies. Science Scope 10 (Apr/May 1987): 12–14. Reprinted with Permission from Science Scope, a publication of the National Science Teachers Association, Washington, DC (1987).

student has a lively curiosity and shows enthusiasm in active learning environments. Student behavior is highly egocentric but often moderated when interacting with classmates or other peers. This student has a broad range of interests and is eager to pursue them. Students are eager to develop skills, but their attention span for doing so may be short. The middle level student is increasingly interested in understanding the meaning and perplexities of life, and is concerned about issues and is learning to discuss them. The intellectual, philosophical, biological, sociological, moral, or ethical nature of topics all have increasing appeal.

Developing Breadth of Understanding. Although the teacher has little control over invoking vertical development, in terms of producing, on demand, a shift of ability from concrete to formal stages of thought, the teacher can do a great deal to extend understanding at a given level in a horizontal sense. We should facilitate learning from the known to the unknown, from simple to complex, starting with hands-on experience—this is the commonly accepted wisdom of the ages. With this approach students progress from manipulating objects and engaging in physical experience to representing ideas through pictures and diagrams to utilizing words and symbols in communication; and learning develops horizontally through stages of understanding based on levels of abstraction: from concrete to pictorial to symbolic.[6] Examples of this horizontal progression are shown in Table 3.4.

Middle level students can recognize and organize objects and ideas that are subordinate to one another. They can, therefore, outline stories, find key concepts, distinguish tree from evergreen from fir, and learn terms such as "free-

TABLE 3.4. HORIZONTAL STEPS IN CONCEPT LEARNING

Concrete Level of Abstraction	→	Pictorial Level of Abstraction	→	Symbolic Level of Abstraction
Direct experience, object, role playing		Picture, diagram, graph		Vocabulary term, formula, equation
Example: Electricity travels in a completed circuit.				
Exploring ways to connect wires and dry cells to light bulbs. Demonstrating variations by manipulating materials directly.		Using diagram of circuit with components and connections. Drawing as-you-see-it diagrams.		Using specialized terms: circuit, positive and negative poles, circuit breaker. Using symbols in circuit design. Discussing consequences of layouts.
Example: Environmental decisions can have and should take into account multiple impacts.				
Roleplaying community factions and their interests in a proposed new highway past your school.		Producing chart or diagram to compare stands on common issues or concerns related to the highway project.		Debating and determining priorities. Formulating rationale for accepting or rejecting proposal.

dom" and "justice," as long as proper experiences are provided for students to construct lasting and transferable conceptualizations. Early adolescents have an increased ability to analyze situations and search for correlations and cause-effect relationships. For learning advanced concepts and promoting objectivity, it is essential that multiple examples be used to allow students to abstract communalities and formulate generalizations. Since textbooks and other resources typically feature one case to represent any given concept, the teacher must understand the concept well enough to recognize and provide additional examples.

Instruction appropriately designed for the middle level provides opportunity for vertical development for those who are ready and, for all students, promotes knowledge acquisition and understanding of concepts through multiple examples and a progression through several levels of abstraction founded first on concrete experience. Middle school is a time for consolidating and refining thinking skills previously learned.

A variety of approaches and materials should be used in the teaching-learning process in order to address the broad range of abilities, intelligences, personality types, interests, and skills. Avenues should be maintained for self-expression, creativity, articulation, and clarification of ideas through discussion with peers, and for achievement through cooperative learning. Both student-centered and teacher-centered instruction should be employed, with tasks designed to include guidance for independent work, appropriate cognitive demands, and time periods that allow optimal focus. In addition, students should be allowed to work in groups as well as alone.

Evaluation of learning should be based on individual progress rather than group norms. In addition, assessment should be designed to allow students to demonstrate knowledge in a variety of formats, utilizing a variety of talents such as spatial, musical, and kinesthetic as well as the traditional verbal and analytical. Chapter 10 addresses a variety of assessment possibilities.

A *word of caution:* There is a temptation to categorize students into one of the personality types, one of the intelligences, or as right or left brain dominant. We must remember that, although individuals exhibit strengths in certain categories under certain conditions, they function in all areas. Opportunities must be made for students to succeed in their areas of comfort and natural talents as well as to exercise other ways of knowing.

Implications for the Curriculum

No doubt experiences we give children in school affect cognitive development, but there is no conclusive evidence that we can specifically precipitate its timing. It seems that if the student is ready, the leaps are made; if not, they aren't. Curriculum is planned, therefore, to match general patterns of cognitive growth and capacities. These patterns are based on trends reflected by large numbers of students tested formally and informally over many years. An individual teacher planning day-to-day lessons, however, has a small sample of this population, a sample that usually reflects a wide range of abilities and demands adjustment to the entire range.

The middle level program should be exciting and meaningful to the student in terms of content, and should include real-life problems such as conflict, competition, peer group influence, and community and environmental concerns. Prerequisite knowledge and ability to carry out thinking processes must be considered to ensure success by students at various levels. Interdisciplinary treatment of concepts presents multiple examples necessary for self-conceptualizing and generalizing. The middle level curriculum provides an environment for broadened exploration of content areas that serves as a transition from the skill-based elementary program to the in-depth treatment of subject matter at high school.

SOCIAL AND EMOTIONAL DEVELOPMENT

The change in thinking abilities changes the early adolescent's outlook on life in general, and affects social interactions.[7]

The socialization needs of the early adolescent shift from being primarily family-centered to including the peer group. For the early adolescent, it is increasingly important to have opportunities to interact with both peers and adults in informal settings. Submitting to peer pressure at the expense of individuality is common. The influence of family norms, however, still functions, even though early adolescents may outwardly decry them. The adolescent values adults as resources and for guidance, although they often express rejection of adult standards, criticism, "wisdom," and conventions. The early adolescent follows fads and worries to the extreme about measuring up to idealized standards. Peer and media expectations strongly influence attitudes and self-assessment, particularly as related to sexual development.

The early adolescent can be argumentative and, driven by egocentrism, attempts to convince others in the process of clarifying personal ideas. Arguing for the sake of arguing is typical, and wanting to know the reasons for the expectations put upon him or her rather than accepting rules at face value is another manifestation of the new level of thinking being incorporated into his or her mental capabilities.

Early adolescents are very self-conscious and overly concerned about other people's reactions to them. David Elkind refers to the "imaginary audience," all of those people the individual assumes are aware of every move she makes and every detail of her appearance. The wisdom that comes from realizing that most people in the world are so concerned about their own problems and functioning that they do not concentrate on us for more than a few nanoseconds, is not acquired for a few, or many, years after middle level life. The imaginary audience affects us to some extent throughout life. Feelings of ineptitude, manifested in shyness, anxiety, and fear, are often compensated for by opposite behaviors such as bravado, overt demonstrativeness, noise-making, and other exaggerated responses. Selfishly monopolizing time, objects, and space at home, including the telephone, communal mirror, bathroom, and television, is characteristic behavior. The early adolescent has strong desires for independence and wants to make decisions for self while, at the same time, revealing a great need for adult reassurance and direction.

Optimism and self-centeredness are often associated with a student's "personal fable," a term also provided by David Elkind. The personal fable refers to the assumption of one's uniqueness, specialness, and immortality. Results can include the sense of being the teacher's favorite student, of being very attractive to a member of the opposite sex (in the imaginary audience) after only a brief encounter, or of being impervious to the dangers of trying out drugs. The personal fable provides hope at a time when so many other facets of life are threatening. We carry a personal fable of some form with us our entire lives.

TALKING WITH TEACHERS: ABOUT SELF-CENTERED PERSPEC-TIVES Students entering our seventh grade from three or more feeder elementary schools were challenged to adjust from a known social "pecking order" to a new amalgamated one. One young man announced to me on opening day, "If I'm in your class, you won't last more than two weeks." "Ah," I said, "but I've been a teacher here longer than you've been going to school." "Oh," he said, realizing, probably only briefly, that there was life before he arrived on the scene. I should have assured him that I knew he was very special and that we looked forward to his contributions, but he, the center of the solar system, was off down the hall and didn't wait for further conversation.

—Seventh grade teacher

Middle level students have high energy as a group and can be caught up in team spirit events and bandwagon movements. Objectivity is not always apparent. They are willing to work hard and are motivated by external rewards of social value such as individual or group recognition.

Implications for Teaching

Students at the middle level need a balance of guidance and independence. Organized discussions in peer groups of feelings and ideas can lead to understanding of self. Adults are important for guidance and advising even though the advice might be rejected. Teachers need to exercise patience and should base assessments of their own effectiveness on more than immediate reactions from students. Students need to be able to work in both mixed sex and same-sex groups. Teachers must continually promote consideration of others besides self and social group, and be prepared to deal with fluctuation in moods, sensitivity to implied criticism from adults, and feelings of personal inadequacy.

Modeling is a powerful teaching technique. Modeling exemplary behavior should include demonstrating the importance of knowing your limitations. Teachers do not know all, and should not pretend to. Students need reinforcement to accept the idea that it's all right not to know something and that finding out is more important than faking it or giving a flip answer. Equally important, students need examples of how to escape or handle situations in which they feel pressured to prove themselves. Teachers can point out times when one needs to say, "I don't know," "I'll find out," or "I need to check on that before I say more."

TALKING WITH TEACHERS: ABOUT DRAMATIC CHANGES IN SO-CIAL INTERACTION What differences do I see between our sixth, seventh, and eighth graders? The sixth graders, when given a choice of where to sit in class, will distribute themselves with boys on one side of the room and girls on the other, with empty tables or seats down the middle if possible. The seventh graders do the same but with a mixture of boys and girls in the center. And with the eighth graders you start having to pull them off each other's laps before starting class!

—Middle level math teacher

TALKING WITH TEACHERS: ABOUT BEING SENSITIVE TO PER-SONAL FEELINGS It's important to be sensitive to student responses in terms of personal feelings. They can say, "I pass" in a variety of ways, and you need to be sure not to push them into a corner where they feel uncomfortable or threatened. Over the years I found that too many times when a student "lost it" and became upset or behaved in what we call an unacceptable manner because of a particular situation in class, it was because I missed the cue that said, "Back off and give me space, give me an escape route, let me save face."

—Seventh grade teacher

TALKING WITH TEACHERS: ABOUT PRIVACY Privacy is important. Students often need an adult ear and need to know that you're not going to think what they feel is funny or trivial, or announce things they say in class or tell other teachers. Even something as simple as catching kids passing notes which I don't allow in class: I take the note and immediately dispose of it. The little information I would gain by reading the note is not worth the trust I lose by nosing into personal affairs uninvited.

—Eighth grade teacher

Implications for the Curriculum

The school experience is powerful in helping to mold attitudes that affect how individuals function in our multicultural, multiethnic society. At the middle level, students are ready to address the consequences of personal behaviors and attitudes. It is appropriate for them to engage in conflict resolution and develop decision-making strategies that include gathering data and establishing priorities. Students at this age can perceive issues in terms of "shades of gray" rather than only in "black and white." Students tend to be altruistic. Their high ideals lead to interest in issues of social relevance and in action-based projects such as those involving service in the community and concern for disadvantaged or oppressed groups. Promoting self-esteem and intrinsic motivation through special awareness programs is effective and important for this age.

PHYSICAL AND PHYSIOLOGICAL DEVELOPMENT

The middle years are marked by distinct physical changes. Shifts in hormone production affect metabolism, body growth, and sexual maturation. Students gain an average of 3.6 to 4.5 kg (8 to 10 lbs) in weight and 5 cm (2 in.) in height during the middle level period.[8] Girls tend to be taller and physically more mature than boys. Temporary physical awkwardness occurs when bone growth exceeds muscle development. Although previous levels of physical coordination are reinstated as this growth plateaus, the transition period is destructive to self-esteem. Restlessness often can be attributed to the ossification of cartilage at the ends of long bones that results in discomfort when sitting on hard surfaces for extended lengths of time. The early adolescent can dramatically fluctuate between a nearly hyperactive state and lethargy or fatigue as basal metabolism varies. The need for frequent nutrition breaks is in response to the alteration in blood sugar stability and a daily need to release energy. This is the junk food age.

Physical development, particularly evidence of sexual maturation, seems to be of disproportionate concern for the early adolescent. At work here is the imaginary audience previously mentioned in the discussion of social development. The growth of breasts, genitalia, and pubic hair are monitored and compared against perceived ideals. Voice change in boys precipitates both pride that comes with entering "manhood" and embarrassment with the lack of control of the indicator. Those who feel that they do not "measure up" experience considerable anxiety. Acne, moles, birthmarks, and other physical features cause self-consciousness. In addition, exaggerated levels of self-consciousness are precipitated by the awareness of changes in one's own physical growth and of changes in others as well as by preoccupation with these differences among peers.

Implications for Teaching

Students benefit from active learning that includes physical movement. Moving to various learning stations and frequent changes of pace are appropriate. Periods in which students lack energy should be expected. Students need opportunity for discussions with peers as part of a process of grasping for self-understanding. For some students, kinetic learning opportunities correspond to the preferred learning styles indicated by Gardner and Jung, and not just because of the physical need for movement. Promoting acceptance and discouraging ridicule or rejection of individuals among students, particularly for reasons related to physical variation, is a constant challenge for teachers. Students do not all experience physical growth at the same rate, a phenomenon shared but not correlated with growth rates in other areas. Just as we do when addressing uneven growth in other areas, we should encourage early adolescents as individuals rather than judge them on a comparative basis, one with another.

Implications for the Curriculum

Health education is recommended as is learning about those systems of the human body that account for the observable changes occurring among peers. Sex education and substance abuse education should be included to provide an understanding of self and a base of factual knowledge for making life decisions. Bringing about self-esteem and awareness of others is essential for prevention programs to succeed.[9] Students who do not value their futures or project beyond themselves to see the effects of their actions on others will not relate to the importance of preventative behaviors.

TALKING WITH TEACHERS: ABOUT HUMAN BODY AWARE-NESS Once I went through the routine of eliminating some note-passing activity, but when glancing at the outside of the folded piece of paper, I saw a drawing of what was obviously me with great care having been taken in detailing the clothes I was wearing that day. One of the students said, "Open it!" and since I heard no protests, I did. On the inside was an identical portrait of me, but naked, with every pertinent detail of female anatomy and including my unmistakable bulging thighs. Those who had seen the drawing waited for my explosion and the expulsion of the pornographer. I responded with, "That's a very good drawing! You certainly observed my body shape correctly. You have talent. If you don't mind, I'd like to keep this to show my mother who is an artist." I didn't wait for an agreement, but just put the drawing in my desk and returned to the topic of the day and teaching task at hand. I had no intention of giving back the drawing for circulation among a giggling group of boys, and my mother really is an artist who really would (and did) get a chuckle out of the drawing which was actually pretty good. There is no gain in showing anger or embarrassment in a situation like that. Defusing is the best way to handle a bomb. One just has to be ready for the full range of normality. What early adolescent hasn't mentally undressed his or her teachers? And remember that it's usually the timing, not the event, that gives you the surprise.

—Eighth grade science teacher

ADAPTING TO MIDDLE LEVEL STUDENTS

Knowing about and being sensitive to how early adolescents function is essential for designing and implementing the middle level curriculum. In this section we look at a number of situations in which this knowledge and sensitivity play key roles in making decisions that lead to success. We recommend that you consider them now and then return to these situations after reading the other chapters.

Activity 3.1: Matching Teaching to Student Characteristics

The decisions that teachers make about instruction and organization are affected by the characteristics of middle level students. We have described and grouped these characteristics into three main areas of development: cognitive/intellectual, social/emotional, and physical/physiological. Some teacher decisions address only certain student characteristics, and some involve combinations. Six teaching situations are described. As you review them, consider how they relate to the main areas of development. Discuss reasons for your choices with a colleague and add to comments to the reflections provided.

Situation 1. In physical education, Miss Halligan gave individual performance tests in running and jumping before the beginning of a unit on track and field, and again after the training period. Achievement was based on individual improvement in performance as well as ability to analyze technique.

Reflections: Miss Halligan reinforced the acceptance of students as individuals and encouraged them on that basis. She included relevant intellectual challenges so that achievement was not based solely on physical coordination.

Situation 2. Mr. Spears assigned four students to each social studies team, with at least one member from each of three ability groups and with a balance of what he privately called "earthlings" and "space travelers."

Reflections: Mr. Spears recognized the value of peer interaction and had set up a basis for cooperative learning. His labeling of student types was a personal means of maintaining an internal sense of humor and/or calm when interacting with students and their changeable moods.

Situation 3. At the beginning of the year Ms. Tolman allowed students to choose different sized desks by "comfort fit." She then moved the desks into clusters, each of which had a mixture of boys and girls.

Reflections: Ms. Tolman wanted to accommodate the broad range of physical stages of growth prior to grouping the students. Clusters of desks often had uneven topography, but students were not force-fit into physically uncomfortable furniture.

Situation 4. Mr. Garcia selected three of his students for the district's gifted science camp.

Reflections: Teachers often are instrumental in providing opportunities beyond the classroom for students with special talents or needs. He or she will need to support the program without making the students left behind feel less adequate.

Situation 5. Ms. Lane's students were allowed to choose mathematics projects from among 15 topics and encouraged to pursue a variety of investigation strategies. Every student's mathematics project was displayed for open house.

Reflections: Students were provided opportunity to make personal choices within certain guidelines and limits. Projects, which are perceived as direct reflections of the students themselves, were neither selected nor rejected for presentation to the public.

Situation 6. Mrs. Booth ordered unbreakable plastic beakers and graduated cylinders for the science lab.

Reflections: Physical growth resulting in a temporary lack of coordination can be costly in terms of self-esteem and the equipment budget.

Activity 3.2: Comparing Teacher Strategies

Just as there are a wide range of student responses to situations that occur at the middle level, there are many different approaches taken by teachers who must address them. Here are several potentially sticky situations that occurred at Justforexample Middle School. What student characteristics are addressed in each of the examples and in the possible solutions? For each example, which solution(s) do you support and why? Do you have a better idea? Discuss your thinking with a colleague and add to the comments provided.

Situation 1. A new clothing fad involved sewing some rather expensive synthetic material to jeans jackets. Students sporting this new style were considered "in." Several students could not possibly afford to buy the synthetics for their clothing. Therefore, not only were they "out" but their poverty was more apparent than usual, as "in" peers were quick to perceive.

a. Ms. Ahn banned the new clothing from her classroom.

b. Mr. Becker led a discussion on the social impact of fad clothing and had students brainstorm ideas for improvising ways for students to accommodate when they couldn't afford the "in" thing.

c. Mrs. Cantera bought some of the synthetic material for her poorer students and had them earn it by helping before and after school.

d. (your idea)

Reflections: This situation is about learning to deal with social pressures to conform to a standard in appearance. Ms. Ahn "provided guidelines" and made the decision for the students. Did she remove the pressure for social conformity? How will her students learn to handle it? Mr. Becker addresses the bigger issue and suggests that there are substitute ways to conform. Will the students buy that? What about learning when to conform as well as how? Mrs. Cantera, who must be wealthier than beginning teachers, supported the fad with a self-help program. Is this appropriate compensation, or is compensation appropriate for helping before and after school?

Situation 2. It was always a struggle to get this year's seventh graders to stand in front of the class to give reports.

a. Ms. Ahn let students who felt uncomfortable in front of the class give their reports from their desks.

b. Mr. Becker had students present in pairs in front of the class.

c. Mrs. Cantera had students give reports in front of a video camera and then had the class view the videotape.

d. (your idea)

Reflections: Early adolescents often exhibit acute levels of self-consciousness. These teachers use a variety of techniques to build self-confidence and ease students into risk taking positions.

Situation 3. As part of an internal school assessment program, the entire grade level was given a set of ten prealgebra problems in math class. The students had to read each situation, identify the problem, and suggest a way to find the solution. They did not have to produce answers, but could work out the solutions on an optional basis. The teachers had to record results for their own classes in their grade books.

a. Ms. Ahn gave each student an "A" for trying and gave bonus points to worked-out solutions.

b. Mr. Becker gave five points for each correct identification and five points for each plausible solution.

c. Mrs. Cantera used the same point system as Mr. Becker but added two points for each completely worked-out solution. She then ranked the total scores and assigned an "A" to the top five students, a "B" to the next ten students, and a "C" to the rest if they at least tried to complete the problems.

d. (your idea)

Reflections: Mrs. Ahn rewarded the affective domain more than the cognitive domain. Whether the "A" was meaningful to the students might depend on past work habits. Mr. Becker also rewarded extra effort if results were correct. Mrs. Cantera compared students to each other to determine achievement level rather than considering individual progress related to ability. Of all the teachers, her expectations most contradicted the optional nature of the second portion of the assignment.

Situation 4. John Jeffreys had grown several centimeters over the summer and now was a pretty awkward human being who constantly bumped into desks and seemed to trip over his own feet. The students called him "Bo Gangly" and laughed every time he stumbled.

   a. Ms. Ahn gave students detention for laughing at others. She told them that John couldn't help it and that it wouldn't last long.
   b. Mr. Becker admonished the students and told John he was a good sport and explained to the class how he himself was an awkward early teenager but became a basketball star in high school.
   c. Mrs. Cantera asked the students if they really thought that was a fair way to treat a classmate and then explained how the bones can grow in relation to muscle at this time of life. She congratulated John on his progress toward adulthood.
   d. (your idea)

Reflections: Many middle level teachers develop means of providing information for understanding the elements that contribute to problematic situations and thus not only support specific expectations for student behaviors but provide transferrable models to related situations.

Situation 5. Students were given cooperative group assignments to research and report on the life cycle of a specific insect and its economic importance. A different insect was assigned to each group.

   a. Ms. Ahn gave directions that each member of the group was to write about a portion of the insect's life and then put the parts together in a booklet. Every student in the group got a copy of the booklet.
   b. Mr. Becker assigned specific portions of the life cycle to specific students and directed them to write up their portion of the report and teach the remaining members of the group. Each group would be tested on its knowledge.
   c. Mrs. Cantera directed that groups were to produce displays that included models, drawings or graphics, and written descriptions. Each group had

to decide which members would work on which parts of the assignment. All group members had to be able to pass a test on the collective knowledge related to the assigned insects.

    d. (your idea)

Reflections: Each teacher provided opportunities for students to work together or contribute to a task or final product. Differences lie in the roles students played in deciding individual responsibilities and in the level or nature of cooperation required for the project as a whole to succeed. Ms. Ahn facilitated cooperative effort, but students were not required to interact with other students nor influence the quality of learning or product output of their peers, as was the case among Mr. Becker's students. Mrs. Cantera's students took on responsibility not only for the quality of learning among their peers but also the initial decisions of role allocation.

Situation 6. The school policy requires that seventh graders be assigned homework four days each week. Policy on follow-up is determined on a class-by-class basis by the individual teachers.

    a. Ms. Ahn assigns the homework but does not grade the students on the work since not everyone turns it in.

    b. Mr. Becker assigns homework to those students who request it or whose parents insist on it.

    c. Mrs. Cantera assigns homework to all students and incorporates the results in daily lessons.

    d. (your idea)

Reflections: Mrs. Cantera's students experience a payoff for completing homework that is associated with regular classroom work. Mr. Becker's system relies on students' self-motivation and community pressure, an approach that probably would not yield identical results in all school situations. Ms. Ahn does not seem to place much value in the homework process or in the role of homework in developing independent learning habits.

Review the approaches used by Ms. Ahn, Mr. Becker, and Mrs. Cantera. What examples can you identify of a teacher's facilitating an environment that accommodates individual learning styles? In which instances do these teachers develop responsibility and positive self-esteem? When do they seem sensitive to peer pressure, to cognitive levels, and to self-consciousness due to differences in physical growth? Compare and discuss your examples with a colleague.

STUDENTS AT RISK

Besides the abundance of variables related to cognitive, social, and physical development that affect the minute-to-minute existence of the early adolescent, there are environmental influences that enhance or complicate a student's chances of successfully navigating this period of transition. Conditions at home, support from the community, and personal and cultural background all affect student attitudes, behaviors, and propensity to profit from school experiences. Students who are at a disadvantage in relation to the mainstream are considered at risk. Students potentially at risk in terms of succeeding in school include those who do not speak English as a first language, are members of minority groups, are gifted or highly talented but unchallenged, are children of alcoholics or drug abusers, do not read and write at grade level, do not eat breakfast, are latchkey children, and must face other adverse conditions beyond their control. At-risk students include children of poverty, victims of stress, and social delinquents. The school environment and middle level teacher play key roles in the lives of all students, but possibly even more important are their influences on at-risk students. (See chapter 7 for more on at-risk students.) Justifiable or not, schools and teachers have been mandated by society to take on an ever-increasing responsibility for extra curricular factors in students' lives. Learning to accommodate environmental factors and weaving them into your understanding of the nature of the early adolescent is an ongoing process.

CONCLUSIONS

The early adolescent is in transition from childhood to adulthood. The change is characteristically one of continued intellectual development, contrasts in thinking abilities, social behavior, rapid physical growth and physiological adjustment, and continued but not uniform intellectual development. Although each individual passes through this period of life in familiar steps, not all do so simultaneously nor are they consistent on a day-to-day basis. Shepherding one individual through this period of life can actually seem fairly straightforward. The classroom teacher, however, is blessed with 30 or more individuals during any given part of the day. Few, if any, are at the same level at the same time. This wide range of stages makes every classroom scene very lively and the task of educating one of great challenge.

Success in designing an appropriate curriculum for the middle level and carrying it out is dependent on recognizing and accounting for the characteristics of early adolescents. The curriculum for this age group must serve to open doors and enhance opportunity. Instruction must take many forms, in both student-centered and teacher-centered arenas, and must nurture growth and promise success for students at different stages of cognitive, social, and physical growth. Evaluation should emphasize measurement of individual progress and should accommodate the variation within any group of middle level students in terms of cognitive development as well as optimal modes for demonstrating knowledge.

In the chapters that follow, we address various aspects of the middle level curriculum and its implementation. As you read, discuss, and participate in the activities, notice in what ways the characteristics of the early adolescent play crucial parts in determining the effectiveness of curriculum design, instructional decisions, school climate, and evaluation.

EXTENSIONS

You can find out more about how early adolescents think, and what they think about, by asking students directly or by engaging them in activities that reveal their views of the world. Below are a few ideas that you can try with individuals, small groups, or a whole class. Be careful to respect individual privacy.

1. Observe a break time on a middle school campus. What kinds of social interaction do you see between sexes? Different ages? Different racial or ethnic or economic groups?

2. Observe a physical education class in a middle school. Describe the physical size and ability ranges in categories such as height, weight, posture, and hand-eye coordination.

3. Choose one of the following concepts and ask several different students to explain it orally, in writing, and/or with drawings. Check for reasoning and transfer of understanding using questions such as "How did you figure that out?" or "How could you explain to someone who didn't understand?" or by presenting other situations in which transfer of understanding could be demonstrated.
   a. What causes us to have seasons?
   b. When you place a playing card over a glass of water and then turn and hold the glass upside-down, why doesn't the card fall off and the water pour out?
   c. How can a heavy steel-hulled ship float?

4. Ask students to express their views on an issue or special topic such as rap music, competitive sports in middle school, or American energy policy. Be sure to pick one topic that is "hot" for early adolescents, one that is of "campus" interest, and one of national concern. Relate their responses to what stages they may be in social and/or cognitive development.

NOTES AND REFERENCES

1. H. T. Epstein, Phrenoblysis: Special Brain and Growth Periods I—Human Brain and Skull Development. *Developmental Psycho-biology* 17 (1974): 207–216.
2. Marion Diamond, Address on the brain at NSTA Regional Convention. Anchorage, Alaska, 1986.
3. H. Gardner, *The Mind's New Science: A History of Cognitive Revolution.* New York: Basic Books, Inc., 1987.

4. R. Driver, E. Guesne, and A. Tiberghien, *Children's Ideas in Science*. Philadelphia: Open University Press, 1985.
5. R. W. Sperry, Lateral Specialization of Cerebral Function in the Surgically Separated Hemispheres. In *The Psychophysiology of Thinking*, edited by F. J. McGuigan and R. A. Schoonover. New York: Academic Press, 1973, pp. 209–229.
6. Jerome Bruner, Edgar Dale, and others have utilized this model to explain natural progression in acquiring knowledge.
7. D. Elkind, *All Grown Up & No Place to Go: Teenagers in Crisis*. Menlo Park, CA: Addison-Wesley, 1984.
8. *This We Believe*. A publication of the National Middle School Association, 1982.
9. Joan Lipsitz, "The Middle School Years." In *Toward Adolescence*, edited by Mauritz Johnson. Chicago: University of Chicago Press, 1980, p. 18.

FOR FURTHER READING

Ames, L. B., Ilg, F. L., and Baker, S. M. *Your Ten- to Fourteen-Year-Old*. New York: Dell Publishing Co., 1988.

Driver, R., Guesne, E., and Tiberghien, A. *Children's Ideas in Science*. Philadelphia: Open University Press, 1985.

Edwards, B. *Drawing on the Right Side of the Brain. A Course in Enhancing Creativity and Artistic Confidence*, rev. ed. Los Angeles: Jeremy P. Tarcher, Inc., 1989.

Eichorn, D. H. *The Middle School* (Special 1987 printing for NMSA and NASSP). New York: Center for Applied Research in Education, Inc., 1966.

Elkind, D. *All Grown Up & No Place to Go: Teenagers in Crisis*. Menlo Park, CA: Addison-Wesley, 1984.

Gardner, H. *Frames of Mind: The Theory of Multiple Intelligences* (1985 paperback with new introduction). New York: Basic Books, Inc., 1983.

Gardner, H. *The Mind's New Science: A History of Cognitive Revolution*. New York: Basic Books, Inc., 1987.

Johnson, M. *Toward Adolescence: The Middle School Years*. Chicago: University of Chicago Press, 1980.

Lowery, L. F. *Thinking and Learning. Matching Developmental Stages to Curriculum and Instruction*. Pacific Grove, CA: Midwest Publications, 1989.

McCoy, K., and Wibbelsman, C. *Growing and Changing. A Handbook for Preteens*. Los Angeles: The Body Press, division of Price Stern Sloan, 1987.

McCoy, K., and Wibbelsman, C. *The New Teenage Body Book*. Los Angeles: The Body Press, division of Price Stern Sloan, Inc., 1987.

National Middle Schools Association. *This We Believe*, 2nd ed. Columbus, OH: NMSA, 1988.

CHAPTER 4

Curriculum-Building Basics

The illustration on this page presents critical issues involved in curriculum building. The scene depicted exaggerates the book-dependent, look-but-don't-touch, rows-and-columns, teacher-as-expert environment that cries for reform. It portrays the importance of keeping what we teach current and the importance of

recognizing the needs of contemporary learners when organizing the content of the curriculum.

As teachers of young adolescents, we need to examine the basics of schoolwide curriculum. With this chapter we shift our focus from knowing about the middle level learner and the educational history of middle level schooling to examining the components of curriculum. One way to see this chapter is to look at it as learning the tools a designer uses to assemble a curriculum, and the remaining chapters as the architectural plans from which to gain ideas about how to employ the tools of this chapter. First we will look at the traditional basics of curriculum development. That is, we will review a set of organizing ideas that have been useful to teachers as they decide what to teach. Then, we leave the technical level and proceed into the bureaucratic arena of curriculum building.

In this chapter, we:

- Review the basic elements of curriculum design,
- Consider the relationship between the design of the curriculum and selected organizational components of the school program,
- Explore ways that teachers influence curriculum building, and
- Compare selected schools and their curriculum designs.

WHAT IS CURRICULUM?

Although the dictionary suggests that a curriculum is a fixed series of studies required for graduation from a particular institution, or all the courses, collectively, offered in that institution, educational scholars do not always agree on the finer points of this definition. Some say it is an organized set of intended learning outcomes leading to the achievement of educational goals, but others argue that curriculum is everything that happens inside a school. Many separate curriculum from instruction; curriculum is simply a course outline, and instruction is whatever teachers do to assist students in learning what is in that outline. John Goodlad offers five separate conceptual levels: (1) the ideal curriculum is that which a group of specialists proposes as desirable; (2) the formal curriculum is that which a state department of education prescribes; (3) a perceived curriculum is that which teachers do to attend to the needs of their students; (4) an operational curriculum is what really happens in the classroom; and (5) an experiential curriculum is that which students perceive is being offered them and to which they relate.[1]

For us, curriculum is the planned school program that includes a set of general goals for all students. These goals are pursued through the activities of schooling, in the content of what is studied, and they provide the criteria used for scheduling, grouping, and organizing the guidance plans for students. Instruction is the implementation of that curriculum. To oversimplify—and to reiterate our original definition—curriculum equals what is taught and instruction equals the methods by which it is taught.

GUIDING QUESTIONS FOR CURRICULUM DEVELOPMENT

How does a teacher, a school, or a school district decide what students will experience during the time they are supervised by teachers? Most of us have never asked this question. We take for granted that students will work on developing their basic literacy and numeracy skills while increasing their knowledge about the world and experimenting with modes of artistic expression and work.

We develop educational purposes or goals, typically, from the study of (1) who our learners are, (2) the society in which they will find themselves, and (3) the knowledge that seems important for young adolescents to have. These three sources are the foundations for a curriculum. They evolved from the basic questions organized by Ralph Tyler in 1949 as helpful guides for school districts and staffs to use in rethinking their educational programs:

1. What educational purposes should the school seek to attain?
2. How can learning experiences be selected which are likely to be useful in attaining these objectives?
3. How can learning experiences be organized for effective instruction?
4. How can the effectiveness of learning experiences be evaluated?

These questions correlate with the curriculum development process of Figure 4.1. They are not meant to be followed, necessarily, in order from beginning to end, but rather to serve as prompts for keeping the dynamic, multilayered process of curriculum development focused on basic issues.

Curriculum must evolve and change to account for new conditions of society and differing needs of today's young people. Setting the philosophy and goals is the basic step in the process of curriculum development. The more a school community works together to establish what it sees as the purpose and goals for middle level education, the more coherent the professional responses to the remaining three curriculum development questions can be. The starter statement most often used by middle level school communities to establish local or district philosophy and goals comes from the statement published by John Lounsbury and Gordon Vars in their groundbreaking 1978 study on middle schools.[2] They suggested that every middle level student:

1. Should have access to at least one adult who knows and cares for him or her personally, and who is responsible for helping him or her deal with the problems of growing up.

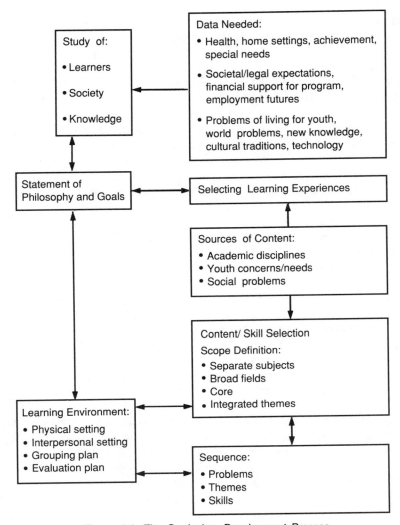

Figure 4.1. The Curriculum Development Process.

2. Should have the opportunity to deal directly with the problems, both personal and social, that surround him or her.
3. Should have the opportunity to progress at his or her own rate through a continuous, nongraded sequence of learning.
4. Should have access to a rich variety of experiences, both required and elective.

Lounsbury and Vars did not propose these points as a complete statement of goals, but simply as a minimum set of requirements. What is striking is their emphasis on the learner as the primary source from which to build curriculum. We agree. We think that the first question to be asked in developing a middle level curriculum is, "Who is the young adolescent?" Any effective curriculum must derive from the learning needs—cognitive, social, emotional, and physical—of the 10- to 14-year-old learner. We discussed these needs briefly in Chapter 3, and the reading list at the end of that chapter provides some excellent resources.

The division of labor in curriculum development needs to be emphasized. To reiterate, the formation of philosophy and goals in the American system of public education requires that the school public be consulted and engaged and convinced to finance their goals. Local districts and schools within those districts are guided by the statements of goals and program suggestions, or mandates, from the state level. Recently, the input from the state level in local curriculum development has grown to the point of requiring districts to become accountable for goals defined at the state level in order to continue to receive full state and federal funding. These requirements come through a set of learning objectives backed up by mandated achievement tests and school program reviews. Table 4.1 highlights recent state middle level curriculum development efforts.

The day-to-day aspects of the development process, regardless of the degree of state-level control and guidance, are a professional activity that needs to include specialists in planning and evaluation, specialists in academic disciplines

TABLE 4.1. RECENT STATE MIDDLE LEVEL CURRICULUM GUIDELINES

State	Curriculum Statements	Special Programs
California	*Caught in the Middle*	Partnership school network
Delaware	In progress	
Florida	*The Forgotten Years*	Regional technical assistance centers
Hawaii	In progress	
Indiana		Center for School Improvement
Maine	*Schools in the Middle*	Dropout prevention
Maryland	*What Matters in the Middle Grades*	
Minnesota	In progress	
Montana		Standards for middle schools
New York		Regents middle level school improvement
Ohio	In progress	
Virginia	In progress	
Washington		Pilot programs

Note: Most states have general guidelines or curriculum standards K–12 that apply to middle levels. Table based on 1989 data.

and technology, and classroom teachers. Typically, a board of education in a school district engages the school administration to organize the initial phases of reassessing the philosophy and goals, or mission statements, for middle level education. Then the detailing and reworking of the school curriculum, or program, is assigned to committees composed of appropriate specialists and classroom teachers. After study, debate, and experimentation, the committees report their results and recommendations for the board to consider and adopt. If adopted, the task of implementing the curriculum, or program, is carried out by district administrators, specialists, and teachers who worked on the development phase. This last phase usually involves in-service activities with teachers who then become responsible for classroom and school level implementation of the program.

GUIDING CONCEPTS OF CURRICULUM DEVELOPMENT

To expand our criteria for looking at a school's curriculum, let us look at some ideas for thinking about how to organize a program. Program or curriculum development proceeds in various manners and arenas, most of which are not perceptible to someone who observes in a school. These planning and designing phases take place outside the classrooms in committee meetings, through individual teachers' personal efforts, and at public meetings. Experts in curriculum recommend a series of procedures and structures as tools for curriculum construction. Added to this ideal set of suggestions is the real set of policies that orient curriculum building. Let us first look at the ideas experts offer.

Selecting Content

A school program must use content and skills that are coherent with the stated philosophy and goals of the district. There are three approaches to the selection of what is to be taught. One is to examine the life and social needs of young adolescents. In his provocative listing, which certainly will be used to stimulate the considerations of program planning groups, James Beane's thesis is that middle schools should focus on the common elements of personal and social concerns. The curriculum themes he suggests are a result of the intersection of early adolescent and social concerns (see Table 4.2).

Beane contends that this priority for selecting content will avoid the pitfalls of more traditionally used schemes of subject matter compartmentalization which inhibit connecting school knowledge and skills to real-life concerns and problems.

The academic disciplines are a contrasting and traditional source from which to select content and skills. Input for content, using this scheme, comes from professional subject matter organizations. A recent publication by the

TABLE 4.2. INTERSECTIONS OF PERSONAL AND SOCIAL CONCERNS

Early Adolescent Concerns	Curriculum Themes	Social Concerns
Understanding personal changes	TRANSITIONS	Living in a changing world
Developing a personal identity	IDENTITIES	Cultural diversity
Finding a place in the group	INTERDEPENDENCE	Global interdependence
Personal fitness	WELLNESS	Environmental protection
Social status	SOCIAL STRUCTURES	Class systems
Dealing with adults	INDEPENDENCE	Human rights
Peer conflict and gangs	CONFLICT RESOLUTION	Global conflict
Commercial pressures	COMMERCIALISM	Effects of media
Questioning authority	JUSTICE	Laws and social customs
Personal friendships	CARING	Social welfare
Living in the school	INSTITUTIONS	Social institutions

From James Beane, The Middle School Curriculum: From Rhetoric to Reality. *Columbus, OH: National Middle School Association, 1990, p. 41. Reprinted by permission.*

Association for Supervision and Curriculum Development invited representatives of different national subject matter organizations to suggest a focus for each area that was in tune with the nature of society. Each author attempted to distill principal content focuses in his or her subject. The synthesis in Table 4.3 provides a second way of looking at middle level content. Not all the leadership of the professional organizations represented would concur with these authors. But the focus each provides forms a very general base for us as we discuss the goals within a given subject and how they might relate to each other.

As we look at both these tables we see the results of widely differing points of departure. Table 4.2 presents a more open, problematic perspective. Skills and content will flow from a development of themes which are not meant to be mutually exclusive. This provides opportunities for organizing knowledge expectations in a curriculum under different titles, or integrating two subjects for certain topics. We can imagine that conflict resolution and interdependence would naturally blend with each other as the ying and yang of a larger theme. Indeed this could be said of most themes listed. Possibly the most innovative aspect of Beane's curricular proposition is its congruence with the foundational questions—Who is the learner? What are social concerns? —deriving from Tyler's now classic curriculum development scheme. The focus in Table 4.3, on the other hand, accepts the traditional division between academic disciplines and

TABLE 4.3. SUBJECT MATTER FOCUS FOR CURRICULUM DEVELOPMENT

Subject	Focus
Social studies	The study of how citizens in a society—past, present, and future—make personal and public policy decisions.
English	The ordering of personal and vicarious experience through language
Mathematics	A language for expressing relations among quantitative factors in a situation
Science	A body of developing ideas, a way of thinking and conducting inquiry, an outlook on the universe, and a complex social and cultural enterprise. Science is concerned primarily with understanding how the world works, technology with figuring out how to arrange things to happen in the way we want.
Foreign language	Meaningful use of a foreign language
The arts	Education in the disciplines of music, art, theater, and dance. Drama/theater is the metaphoric representation of human behavior. Dance is expressive movement.
Technology	A comprehensive, action-based educational program concerned with technical means, their evolution, utilization, and significance with industry, its organization, personnel, systems, techniques, resources and products, and their social impact
Home economics	Preparation for family and home living
Physical education	The study and refinement of human movement
Health	The development of health skills, attitudes, and practices that are conducive to wellbeing.

From Ronald S. Brandt, (Ed.), Content of the Curriculum. *Alexandria, VA:. Association for Supervision and Curriculum Development, 1988. Reprinted by permission.*

attempts to synthesize them. Using this list as the sole definition of content will probably lead to slighting the student-oriented nature of the learning experiences.

A third way to conceptualize the content of the program is from a skills perspective. Listing skills—ability to think critically, to work with groups in social action projects or to solve problems involving arithmetical computation, to communicate effectively—is an approach popular when curriculum developers focus first on being accountable for achievement results in skills testing. We would argue that to begin the process of selecting learning experiences with lists of skills is to invert the logical order of content development. In truth, any topic from the study of the solar system to the war on drugs in the local community can be employed to develop communication skills. The contrary is also true. In other words, a listing of themes without the subsequent elaboration of the skills that can be developed via these themes runs the risk of not taking full advantage of the skill development potential within a theme or choosing a set of themes or subjects that ignores or inadequately addresses vital skills.

As you can sense, selection of content requires that we be sensitive to what social perspective is implied by the kind of organizing scheme we choose. Choosing any one of these schemes—problems or theme-based, academic disciplines or skills—to the exclusion of the others can limit a program. A balanced curriculum needs to incorporate all three of these content selection perspectives.

Scope

Deciding how much of a topic or theme or subject to include in the program is a major task in curriculum development. The "how much" is known as the scope of the curriculum. When you make choices between, for example, an in-depth look at medieval England versus studying the same period in Shogunate Japan, the American Southwest, and Moslem Africa, you are resolving questions of scope. We have used the term *subject* to talk about the *what* of the curriculum. However, there are various ways of organizing the *what* that we need to define and will consider more closely in Chapter 5. Separate subjects, broad fields, core curriculum, and interdisciplinary curriculum are several common approaches to organizing curriculum scope. Let us define each.

1. Separate Subjects. The most traditional manner of defining curriculum scope is by subject area. The back-to-the-basics proponents argue that some subjects are more useful than others. Typically, a separate subject program will have periods of time during a school day when the student studies math or English.

2. Broad Fields. This way of defining program scope fuses two or more subjects. For example, a social studies class studying the civilization of ancient Egypt would learn from art the difference between two- and three-dimensional painting; from technology, they would learn the craft of making paper from papyrus reeds; from science and math they would form hypotheses about how the pyramids were constructed and design models to test them; from language studies they would learn to make a cartouche from a phoneticized set of hieroglyphs. All this would be done in conjunction with studying a series of readings from texts and other resources and videos. Therefore, the students would learn something about the location in time and space of this social system in addition to recognizing some examples of ancient Egyptian art and culture and famous people.

3. Core Curriculum. In practice, core curriculum is a version of broad fields. Middle schools use the term *core* in several ways. Core may be that content essential for all students, or core may refer to blocks of time where students remain in the same setting, typically with one teacher or a team of teachers. Core programs often place language arts and social studies together and less often integrate content from all the basic subjects. The topics studied serve to integrate the separate subjects using a theme such as Life in the Sixties or a problem area such as Making Better Use of Water Resources. Typically, a core program attempts to choose themes or units that foster the study of content and skills from more than one subject area. Projects, designed by students or by teachers, are produced. The scope of the curriculum is then defined by the themes or topics chosen and by the skills necessary for students to develop their projects. Chapter 5 will explore these possibilities more fully.

4. Interdisciplinary Curriculum. The themes suggested in Table 4.2 such as interdependence could lead to an interdisciplinary curriculum. Under this scheme the theme could call on topics from any of the disciplines as they made sense to the development of the theme. For example, the theme of caring from Table 4.2 could involve exploring the attachments adolescents form using literature such as *Solitary Blue* or film such as "Stand by Me," and incorporate a study of the politics and history of local social welfare as it relates to early adolescents and their families. Personal and family budgeting could also be part of the development of this theme. As with the core curriculum, skills would depend on the way the theme was developed with, possibly, agreement to develop aspects of several broad skill clusters such as interviewing and essay writing through all themes studied.

Selecting Topics

Which way of organizing makes more sense? Does a program organized around separate subjects necessarily ignore the needs and concerns of early adolescents and society? Would an interdisciplinary program, such as Beane proposed, fail to develop math and science knowledge and skills? Would it be possible for teachers specialized in one subject to be effective in a program that rearranged or combined or blended subjects? As a teacher you will be involved in evaluating the content model most appropriate to your setting.

Whatever content model or constellation of models a school or district chooses, the next step in the curriculum process is listing the topics within each subject or the themes and their possible subcomponents. In an unexamined program, the units of a course or subject are often defined by the table of contents of the textbook used. Although there are fine texts in every subject, we feel that teachers and school staff will produce a more cohesive program that is tailored to school and/or district needs if they use various sources for devising content topics for each level of the program. Such sources include professional subject matter organizations, state curriculum guidelines, district curriculum guidelines, published text series and curriculum packages, professional periodicals, and educational research findings.

Once the topics are generated, they need to be discussed and evaluated by the group charged with building a program to meet the philosophy and broad goals set out in the initial phase of the curriculum development process. A set of criteria based on the broad goals should be used to rate the list. Table 4.4 illustrates a sample content rating sheet. The criteria employed should reflect the broad program goals.

Other criteria may flow from the philosophy and goals statements of districts, but these three are most common and merit further discussion. Evaluating a topic on the criterion of learner concern and interest places the evaluator in the position of assessing what is best for a student or reflects the interests of students. If students themselves could vote, they might leave out social studies or math. But this kind of result probably says more about how the students have experienced these topics than anything about the enduring value they might have in the students' lives. We must guard against judging the way these topics have been or are presented in favor of assessing the importance they can or could have for student current and future needs.

The criterion of importance with a subject area asks us to consider picking and choosing the most important topics of a subject since time does not permit coverage of all within an area. Proponents of interdisciplinary studies might choose a criterion not related to academic disciplines. From their perspective, a more important criterion would be the generality of the topic. In other words, is the topic one that everyone needs to know or be able to do?

The criterion of societal value causes us to consider whether the topic being

TABLE 4.4. SAMPLE RATING SHEET FOR CONTENT SELECTION

Here is a list of topics to be ranked for inclusion in the seventh grade. Mark each column with a 1 for *highest value* and a 3 for *lowest*. We will use your ratings to begin our content selection meeting.

Topic	Learner Interests	Sources of Value	
		Academic Importance	*Societal Value*
Computer literacy			
Kinds of pollution			
Earth science			
The sixties			
Mathematical problem solving			
Contemporary world geography			
African-American poetry and prose			
Science fiction			
French			
Ceramics			
Folk dance			
Home life skills			
Wood shop			

examined promotes study of various points of view. Topics useful to sustaining a democratic society should advance human dignity and the issues of freedom and responsibility. They should promote cultural diversity as well. This criterion may be more relevant when we consider the ways the content is presented. School programs should be organized to promote student participation in decision-making at school and classroom levels. Recent research findings suggest that cooperative learning strategies may be the most powerful way of providing students with a structure that teaches them not only to contribute to solving a problem in a group setting but also to appreciate students who are different than they are as individuals with whom they can get along in a work or study setting.

In many states the scope as well as the content of the curriculum is prescribed. Where this kind of topical listing exists, the staff of each school will profit from discussing which are the most important topics and exploring how the content from the state outlines can be adapted and integrated to meet student needs and interests more effectively. We will return to this aspect of curriculum development when we discuss the bureaucratic perspective in the last part of this chapter.

Sequencing Topics and Skills

Where do we start with a topic? In what order should subtopics be presented? How do we articulate between grade levels? Can we assume that if sixth graders learn to solve problems involving percentage, that seventh graders are ready for ratios? Or, that library research skills must be taught every year? As we mentioned before, the most unexamined way to sequence a program is to use the tables of contents of the textbook series currently being used in the school. The strength of this approach to sequencing is that the authors of the texts have given a great deal of thought to the order in which they present material. For beginning teachers this structure lends support to the planning process. The difficulty is that most texts may present a vast array of material. We feel guilty if we do not cover it. Yet, we do not have the time to explore a topic in depth if we try to get through the entire text. Another sequencing rationale is based upon your preferences and strengths as a teacher. You may not like measurement in math or poetry in language arts, so you skip it. Hopefully, you will be working in a team of teachers so that your preferences and weak spots are balanced by those of others.

More sophisticated rationales for sequencing include the structure of the subjects, learner interest or community needs, learning hierarchies, and developmental appropriateness. Let us look briefly at each. The *structure of a subject* relates to skills that students must have before they can progress to more difficult ones. Students must understand addition and subtraction before they can do long division. John Dewey advocated the use of *learner interest* as the way to get students involved in a topic or subject. He would have approved, for example, the use of real-life problems such as following a recipe as a way to interest students in conversions to the metric system. Progessive educators of Dewey's period advocated using *community problems* such as police protection or environmental concerns as rationales upon which to sequence content. Under this approach skill development emerged as needed, moving from problem definition to data gathering to comparing alternatives and deciding on action steps. Learning theorists disagree on which way to sequence material. Some propose *learning hierarchies* that move from the generalization to the component parts. Other theorists recommend teaching the elements, then building to a generalization, or from the concrete to the abstract, or from the reality close to the child to that which is distant in time or space. These propositions are often allied with sequencing that attempts to tailor content to the developmental level of the child. Each of these rationales for the sequencing should be considered as we design programs. They are valid considerations regardless of the kind of scope we choose to give the content.

Learning Environments

Giving a well-considered structure to the learning environment is one of the major tasks of program development. Middle level educators have rightfully placed great emphasis on the importance of this aspect of the school program. We will survey two aspects of the learning environment—the physical or material setting and the interpersonal environment—to achieve increased familiarity with the concepts, or tools, of curriculum development. Let us look briefly at each element.

1. Physical Setting. Sometimes a school staff has the opportunity to design a new school to suit its goals and program. Most of us do not. We must learn to work within a school that exists. This does not mean, however, that we should let our physical surroundings dictate the program. As individual teachers, we need to consider the way we arrange our instructional setting. Desks in columns and rows, for example, make little sense for most program goals and objectives. Ideally, your teaching space should be designed to fit your curriculum. That is, science needs lab facilities such as work tables and storage areas for supplies and equipment, while multipurpose instructional areas need word processing equipment, video access, individual places for students' supplies and books, furniture that can be used for flexible instructional groupings. Materials for instruction should support the program. Before computers are purchased, for example, their place in the program should be defined. Are they to be used by every student for word processing? Are they to be used only in specialized labs that teach programming? Our bias is that few students will become programmers and that all students need to have skills that will allow them to use the computer as a writing and research tool. It is unfortunately true that placing such equipment in unsecured areas of many schools invites theft. Computers, then, are a contemporary example of trade-offs that must be resolved between the ideal program usage and the safety of students and the security of the equipment of the school.

2. *Interpersonal Setting*. This is the most dynamic element of the learning environment. The organization of teachers and students truly influences what happens to a program written on paper. Age and achievement factors—age, previous schooling or grade level, scores on standardized achievement and intelligence tests, marks or grades from previous work, and fluency in English—are used in conjunction with factors of teacher expertise, the kind of space available, and the goals of the school program to group students for instruction. Let us focus here on two interpersonal issues—grouping for instruction and advisement—that influence the learning environment.

    a. Grouping for Instruction. Pre-adolescent students, as we saw in Chapter 3, are consumed with finding out who they are and how to relate to the rest of the world. The ways we group them for instruction throughout their school day can influence the conclusions they reach about themselves and their ability to get along in the world. Often we have relied on achievement levels to form class lists, placing the faster or higher achievers together and the slower or lower achievers together. This system is known as tracking. When it is used as the primary basis for instructional grouping, it has the effect of a label. Students know which are the "honors" classes and which the "retards" or "dumb kids." And, what is worse, they usually perform according to their labels.

    Critics of tracking charge that the practice does not provide all students with equality of access to knowledge and is based on several assumptions that are psychologically questionable and socially unacceptable in a democratic society. The assumptions that researcher Jeannie Oakes points out merit our consideration when we are laying out the interpersonal environment or a school's program. Oakes questions the common rationales for tracking. Her reading of relevant educational research argues that students do not learn better when they are with other students who are like them academically. This is contrary to the tradition of ability grouping on math and reading skills so that bright students are not held back and slower students are more easily remediated. Another tracking rationale is that slower students develop more positive self-concepts and attitudes about themselves as learners when not in classes with much more able students. Oakes reminds us that most tracking is based on the assumption that test scores are a valid and reliable way to estimate a student's achievement and potential. To the common justification of basing placement decisions on individual achievement test scores because they are accurate, fair, and appropriate for future learning, Oakes cautions us to keep in mind the limited and transitory nature of individual achievement test scores. A final reason used to favor tracking is that teachers are better able to accommodate individual differences in homogeneous groups that are easier to teach and to manage. Oakes' perspective is that teachers, in fact, do not tailor their instructional procedures to meet the group. Furthermore, within any group with, say similar test scores, there are individual differences in English comprehension, social adjustment, and interests that are more significantly related to successful achievement.[3]

Recent research by Slavin and his associates suggests that we need to rethink the criteria we use to group students. In an analysis of many studies on ability grouping in the elementary grades, which included eighth grade data but concentrated on earlier grades, Slavin concluded that assigning students to self-contained classes on the basis of general ability or past achievement does not enhance their achievement. From this meta-analysis Slavin proposes five elements of effective grouping plans[4]:

1. Students should remain in heterogeneous classes at most times, and be regrouped by ability only in subjects (e.g., reading, mathematics) in which reducing heterogeneity is particularly important. Students' primary identification should be with a heterogeneous class.
2. Grouping plans must reduce heterogeneity in the specific skill being taught (e.g., reading, mathematics).
3. Grouping plans must frequently reassess student placements and must be flexible enough to allow for easy reassignments after initial placement.
4. Teachers must actually vary their level and pace of instruction to correspond to students' levels of readiness and learning rates in regrouped classes.
5. In within-class ability grouping, numbers of groups should be kept small to allow for adequate direct instruction from the teacher for each group.

We feel that these principles apply to young adolescents as well. Chapter 9 discusses strategies for organizing classroom learning with heterogenous groups.

The challenge of making a common curriculum, accessible to all adolescents, is real. This challenge was issued by all the school reform legislation and reports of the eighties. Let us look briefly at some broad criteria for grouping in the middle level. First is the possibility of regrouping for instruction in basic skills such as reading or mathematics. According to the Joplin Plan for elementary schools, students were shuffled across grade levels in reading or math. This meant that all classes would have math during the same time. Favoring this plan is the argument that teachers can more easily plan instruction for a homogeneous group. On the other hand, this plan restricts every teacher's schedule into a bell-dominated routine and, if reassessments and reassignments are not frequent, can serve to lower expectations rather than accelerate learning for some students.

Next, take the case of departmentalization by separate subject where students change classes every 50 minutes and have a different teacher and subject in each period. For teachers specialized in science, this may be a preferred mode of operation. They feel secure in what they are prepared to teach. And teachers not specialized in science feel relieved that they do not have to teach in that area! On the other hand, this kind of schedule may not fulfill the young adolescents' need for stability and getting to know one group of students and one or two teachers well.

Nearly every proposal for grouping students for instruction has positive and negative aspects. Teachers have the task of weighing these possibilities when they make decisions about program scheduling.

b. Advisement and Guidance. Moving from an elementary school to a junior high or middle school environment is yet another transition with which the young adolescent must cope. Accumulated knowledge of students at this age prompted leaders of the middle school movement to make guidance of students one of the cornerstones of their curriculum proposals. Recent studies of excellent schools and the national reports by the Carnegie Council on Adolescent Development support the emphasis on guidance as a fundamental element of the pre-adolescent school curriculum.

Middle level guidance programs begin with the standard that every student will have a close, daily relationship with at least one adult. Building this standard into the school program can take a variety of forms that involve all teachers on the staff as advisors. Most schools schedule a set time, called homeroom or advisement, each day to pursue the goal of providing adult guidance for every student. Three kinds of issues are incorporated in this program: academic or study assistance, social issues as they relate to the students within the school or from the greater world, and personal issues of growing, changing, and relating. Some programs schedule their guidance programs as small-group or class sessions. Others manage to schedule individual teacher time with each student on a rotating basis. Often the school counselor will collaborate with teachers in developing a guidance program. Teachers refer individual cases requiring greater expertise to the counselor while conducting their general sessions with their small groups.

Activities developed in these teacher-led sessions are as diverse as the teachers themselves. Popular ones include SSR (Sustained Silent Reading), community service coordination, peer tutoring, teacher conferencing, socializing games and values clarification exercises, interpersonal programs that teach decision-making skills, and general team-building activities that develop citizenship skills while involving the group in contests with other groups or that lead to an out-of-school group activity. This vital element of the curriculum is discussed in greater detail in Chapter 7.

Structuring the interpersonal environment of a school is an ongoing process that is never finished and can always be improved. Lack of attention to this element in curriculum planning can sabotage a program that has every other characteristic required for excellence. Too much attention to the interpersonal environment can short-circuit the possibility of a well-articulated and coherent program. Beane coins a new term for this in his critique of the reality of many middle level programs. He identifies the combination of overattention to the elements of interpersonal environment with little thought and/or revision directed to the curriculum content as the "curriculum hole."[5] By this he means that the basic issues connected to selecting learning experiences are not debated in the formulation of many programs.

Before we move into considering how teachers influence curriculum in the bureaucratic arena, let us emphasize that even though the curriculum development process as outlined in Figure 4.1 and elaborated on in this section seems complex and cumbersome, it is a time-tested model that can guide construction of a program that is internally consistent.

TEACHERS AND CURRICULUM DEVELOPMENT

Is it realistic for a classroom teacher to expect to be engaged in curriculum planning as outlined in the first section of this chapter? Can new teachers actually implement their ideas about how to integrate language arts and social studies? To these questions the answer is both "yes" and "no." In this section we will explore the ways teachers can influence curriculum by looking at the structure of decision-making responsibilities, directives from state and district educational bureaucracies that influence curriculum, opportunities for teacher input in curriculum development, and challenges of school restructuring.

Decision Making and the Institution of Education

You may not be acquainted with the scale and degree of educational planning and decision making that takes place before the individual teacher meets students. Establishing and maintaining the public school teacher's workplace engages hundreds of people ranging from state legislatures to local taxpayers, from workers of the state office of education to local bus drivers and cooks. In fact, if the amount spent for salaries and capital investment for education in your state were totaled, it would represent one of the state's biggest industries. The list below outlines the hierarchy of responsibilities for making educational decisions and developing curriculum in the institution of education.

Levels of Responsibility in Curriculum Development

State: *Legislative* sets policy concerning financial support, required topics, minimum amount of time spent, general goals for content

           Administrative implements state and federal legislation, serves as consultant to local level, develops curriculum guidelines and materials to illustrate legislative intent

District: *Legislative* sets policy concerning financial support and curriculum following federal and state guidelines and local administration recommendations

Administrative implements local board policy using curriculum renewal process

School: *Legislative* sets policy concerning distribution of resources and rules for organizing staff and students

Administrative organizes program to implement federal, state, and district curricula guidelines in light of student needs, staff capabilities, building and grounds, instructional resources

Teacher: *Legislative* sets policy concerning classroom rules with students and policies within teacher team

Administrative implements school program according to designated responsibilities

Traditionally, school districts have been charged with all aspects of the curriculum development process, with the states setting general goals for education and high school graduation requirements. Some states require that districts follow state syllabi listing the curriculum content and scope and objectives. Others do not. Some states allow districts to select their own educational materials; others require that materials be selected from an approved list.

All states supervise the use of special federal and state funds in local school districts. Districts must guarantee that categorical funds designated to give special assistance to the non-English-speaking or refugee or disabled or low-income students are actually used with these students.

An informal network influences the decisions made at every level of the educational decision-making hierarchy. Studies and critiques of schools written by university scholars, think-tank experts and public authorities inform and sway educational decision makers. The work of E.D. Hirsch (*Cultural Literacy*, on the bestseller list in the late 1980s) is an example.[6] Hirsch, an English professor, compiled lists of factual knowledge pertaining to Western, particularly American, civilization that he advocated all students should learn in order to comprehend a shared set of references and thus become members of a common culture. Many educators incorporated his ideas, increasing the emphasis on American history and literature, at various levels in the decision-making structure. Trends from standardized achievement test data, think tanks, and special commission studies all bombard educational decision makers who are shaping and redirecting the goals and requirements for local schools, teachers, and students.

State Influences on the Curriculum

In the past two decades, states have assumed more specific direction of the curriculum. They have gone beyond setting broad goals for education and have begun to centralize many curriculum decisions. Figures 4.2 and 4.3 are samples

1. **Each student will master communication and computation skills as a foundation to:**

   1.1 *Think logically and creatively.*
   1.2 *Apply reasoning skills to issues and problems.*
   1.3 *Comprehend written, spoken, and visual presentations in various media.*
   1.4 *Speak, listen to, read, and write clearly and effectively in English.*
   1.5 *Perform basic mathematical calculations.*
   1.6 *Speak, listen to, read, and write at least one language other than English.*
   1.7 *Use current and developing technologies for academic and occupational pursuits.*
   1.8 *Determine what information is needed for particular purposes and be able to acquire, organize, and use that information for those purposes.*

2. **Each student will learn methods of inquiry and knowledge gained through the following disciplines and use the methods and knowledge in interdisciplinary applications:**

   2.1 *English language and literature.*
   2.2 *History and social sciences.*
   2.3 *Mathematics.*
   2.4 *Natural sciences and technology.*
   2.5 *Language and literature in at least one language other than English.*

3. **Each student will acquire knowledge, understanding, and appreciation of the artistic, cultural, and intellectual accomplishments of civilization and develop the skills to express personal artistic talents. Areas include:**

   3.1 *Ways to develop knowledge and appreciation of the arts.*
   3.2 *Esthetic judgments and the ability to apply them to works of art.*
   3.3 *Ability to use cultural resources of museums, libraries, theater, historic sites, and performing arts groups.*
   3.4 *Ability to produce or perform works in at least one major art form.*
   3.5 *Materials, media, and history of major art forms.*
   3.6 *Understanding of the diversity of cultural heritages.*

4. **Each student will acquire knowledge about political, economic, and social institutions and procedures in this country and other countries. Included are:**

   4.1 *Knowledge of American political, economic, and social processes and policies at national, state, and local levels.*
   4.2 *Knowledge of political, economic, and social institutions and procedures in various nations; ability to compare the operation of such institutions; and understanding of the international interdependence of political, economic, social, cultural, and environmental systems.*

5. **Each student will respect and practice basic civic values and acquire the skills, knowledge, understanding, and attitudes necessary to participate in democratic self-government. Included are:**

   5.1 *Understanding and acceptance of the values of justice, honesty, self-discipline, due process, equality, and majority rule with respect for minority rights.*
   5.2 *Respect for self, others, and property as integral to a self-governing, democratic society.*
   5.3 *Ability to apply reasoning skills and the process of democratic government to resolve societal problems and disputes.*

Figure 4.2. Goals of the Board of Regents for Elementary and Secondary School Students in New York State (approved 1984). (New York State Education Department, Albany, 1984. Reprinted by permission.)

(continued)

6. Each student will develop the ability to understand, respect, and accept people of different race; sex; ability; cultural heritage; national origin; religion; and political, economic, and social background, and their values, beliefs, and attitudes.

7. Each student will acquire knowledge of the ecological consequences of choices in the use of the environment and natural resources.

8. Each student will develop general career skills, attitudes, and work habits and make a self-assessment of career prospects. Students not directly pursuing postsecondary education will acquire entry-level employment skills.

9. Each student will learn knowledge, skills, and attitudes that enable development of:

    9.1 *Self-esteem.*
    9.2 *The ability to maintain physical, mental, and emotional health.*
    9.3 *Understanding of the ill effects of alcohol, tobacco, and other drugs.*

10. Each student will develop a commitment to lifetime learning with the capacity for undertaking new studies, synthesizing new knowledge and experience with the known, and refining the ability to judge.

Figure 4.2. (continued)

of how New York is assuming a more directive role in curriculum reform. Note that Figure 4.2 sets broad goals for elementary and secondary grades. Such state lists are within the tradition of broad state delineation of educational goals. In contrast, the excerpt of the Regents Policy Statement on Middle Level Education and Schools with Middle Grades (presented in Figure 4.3) goes much further toward actually defining how the program will be delivered. In addition to the excerpt given here, the policy statement discusses other curricular reform aspects of philosophy and mission, educational program, classroom instruction, student support, and professional training and staff development.

To implement these goals, New York designed a Regents Challenge for Excellence Program. Individual schools may receive special state funds for developing programs that reorganize the middle grades according to the criteria of the special program which includes areas of organization and structure, classroom instruction, student support, and professional training/staff development. Many other states have programs that provide special funds and recognition to schools that propose to engage in school and curriculum reform.

Tied to state-instigated curriculum reform is the concept of teacher and school accountability for student learning outcomes. By becoming accountable for results, reformers of the 1980s argued, teachers would focus more sharply on improving student knowledge and skills. Typically, student achievement is measured by scores on standardized tests of basic skills. The fatal difficulty with this kind of accountability scheme was that it avoided the discussion of goals students should achieve and merely accepted the test-makers' vision of what was most important to be learned.

Schools enrolling middle level students should:

- Contain at least three grade levels. Schools with fewer grades may have difficulty fostering a feeling of belonging as there is no permanence—students are either entering or leaving; they are never "just there."
- Have comparatively small student enrollments so that every student is viewed as an individual and receives personal attention.
- Where the total student population is large, have "houses" within schools or schools-within-schools to promote a feeling of family and to reduce the feeling of anonymity among students.
- Have established procedures such as multiyear assignment of advisor-teachers, classroom teacher(s) or teams of teachers for the same students designed to develop long-term personal relationships.
- Use student grouping strategies that maintain heterogeneous classes but group for specific purposes and for brief periods.
- Have teacher teams sharing responsibility for the education and personal development of a common group of students.
- Have common planning time for those teachers and teacher teams sharing responsibility for a common group of students.
- Have schedules with flexible time assignments within blocks of time to encourage interdisciplinary programs and creative time use.
- Provide a gradual transition from the more self-contained classrooms of the elementary school to the more departmentalized structure of the high school.
- Provide a variety of cocurricular and extracurricular activities.
- Promote and encourage appropriate participation of pupils with handicapping conditions in all curricular, cocurricular, and extracurricular activities.
- Have students with disabilities or other special needs, as well as their programs and services, integrated throughout the school building rather than clustered in a separate area.
- Provide support services such as guidance, counseling, and health-related services to all students.

Figure 4.3. Regents Policy on Middle Level Organization and Structure (Excerpted from *Regents Policy Statement on Middle-Level Education and Schools with Middle-Grades.* New York State Education Department, Albany, 1989, p. 6. Reprinted by permission.)

The trend toward more state requirements began to be questioned in the late 1980s. By 1989, according to a National Governors Association survey, 21 states offered ways for school districts to regain curriculum development initiative by applying for waivers to state regulations that blocked their attempts. A new version of accountability grew, called *restructuring*. Under this title the direction of educational decision making began to transfer from the state to districts, and particularly to schools, placing more power over resources with the principal and teachers. Professional organizations supported this building level approach to more relevant schooling. The National Governors Association provided a framework for school restructuring (presented below) that discarded the Carnegie unit (180 minutes per week throughout the school year) view of selecting and organizing content in favor of more flexible use of learning time.

National Governors Association Areas of Restructuring

1. Curriculum and instruction must be modified to support higher order thinking by all students. Use of instructional time needs to be more flexible, learning activities must be more challenging and engaging, and student grouping practices should promote student interaction and cooperative efforts.
2. Authority and decision making should be decentralized so that the most educationally important decisions are made at the school site. Teachers, administrators, and parents should set the basic direction of the school and determine strategies as well as organizational and instructional arrangements needed to achieve them.
3. New staff roles must be developed so that teachers can more readily work together to improve instruction and so that experienced and talented teachers can implement staff development. Greater use of paraprofessionals should be considered. Principals will need to provide the vision to help shape new school structures, lead talented teachers, and take risks in an environment that rewards performance rather than compliance.
4. Accountability systems must clearly link rewards and incentives to student performance at the building level. Schools must have more discretion and authority to achieve results and then be held accountable for results. States must develop measures to assess valued outcomes of performance of individual schools and link rewards and sanctions to results.[7]

Of equal importance, the governors recognized the discretion of schools to design accountability systems coherent with their curricula. As a counterpoint to restructuring, discussion in the national political arena of instituting a national curriculum and testing continued to appear at the same time that the trend toward more local power received support. Tradition is on the side of local decisions. Perceived decline in educational results combined with harder economic times encourages the seeking of measures, like a national curriculum, that promise quality results in student achievement. Clearly, the debate will continue about where the power lies for determining what will be taught in middle level education, as it will at all levels of education.

Opportunities for Teacher Input

Opportunities for teacher input in the school program have always been present despite trends of more or less state control. In fact, most teachers welcome the guidelines about goals, viewing them as generalized maps that can be used for global reference. Their complaint is that these maps do not give enough support, however, to chart their yearly activities. They want a more detailed orientation to plan where they will lead students during the middle grade years. To fill this need, states develop subject frameworks, or outlines, that describe topics and suggest readings and activities. Some school districts develop curriculum guides that give even more detail to the state level outlines. Table 4.5 plots responsibilities for program development. Note the roles of the teacher in program decision making and implementation.

Just how much can a teacher do? Teachers are closest to students and most

TABLE 4.5. PROGRAM DEVELOPMENT RESPONSIBILITIES

Program Element	Decision Level		
	District	*School*	*Teacher*
Goals	May set or adopt state version	May refine	Uses as reference
Funding	Sets salaries, capitol investment, individual	Principal +/or teacher-parent board allocates school budgets, distributes federal-state aid	Discretionary allotment for supplies, events
Program content	Syllabus, tests Grad requirements	Set scope, sequence for grade levels	Select themes, develop units, organize and implement instruction
Materials	Select, purchase texts and supplemental	Teacher team, librarian make purchase lists	Shares, develops, begs, borrows, bake sales
Scheduling	Defines school year, bussing schedule	Defines grade schedule	Teams to refine grade schedule
Student placement	Provides specialists, organize testing	Counselor, teacher team, parents set groups	Monitor-advise students, parents, team members
Program evaluation	Set objectives/ competencies, select tests, evaluation calendar	Check program against district, school specifications	Organize activities that meet district/school objectives/competencies, evaluate students
Physical setting	Building maintenance, repair, improvements	Design best use, plan labs, set grade level "homes"	Arrange equipment and materials in designated settings
Interpersonal setting	Set goals, provide specialists	Set general student-teacher, student-student guidelines	Implement school policy, advisor role

able to sense and respond to their needs. Structuring that response is best done at the building level. By the same token, teachers do not have time to create all the instructional materials they will need or involve themselves with the entire scope of program planning. To help meet this need is the main curricular task of the school district. Objectives and syllabi and evaluation strategies elaborated cooperatively by groups of teachers and administrators are essential supports for instructional planning.

It is also true that programs planned at a state level run the risk of not attending to local circumstances and student needs. However, the support that general guidelines such as broad goals and subject frameworks or syllabi provide is most helpful to orient program planning.

A balance must be struck between the extremes of programs mandated from the state level and of schools asked to develop programs almost without outside assistance. School districts and teams of teachers and administrators at each school site can provide the necessary articulation between these extremes. That point of balance is the middle level of the educational bureaucracy. School districts that call together teachers and administrators from representative schools to develop program elements, pilot them, and then provide staff development for teachers to implement the successful programs are returning to the tradition of curriculum construction as it was envisioned and developed 40 years ago.

As a teacher you may be asked to serve on district committees. If you accept, you should solicit advice from colleagues at your school and keep them informed about the issues being discussed at the district level. Your participation at this level of educational decision making will require extra reading and hours spent in group sessions. This level of program development will probably not be a constant or even yearly part of your responsibilities.

As a teacher, you will engage in building-level program planning to further refine the orientation given in state goals, subject requirements, and district or state curriculum guides. Facilitated by building administrators, you will have various kinds of involvement, some sporadic, some daily, as your school program evolves. Most often you will be working with colleagues in subgroups of teaching teams or grade levels or departments. Sometimes parents will participate in an advisory capacity. You will debate all the elements we have alerted you to in this chapter, and more. Go back to the broad questions proposed by Tyler to help you be clear about what to look at when considering program changes. We hope that you attempt to take a broad, rather than a personal perspective as you engage in program debates.

Activity 4.1: Examining Two Schools

We have surveyed the basic program development and considered some of the issues involved in selecting learning experiences. Let us now look at a thumbnail sketch of two excellent middle schools as a way of seeing how these ideas get put together.

During 1980, Joan Lipsitz of the University of North Carolina's Center for Study of Early Adolescence conducted an intensive study of four middle schools with a reputation for excellence.[8] Her goal was to observe how each school translated its goals into desired outcomes.

As you read these abbreviated descriptions from Lipsitz's study, note your impressions.[9] How are these school programs alike? Different? What scheme(s) do they use to organize content? Fill in the Comparison Chart as a way of keeping track of the two schools. Discuss your reactions to these schools. Would their programs fit in other schools? With other teachers? What is your conclusion about the importance of the teacher in curriculum development?

Samuel V. Noe Middle School, Louisville, Kentucky

Student Body. About 1,000 sixth, seventh, and eighth graders comprise the student body of this school, some bussed in because of court-mandated desegregation, many from low income families identified to receive free lunch and Chapter I funds, 40 percent from single-parent families. There is mainstreaming for the hearing-impaired and orthopedically handicapped, and the program accepts students suspended from other schools for behavior problems. One hundred students are academically gifted. The school is a large, two-story structure, with an open-plan design.

Purposes, Goals, Definitions. Teachers say, "Kids take priority over the curriculum." The central purpose of the school is directed toward helping young adolescents become responsible and self-directed young adults. Teachers meet over the summer to determine their annual goals which are checked, in group discussion, against the school's central purpose.

Organization. The school is highly decentralized into seven semi-autonomous schools: four are multi-aged, and three have single grades with unified arts teachers (home economics, industrial arts, music, physical education, art, media, band, orchestra, Spanish, and independent study) serving the other seven teams. The school day is divided into two blocks of time—team and unified arts—with team including reading, math, language arts, science, social studies, teacher-based guidance, and Spanish. Administrators—principal, assistant principal, instructional coordinator, two guidance counselors, and a practical arts coordinator—are called the Supportive Service Team. They set each group's planning, lunch, and unified arts times. Teams make all grouping and scheduling decisions—for skills, departmentalization, interdisciplinary units, skill subteams, allocation of time, intramurals, teacher-based guidance, and team rules for students. Students in multi-aged "schools" are not known as sixth or eighth graders, and they work with the same teacher team for three years. Students in graded teams stay together as a group for three years, changing teacher teams each year.

COMPARISON CHART

Program	Samuel V. Noe M.S.	Shoram-Wading River M.S.
Purpose		
Organization		
Program		
Results		
Teacher roles		

The principal visits each team daily and is "pleased not to see 55-minute, teacher-directed lessons."

Some Results. Achievement test scores are at the district mean. Scores on the California Test of Basic Skills are above the scores predicted for the socio-economic composition of the enrollment. Fewer than five incidents of vandalism occur annually, much lower than neighboring schools. Ninety percent of students, required to be bussed in for one year for the advanced program class, elect to continue attending Noe. Average daily attendance is from 90 to 93 percent of the enrollment.

Shoreham-Wading River Middle School, Shoreham, New York

Student Body. Numbering about 560, these students come from neighboring Long Island communities. They are predominantly white and middle class: 94 percent of the students come from two-parent homes where only 41 percent of their mothers work outside the home.

Purposes, Goals, Definitions. A printed introduction to the school says, ". . . the approach to education that the middle school takes begins with the fact that it is a middle school, and that it has the opportunity to build a curriculum around the specific needs of 11-, 12-, and 13-year-olds. . . . The school is not, therefore, an 'advanced elementary school' or a 'baby high school,' but recognizes that there is a certain kind of education appropriate to students at this stage of their development."

Organization. The building has four wings opening from the media center. Students are divided into four houses, with two classes each of grades 6, 7, and 8. Grades are kept separate for daily classes in math, English, science, and social studies. Teachers in grades 7 and 8 team for language arts and social studies or science and math. Sixth grade teachers work in teams of two for some activities and across grades for some. Students stay in the same wing for three years.

Program. School begins with a 75-minute advisory for all students which includes a once-monthly individual conference between each student and the advisory teacher. Most students participate in community service activities that take them off-campus, tutor in elementary schools, work in preschools and nursing homes and with retarded children, serve in career apprenticeships in fields as varied as aviation, solar energy, the arts, veterinary medicine, law, politics, and in organizing school-sponsored events for the community as a way of pursuing their goals of developing community responsibility. Students sign up for two-week tours of duty, taking care of a working farm from 7:40 to 8:30 mornings, at lunch, after school, and over weekends. From the farm units on shearing and preparing wool to weave in art, animal breeding and organic gardening in science are developed. Arts are scheduled three times a week in grade 6 and four times in grades 7 and 8. In addition, art rooms are open for students during lunch and before school. Booktalks celebrate reading. Groups of students sign up to read specific titles and then meet every three weeks to discuss one of them in groups of eight students and one adult. Students also write and publish their own books for peers and the public.

Some Results. Teachers are involved in writing grants for new funding. The district invests in staff renewal. Academic scores are well above average, and parents' expectations are satisfied. Discipline is not an issue. No graffiti is on the walls. The one persistent parental complaint is, "How can I get my child to come home from school?"

CONCLUSIONS

We feel that these sketches begin to illustrate several points about curriculum. Effective school programs must be developed by the staff of a particular school in response to that setting and student group. The program elements must be guided by a set of common goals or purposes with which everyone agrees. Program planning uses knowledge from the different subjects and academic disciplines, but teacher creativity and teamwork are required to adapt that knowledge so it will involve students and meet their needs.

The next chapters will explore in greater depth the substantive and procedural issues of curriculum building. In this chapter we have introduced you to some major ideas and ongoing debates about curriculum. To detain you with interesting options for working with groups to set goals and perform the administrative functions of curriculum building has not been our purpose. Rather we hope that you come to the end of this chapter with a greater sensitivity to the effects of grouping and scheduling students, and the effects that collaboration or refusal to collaborate with teaching colleagues in carrying out an interdisciplinary topic can have. How we resolve the basics of curriculum issues greatly affects what students learn.

EXTENSIONS

1. Visit a middle or junior high school. Look at the school as a whole. Try to write a description of the student body, the school's purpose or goals, program, and organization. Report your impression of the school's effectiveness in meeting the needs of early adolescents.

2. Divide Joan Lipsitz's *Successful Schools for Young Adolescents* book into reading assignments among your class and report to the whole group on each school.

3. Analyze *Turning Points: Preparing American Youth for the 21st Century* for data pertinent to developing a program for today's young adolescents. Present your findings to the class.

4. Interview a middle level teacher. Ask about his or her view on the teacher's role in program planning and how it is done in his or her school. Report your findings.

5. Visit a school district curriculum office. Ask to examine their written curiculum for young adolescents. Report your findings to the class.

6. The 1989 Annual Gallup Poll about education found that two-thirds of those surveyed favored national goals for schools and a nationally set curriculum. Do you feel that this is a sound idea? Debate this with your colleagues and with practicing teachers.

NOTES AND REFERENCES

1. John I. Goodlad, What Goes on in Our Schools? *Educational Researcher* (6) (1977): 3–6.
2. J. H. Lounsbury and G. E. Vars, *Curriculum for the Middle School Years*. New York: Harper and Row, 1978.
3. Jeannie Oakes, *Keeping Track: How Schools Structure Inequality*. New Haven, CT: Yale University Press, 1985, pp. 6–7.
4. Robert E. Slavin, *Ability Grouping and Student Achievement in Elementary Schools: A Best Evidence Synthesis*. Baltimore: Center for Research on Elementary and Middle Schools, Johns Hopkins University, 1986, p. 76.
5. J. E. Beane, *The Middle School Curriculum: From Rhetoric to Reality*. Columbus, OH: National Middle Schools Association, 1990, p. 64.
6. E. D. Hirsch, *Cultural Literacy*. Boston: Houghton Mifflin, 1987.
7. National Governors Association, *Results in Education: 1989*. Washington, DC: National Governors Association.
8. Published by permission of Transaction Publishers, from *Successful Schools for* Young Adolescents, by Joan Lipsitz. Copyright © 1984 by Transaction Publishers.
9. Lipsitz's expanded descriptions in *Successful Schools for Young Adolescents* detail more richly the differences in these two schools in addition to portraying two additional excellent schools—Western Middle School of Alamace County, North Carolina, and the Dorothy L. Fisher Magnet Middle School of Detroit, Michigan—is well worth reading in its entirety for a better view of these curricular issues.

FOR FURTHER READING

Alexander, W. M., and George, P. S. *The Exemplary Middle School*. New York: Holt, Rinehart and Winston, 1981.

Beane, J. E. *The Middle School Curriculum: From Rhetoric to Reality*. Columbus, OH: National Middle Schools Association, 1990.

Glatthorn, A. A. *Curriculum Renewal*. Alexandria, VA: Association for Supervision and Curriculum Development, 1987.

Lipsitz, J. *Successful Schools for Young Adolescents.* New Brunswick, NJ: Transaction Books, 1984.

Oakes, J. *Keeping Track: How Schools Structure Inequality.* New Haven, CT: Yale University Press, 1985.

Schubert, W. H. *Curriculum: Perspective, Paradigm, and Possibility.* New York: Macmillan, 1986.

CHAPTER 5

Basic Subjects
of the Curriculum

As teachers of young adolescents we often have uncomfortable instructional expectations placed on us. We might be expected to teach all the basic areas of the curriculum when we have come from a specialized college preparation. Or, we have a broad background and are asked to teach in a specialized area for which we are unprepared. In either situation, part of what we need in order to handle professional expectations is a broad overview of each area traditionally considered as basic to the school curriculum.

Examined in one way, the traditional basic subjects look at different aspects of life. Examined another way, each subject helps us see the same aspects of life through different lenses. English-language arts explores ways to tell about life. Exposure to personal, fanciful, and reportorial voices of the arts and literature, usually addressed in language arts, opens avenues to understanding and expression about any sphere of human activity. History and social science extend our views beyond the immediate into the past, and beyond description into seeking patterns in human affairs. Math permits us to quantify patterns and events. Science leads us to build meaning about how things work and apply our understanding so we can solve problems, create, and invent. As we investigate curriculum through these lenses, we discuss in this chapter the rationale, content perspectives, and skill areas of each of the four traditional subject areas of the curriculum—language arts, math, social studies, and science. Furthermore, we consider what causes subjects to change. Through the chapter activities, we initiate your thinking about the process of integrating subjects in a program. If you enjoy thinking by analogies, you might picture this chapter as learning how to identify the basic food groups. We do not offer you a U.S. Recommended Daily Allowance of each, but you will be equipped to select a more balanced, yet appetizing and varied curricular diet if you can identify each group and know what each contributes to the whole.

In this chapter, we:

- Review the traditional basic subjects of language arts, mathematics, social studies, and science, and their roles in the curriculum,
- Consider causes for change within the subjects, and
- Introduce the process of integrating subjects into a middle level program.

ENGLISH-LANGUAGE ARTS

A middle school principal once said, "Find a teacher who identifies as 'an English teacher' and you'll find a college English major. Find a teacher who identifies as 'a language arts teacher' and you have an education major!" It is true that we bring these conflicting identities and expectations with us from our college preparation. To bridge these differences, we need to acquire a common rationale or set of purposes upon which to develop a cohesive program for young adolescents.

Rationale

The traditional model of English was portrayed as a tripod standing on the legs of literature, grammar, and composition. The competing model of language arts sees the field as a communication model composed of listening, speaking, reading, and writing. One model stresses content while the other emphasizes process. More recent models of the field place literature at the center, as illustrated in Figure 5.1. The model takes literature to be the "stuff" of what is taught in English-language arts. Major literature concepts for middle grades include plot, character, motivation, and theme.

Recognizing that information comes from all kinds of sources, Suhor places literature at the heart of sources of information that can become content. According to this view, content should come from age-appropriate literature. Literature is meant to include not only books, poetry, and plays but also essays, newspaper articles, and documents. Suhor provides a set of criteria for the selection of literature to be included in the school-organized information input in the English curriculum. Selected classics such as *Paul Revere's Ride* by Longfellow should be included for their *cultivation* value. That is, they provide students with exposure to great works of literature. Other works should be chosen for their *connection or carryover* value. Such works provide students with reading material that is relevant to their lives, that gives students connections between their personal worlds and the experiences of others similar to theirs.

Examples are the Judy Blume books as well as teen romances and adventure paperbacks. Suhor suggests a "third c" for selection—the *cut-above* strat-

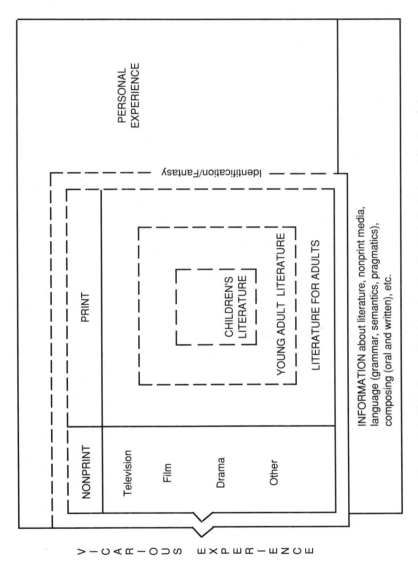

Figure 5.1. The Place of Information in English Curriculum. (Charles Suhor, Content and Process in the English Curriculum. In *Content of the Curriculum*, edited by Ronald S. Brandt. Alexandria, Va.: Association for Supervision and Curriculum Development, 1988, p. 47. Reprinted by permission.)

87

egy. This strategy involves building on what a student finds interesting in popular literature and providing works that are a step up in quality, but on the same theme. Cut-above examples are pet lovers moving from Lassie and Henry's Horse books to *Where the Red Fern Grows* or *The Red Pony*, or girls with relating-to-boys pangs from Sweet Valley High books to *Come a Stranger* or *Solitary Blue*. The difference in these examples is that the cut-above works engage the reader on a variety of planes beyond the plot: character development, a sense of setting, and greater ambiguity and intricacy in the interplay between plot and character motivation in the narrative.

Frequently referred to as the "whole language" approach, the literature-based model employs readings and listening to good writing samples as the springboard to developing the language processes of speaking and writing. Books from various genres are used as themes on which to base integrated units. For example, in eighth grade the social studies topic of political freedoms is stimulated by reading *Animal Farm* and viewing the video *The Wave*, which is about the negative influence on individuality that peer pressure can have.

Nonprint sources of information are the largest contributors to the language arts experience of young adolescents and should be exploited as sources for the English curriculum. The cut-above strategy is especially potent in orienting film, video, and television exposure. Public station and some commercial programming are based on fine literature and significant social issues that can be profitably brought into the classroom with appropriate teacher direction. Discussions of viewing assignments can be used to teach about reporting standards, stereotypes, characterization, theme, and logical argumentation. For example, the Public Broadcasting System's (PBS) transmission of *The Civil War* (now available through Time-Life Enterprises), replete with opportunities to look at any one of these categories, provided a chance to compare the major themes chosen for emphasis in one, or a portion of one, episode and compare them with the topics on the Civil War as presented in various video and/or print sources such as *Red Badge of Courage* or *The North and the South*.

The student's personal experience should be used as a prime source of the English curriculum. It is through processing—writing, speaking about, reading, and listening to—our own experiences that we begin to make sense of them. Expressing how they feel about school or earning money or being part of a group will stimulate many students to speak and write who cannot be reached from the vicarious avenues of books. Finally, the whole language model incorporates information about literature and language and writing as part of the content, but these do not comprise its sustaining element.

Traditionally, students have learned definitions of the parts of speech, lists of spelling and punctuation rules, and then applied them in exercises. They have learned details about authors' lives and figures of speech. According to this approach, the tools of language and skills in identifying and emphasizing them are the primary elements of the curriculum. Information about literature and language are tools for understanding literature, not the major content emphasis. Major literature concepts for middle grades include plot, character, motivation, and theme. The processes of expression are the rationale for sustaining this way of looking at the English-language arts. Developing these processes demands that sources of content be used artistically. Proponents of this version of the subject place less emphasis on core samples of literature as content, preferring to concentrate on developing the skills and processes of expression.

Content Perspectives

As you must have sensed from the rationale for this subject area, not all the experts agree about what content is appropriate for middle grades. Table 5.1 from the State of California comparison of English-language arts programs clearly shows the curriculum perspective of the framework writers.

TABLE 5.1. COMPARISON OF FEATURES IN EFFECTIVE AND INEFFECTIVE ENGLISH-LANGUAGE ARTS PROGRAMS

Effective features	Ineffective features
The framework calls for	*Rather than for . . . .*
A literature-based program that encourages reading and exposes all students, including those whose primary language is not English, to significant literary works	A skill-based program that uses brief, unfocused narratives and work sheets lacking meaningful content or that are constructed to teach independent skills in isolation
Attention to values in literature that reflects the real dilemmas faced by all human beings and that represents traditional and modern classics across all the disciplines	Superficial treatment of values in *safe,* diluted, or sterile texts dealing with trivial subjects or condescending themes
Instructional programs that emphasize the integration of listening, speaking, reading, and writing and the teaching of language skills in meaningful contexts	Instructional programs that focus on only one of the language arts at a time, such as reading without purposeful writing, discussing, and listening
Instructional programs that guide all students through a range of thinking processes as they study content and focus on aesthetic, ethical, and cultural issues	Instructional programs that limit some students, such as the less-prepared or limited-English-proficient, to work sheets and activities addressing only low-level cognitive skills
A systematic kindergarten through grade 12 developmental language arts program articulated and implemented at all grade levels	A fragmented curriculum having little continuity from grade to grade or school to school
A writing program that includes attention to the various stages of the writing process—from prewriting through postwriting and from fluency and content through form and correctness	A writing program in which students are merely assigned low-level tasks and papers are read only for corrections

(continued)

90

TABLE 5.1. (*continued*)

Effective features	Ineffective features
The framework calls for	*Rather than for . . . .*
An oral language program in which all students experience a variety of speaking and listening activities, individual and group, integrated with reading and writing	An oral language program in which only the most verbally skilled students speak often or in which speaking is isolated from other language activities, such as reading and writing
A phonics program taught in meaningful contexts, kept simple, and completed in the early grades	An intensive phonics program extending into the middle and even upper grades
A school environment where teachers of all subjects encourage students to read widely, to write frequently, and to listen and speak effectively	A school environment where teachers of other subjects delegate the responsibility of helping students acquire language arts skills solely to reading and English teachers
A school environment where teachers, administrators, and other adults support the importance of language arts skills to the school program and model effective use of all the language arts, including listening, speaking, reading, and writing	A school environment where teachers, administrators, and other adults demean the importance of language arts skills or offer poor models in their own speaking, reading, and writing
A home environment where parents model effective listening, speaking, reading, and writing and offer appropriate help with their children's homework	A home environment where parents play a passive role as their children are learning the language arts
Teacher preparation programs that provide candidates with (1) a broad background in literature; (2) methods and processes of teaching language arts and higher-order thinking skills in meaningful contexts; (3) awareness of new research about how children learn; and (4) resources offering help in design and implementation of language arts programs	Teacher training programs that emphasize only instructional methodology or the teaching of isolated language skills
An assessment program encompassing the full range of goals of the English-language arts program, aligned with what students are expected to learn in the English-language arts program, and providing alternate strategies and forms of testing	An assessment program emphasizing the testing of narrowly focused, isolated, or low-level skills

Reprinted by permission from pages 3 and 4 of the English-Language Arts Framework, © 1987, *California State Department of Education, P. O. Box 271, Sacramento, CA 95802-0271.*

The Chicago Reading objectives listed on the next two pages emphasize reading skills. In contrast to the literature-based emphasis, this orientation stresses process objectives as the organizing principle. It is important to keep in mind that both these examples are excerpted from longer documents that include, in the case of Chicago, reading lists and further rounding out of this perspective. Nevertheless, Figure 5.2 focuses on reading that lends a skills-based/testing emphasis to language arts instruction.

Table 5.1 highlights school programs that tend to separate reading instruction from language arts instruction and maintain separate strands within language arts that emphasize spelling, usage, and grammar. Proponents of literature-based language programs would make the teacher responsible for deriving spelling lists from what students are reading and/or discussing in all subjects. Usage and grammar exercises would flow from writing and speaking projects based on literature—textbooks in social studies, science, and health; novels; newspaper and journal materials—as the need for learning to handle these forms presents itself in student study of various topics rather than from a set of language texts and workbooks.

What are the difficulties with each of these orientations? The purer form of the literature-based approach imposes a heavy curriculum development responsibility on individual teachers. To remedy this, teachers have begun to develop instructional plans to accompany selected pieces of literature. Typically these plans help the teacher take advantage of the possibilities of theme or character exploration that are imbedded in the work. They also offer suggestions for speaking and writing projects that build on the attributes of the book. These instructional plans have the effect of incorporating skills development activities with the study of high quality samples of literature. Critics of the literature-based approach point out that it opens the door to not exposing students to basic usage and grammar skills in a sequentially organized manner as a consequence of relying on the pieces of literature and/or the individual teacher's ability to extract illustrations and construct reinforcement activities from prose passages.

Activity 5.1: Every Teacher a Reading Teacher

If your special area is not English, compose a list of ways you can develop the skills of literacy in your area. If your special area is English, compose a list of connections you might make between the other areas—math, social science, and science—and yours. Use the excerpted list of reading program objectives from Chicago to assist your thinking. This activity should be done with colleagues of similar special areas and the results presented to the large group.

MATHEMATICS

By the middle grades most students have intense feelings about math. They see themselves as either good or bad at math. They define math as doing repetitive arithmetical operations that are "just for practice" with paper and pencil. By the

Grade 5

LANGUAGE ARTS

Reading

Determine denotative and connotative meanings of words and phrases.
Infer main idea.
Draw conclusions.
Infer meaning from the structure of a word.
Make predictions.
Identify patterns of organization: cause-effect, sequence, and comparison-contrast.
Determine author's point of view.
Identify elements of plot: problem, development, climax, and resolution.
Infer meanings from context.
Identify characteristics of folk literature: myth, tall tale, fable, and fairy tale.
Organize a two-level outline.
Make generalizations from visual aids.
Identify characteristics of expository literature.
Recognize techniques of persuasion.
Identify information through functional reading.
Develop reading skills by using materials written by authors representing different cultures as well as different countries.
Use the library to select appropriate resources.

Grade 6

LANGUAGE ARTS

Reading

Infer meaning from the structure of a word.
Draw conclusions.
Infer main idea from patterns of organization: cause-effect, sequence, and comparison-contrast.
Infer themes.
Interpret poetry and figurative language.
Develop reading skills by using materials written by authors representing different cultures as well as different countries.
Identify symbolism.
Determine character traits and motives.
Obtain information from reference sources.
Infer word relationships in analogies.
Identify author's purpose: inform, instruct, persuade, entertain.
Compare and contrast points of view.
Make generalizations from visual aids.
Interpret functional information.
Provide rationale for predictions and questions before, during, and after reading.
Recognize, recall, and summarize material read.
Infer meaning from context.
Identify characteristics of fiction: science fiction, historical fiction, realistic fiction, and folk literature.
Read for various purposes and identify text to accomplish each purpose.

Figure 5.2. Overview of Reading Program Objectives for City of Chicago. (Excerpted from the instructional program objectives in *Systemwide Objectives and Standards, Grades 4-6,* 1990, and *Systemwide Objectives and Standards, Grades 7-8,* 1990. Reprinted with permission of the Board of Education of the City of Chicago.)

Grade 7

LANGUAGE ARTS

Reading

Relate reading material to prior experiences and learning.
Infer meaning from context.
Make judgments about characters' traits and motives.
Draw conclusions.
Infer themes.
Determine denotative and connotative meanings.
Infer predictions.
Infer word relatlonships in analogies.
Infer main idea from patterns of organizatlon: cause-effect, sequence, and comparison-contrast.
Detect biased viewpoints.
Summarize information.
Use functional information.
Compare information from visual aids.
Identify characteristics of poetic forms: ballad, haiku, limerick, and free verse.
Develop reading skills by using materials written by authors representing different cultures as well as different countries.
Determine author's purpose: inform, instruct, persuade, entertain.
Organize a three-level outline.
Use library resources.

Grade 8

LANGUAGE ARTS

Reading

Read for various purposes and identify types of text that accomplish each purpose.
Infer meaning from context.
Use research sources.
Identify literary devices: flashback, foreshadowing, imagery, sarcasm, irony, humor, figurative language, characterization.
Identify elements of short stories: setting, plot, characters, point of view, theme, and mood.
Provide rationale for predictions and questions before, during, and after reading.
Interpret symbolism.
Interpret poetry.
Compare themes.
Draw conclusions about author's point of view.
Infer word relationships in analogies.
Detect biased viewpoints.
Compare excerpts of literary works from different historical periods.
Develop reading skills by using materials written by authors representing different cultures as well as different countries.
Use functional information.
Infer conclusion.
Interpret parts of a play.
Recall, compare, and summarize information from two or more sources.
Synthesize information.
Understand the textual structure of a selection: vocabulary, content, organization, and author's purpose.

same token, middle grade teachers hold math teachers in some awe because they studied higher math in college while most teachers suffered through an obligatory collegiate course of math for teachers. Yet for the benefit of students and their curriculum, and regardless of our academic backgrounds, we all need to have a sense for the place and importance of math in the curriculum.

Rationale

The National Council of Teachers of Mathematics formulated an agenda for the eighties.[1] Among their recommendations, three lend direction to the rationale for math in middle level schools:

1. Problem solving must be the focus of school mathematics.
2. Basic skills in mathematics must be defined to encompass more than computational facility.
3. Mathematics programs must take full advantage of the power of calculators and computers.

Students must not only be able to perform arithmetic operations, they must be able to understand the mathematical significance of the operations. Students who can perform the basic operations are often only rotely manipulating symbols. By focusing on the "why" behind the algorithmic procedures, we are preparing students for further study of mathematics as well as the quantitative literacy of daily life.

Content Perspectives

Traditionally, math programs for middle grades followed three strands: computation, applications, and geometry. Computation includes the four operations—adding, subtracting, multiplying, and dividing—with whole numbers, fractions, and decimals. Application strands are means to move the basic operations into higher-order thinking by solving problems based on situations dealing with the stuff of daily decisions, not just symbols. Application sections appear sporadically in most programs. Textbooks often use consumer decisions as material for one- to two-step word problems. Step-by-step solutions are modeled in the instruction. Standard geometry topics include shape identification, categorization of angles, polygons, and curves, and comparison of figure size and shape.

In many programs, maintaining skills in computing with whole numbers, place value, fractions, and decimals has taken up the major part of the program for young adolescents. Less time is devoted to estimation, measurement, problem solving, geometry, graphs, descriptive statistics, ratio and proportion, and integer computation. Critics charge that too much time is spent on perfecting long division and percentages, and that mastery of these operations should not be expected until high school. They also criticize the amount of emphasis given to algorithms with fractions, charging that the application is rare for seldom-used fractions with unlike denominators.

The advent of the information age makes imperative the inclusion of calculators and computers as tools for doing middle grade math. Program topics implied in the use of these tools include greater emphasis on decimals, including very large and very small numbers; estimation; scientific notation; order of operations; exponents; and negative integers. Yet many parents and teachers resist hand-held calculators, arguing that students must be able to perform

TABLE 5.2. SUMMARY OF CHANGES IN CONTENT AND EMPHASIS IN 5–8 MATHEMATICS

Increased Attention	Decreased Attention
Problem Solving Pursuing open-ended problems and extended problem-solving projects Investigating and formulating questions from problem situations Representing situations verbally, numerically, graphically, geometrically, or symbolically	*Problem Solving* Practice routine, one-step problems Practicing problems categorized by types (e.g., coin problems, age problems)
Communication Discussing, writing, reading, and listening to mathematical ideas	*Communication* Doing fill-in-the blank worksheets Answering questions that require only yes, no, or a number as responses
Reasoning Reasoning in spatial contexts Reasoning with proportions Reasoning from graphs Reasoning inductively and deductively	*Reasoning* Relying on outside authority (teacher or an answer key)
Connections Connecting mathematics to other subjects and to the world outside the classroom Connecting topics within mathematics Applying mathematics	*Connections* Learning isolated topics Developing skills out of context
Number/Operations/Computation Developing number sense Developing operation sense Creating algorithms and procedures Using estimation both in solving problems and in checking the reasonableness of results Exploring relationships among representations of and operations on whole numbers, fractions, decimals, integers, and rational numbers	*Number/Operations/Computation* Memorizing rules and algorithms Practicing tedious paper-and-pencil computations Finding exact forms of answers Memorizing procedures, such as cross-multiplication, without understanding Practicing rounding numbers out of context

(continued)

TABLE 5.2. (*continued*)

Increased Attention	Decreased Attention
Developing an understanding of ratio, proportion, and percent	
Patterns and Functions	*Patterns and Functions*
Identifying and using functional relationships	Topics seldom in the current curriculum
Developing and using tables, graphs, and rules to describe situations	
Interpreting among different mathematical representations	
Algebra	*Algebra*
Developing an understanding of variables, expressions, and equations	Manipulating symbols
Using a variety of methods to solve linear equations and informally investigate inequalities and nonlinear equations	Memorizing procedures and drilling on equation solving
Statistics	*Statistics*
Using statistical methods to describe, analyze, evaluate, and make decisions	Memorizing formulas
Probability	*Probability*
Creating experimental and theoretical models of situations involving probabilities	Memorizing formulas
Geometry	*Geometry*
Developing an understanding of geometric objects and relationships	Memorizing geometric vocabulary
Using geometry in solving problems	Memorizing facts and relationships
Measurement	*Measurement*
Estimating and using measurement to solve problems	Memorizing and manipulating formulas
	Converting within and between measurement systems
Instructional Practices	*Instructional Practices*
Actively involving students individually and in groups in exploring, conjecturing, analyzing, and applying mathematics in both a mathematical and real-world context	Teaching computations out of context
	Drilling on paper-and-pencil algorithms
	Teaching topics in isolation
Using appropriate technology for computation and exploration	Stressing memorization
	Being the dispenser of knowledge
Using concrete materials	Testing for the sole purpose of assigning grades
Being a facilitator of learning	
Assessing learning as an integral part of instruction	

National Council of Teachers of Mathematics, Curriculum and Evaluation Standards for School Mathematics. *Reston, Va.: NCTM, 1989, pp. 70–73.*

operations without the aid of calculators, or they will become dependent on them and be oblivious to errors in making change or calculating sales taxes.

To highlight the changing perspectives about the content of middle grade math, the National Council of Teachers of Mathematics (NCTM) presented the lists shown in Table 5.2. As you peruse the lists, make mental checkmarks beside topics that were not part of your middle school experience.

Most school programs include some aspects of this list. The list does not resemble the actual math program in many schools in distinctive ways. Strands, or topics, of statistics and probability are often ignored. Instruction is rarely organized around real-life problems that mix topics and integrated subjects.

Skills and Sequence

Increasingly, middle level educators are developing curriculum projects that integrate mathematical operations and concepts with science and social studies topics. Data bases developed from outdoor surveys of flora and fauna apply topics from the areas of pattern and statistics as students graph and categorize their small group findings so they can be compared. Developing time lines and portraying population and other statistics in the various formats—pie graph, bar graph, table, graph—are obvious social studies applications of mathematical topics and tools. Computer-based simulations and data bases comprised of inquiry and problem-solving strategies naturally incorporate the application of mathematical thinking into the problem areas to be investigated.

In summary, we can sense that just as with reading and language skills, in math the idea is spreading that every teacher is responsible for addressing the development of middle level skills. Math specialists address the conceptual development of the content and use a combination of computer-assisted instruction and cooperative learning strategies for operations that need drill and practice and for problem-solving experiences. Math applications in other subjects are needed to round out the vision that students gain of the real-world necessity and power of mathematics in our daily lives.

SOCIAL STUDIES AND HISTORY

Understanding the rationale for social studies is difficult for teachers from other specializations. The kinds of activities they observe going on during social studies are varied: students working on a play about life in classical Greece, students separating aluminium from glass and paper in recycling bins, students drawing their own world maps on graph paper assisted by an overhead transparency image, small groups reading the historical novel *My Brother Sam Is Dead,* a teacher-led recitation on a textbook chapter about the feudal system in Europe, a group session where feelings about the war on drugs are shared. The topics run the gamut from history to current problems. To the untutored eye there seems to be no one thread that ties together this potpourri of activity.

Rationale

Specialists define all these activities as within the realm of social studies. These activities flow from the knowledge bases of history and the social sciences such as economics and anthropology to develop the knowledge, skills, and attitudes necessary to live as a thoughtful citizen in a democracy. This emphasis on citizenship casts a special light on the relationship of information to knowledge. To social studies experts, studying about, say, life in the Roman Empire qualifies as an appropriate social studies topic if students are led to think critically about the information they gather and extrapolate conclusions from their study to our contemporary situation.

The rationale for social studies emphasizes the principles and values of a democratic society that includes study of our national heritage. Increasingly, with the smaller, interdependent world created by nearly instantaneous communication and technology, social studies is moving to include a global perspective that looks at issues from more varied perspectives and helps students to see themselves as citizens not only of a nation but also of the world. Civic problem-solving skills developed around the content of socially relevant issues integrated with developing an understanding of geographical relationships and the span of history coalesce to provide the typical argument for including this subject as a basic one for middle school programs.

Content Perspectives

Since the early part of this century the topics of American history, geography, and government have been studied during the middle school years. Since the 1930s, content for the middle grades changed to accommodate the expanding horizons rationale. According to this content design, younger students studied how the basic needs of life were met in their immediate surroundings such as the family, the school, and the neighborhood. With each successive year the scope of study extended outward from the child to incorporate the state or region, the nation, the hemisphere, and the world. By the sixth and seventh grades, the expanding horizons model included various versions of world history and geography. Typically this translated to sixth grade programs that looked at the contemporary world, seventh grade programs that looked at the ancient world, and eighth grade programs that looked carefully at American history and basic civics. Because this was the last year in school for many students, it was the school's last chance to get them ready for citizenship responsibilities.

Different versions of this traditional content are in operation in the middle level school today. Some states extend the expanding horizons scheme through the seventh grade, focusing on an overview of American regions in the fifth, Western Hemisphere in the sixth, Europe and the Eastern Hemisphere in the seventh, and American history in the eighth. Under this scheme the organizing principle for content comes from geography. Historical focus is kept to a minimum in favor of highlighting contemporary life styles. Another version of middle level content organization keeps the fifth grade as the first general survey of American history, the sixth as contemporary world cultural geography, the seventh as a first survey of world history with greater attention given to Western European and/or Judeo-Christian civilization, and eighth as the second survey of American history and civics.

California is moving to a revision of these traditional approaches to sequencing content. Casting the state framework in terms of various "literacies"—historical, ethical, cultural, geographic, economic, sociopolitical—middle level topics (shown in Figure 5.3) are pre-Columbian to new American nation for fifth grade, early civilizations for sixth grade, the Middle Ages for seventh, and the period from the Constitution to World War I in the United States for eighth grade. Proponents of this sequence point out that it avoids repeating the same American historical survey at three grade levels—fifth, eighth, and eleventh—in favor of giving each level a specific part of the historical chronology to address in greater depth. Further, the scattered nature of looking first at world geography and then at world history is unified by integrating geography and history at the sixth and seventh grades, and employing chronology as a sequencing device.

Many social studies experts oppose giving greater and chronological emphasis to history. Some point out that many students are not ready to grasp notions of the past. Others remind us that most teachers do not have the kind of background in history that will facilitate in-depth focus on history. Still others point out that the California outline throws out some gains made over the previous generation by ignoring most of the developing nations of Africa and Latin America. To overlook contemporary problems that involve the relationships between richer and poorer nations, they feel, is to miseducate students for the world, falling back instead on a Eurocentric version of history. Proponents of greater Western civilization emphasis argue that in order to sustain our American civic culture, all students must be exposed to this version of its historical origins.

Skills and Sequence

At first glance may appear that the skills to be developed in social studies are really from the language arts. Surely, all communication about history-social studies topics is achieved through the basic processes of language. However, in addition to the expressive tools of language, there are three skill clusters that belong to the social studies: spatial and chronological relationships, data collecting, and communicating and decision making. They are all crucial for daily living in our complex world and society.

At the middle level students can grasp the conventions of measuring time and space as well as absorb masses of geographical place-name data. Students need to know not only how to locate Florida. They need to see that state in relation to the Caribbean region to understand weather, immigration, and drug

Grade Five
United States History and Geography: Land and People
America before Columbus
Colonial America
Making a New Nation
Life in the Young Republic
New Nation Expands beyond the Mississippi
Linking Past to Present

Grade Six
World History and Geography: Ancient Civilizations
Early Humankind and Development of Human Societies
Beginnings of Civilization in Near East and Africa: Mesopotamia, Egypt, and Cush
Foundation of Western Ideas: Ancient Hebrews and Greeks
West Meets East: Early Civilizations of India and China
East Meets West: Rome

Grade Seven
World History and Geography: Medieval and Early Modern Times
Connecting with Past Learnings: Uncovering the Remote Past
Connecting with Past Learnings: The Fall of Rome
Growth of Islam
African States in the Middle Ages and Early Modern Times
Civilizations of the Americas
China
Japan
Medieval Societies: Europe and Japan
Europe During the Renaissance, the Reformation and the Scientific Revolution
Early Modern Europe: The Age of Exploration to the Enlightenment

Grade Eight
United States History and Geography: Growth and Conflict
Connecting with Past Learnings: Our Colonial Heritage
Connecting with Past Learnings: A New Nation
Constitution of the United States
Launching the Ship of State
Divergent Paths of the American People: 1800–1850—West, Northeast, South
Toward a More Perfect Union: 1850–1879
Rise of Industrial America: 1877–1914

Figure 5.3. Unit Topics Suggested for Grades Five through Eight in California State Framework for History-Social Science. (Reprinted by permission from pages 57–75 of the *History-Social Science Framework*, © 1988, California State Department of Education, P. O. Box 271, Sacramento, CA 95802-0271.)

traffic news. As they play "Where in the World Is Carmen San Diego?" they are ready to grasp the relationship between longitudes and time zones. They are ready to relate events in time by, for example, sequencing events in Chinese and Amerindian cultures side by side with those of the era of European "discovery."

Data collection and communication is another skill cluster that middle level students are conceptually ready to explore. Indeed, the prerequisites of contemporary citizenship demand a sophistication with social statistics that is new and evolving due to the dramatic changes unleashed by the information age. Hartoonian, in a National Council for the Social Studies bulletin, cogently illustrates the need for social studies programs to develop skills in understanding and judging what he calls "social mathematics." He defines social mathematics to include "abilities that are used when we measure or quantify social phenomena in any way and communicate these measures to others, plus those related abilities that we need when judging the information presented to us as we decide for whom to vote, what car to purchase or what personal economic course to follow."[2]

Statistics and probability from math combined with the data of contemporary and past issues provide possibilities for the integration of math and social studies. The list below suggests some objectives that teachers could use to address this skill cluster.

Social Mathematic Objectives

Grades 4–6

Explore the importance of statistics in society through citing their use in newspapers, magazines, and television.

Become familiar with the use of numbers and graphs in newspapers, magazines, television, and other sources within society.

Using a graphic presentation of a set of data, recognize and describe patterns such as increases, decreases, and trends.

Explore the concept of probability by working with simple models such as dice and coins and also by conducting trial experiments to make probability predictions at home, at school, and in the community.

Explore different kinds of data generated by others and evaluate the sources of those data. Recognize that bias in a question can affect results or interpretations of those data.

Gather data by conducting a survey or by carrying out a simulation.

Grades 7—8

Become familiar with the U.S. census. Know how the census is given, when it is given, what kinds of questions are contained in the census, why the census is given, and what uses are made of the information gathered.

Explore concepts of independent, dependent, and mutually exclusive events. Compare the odds for or against a given event.

Construct scatter plots, circle graphs, frequency polygons, and box plots. State impressions obtained from these graphs.

Distinguish between a survey (sample) and a census (population), and understand when each is necessary, why a survey might be given, and by whom.[3]

The most complex cluster of social studies skills is learning personal and group decision-making skills. Included in this cluster are a variety of strategies from role playing for breathing life into a conflict situation, to simulation games that extend roles by adding rules and more elaborate data or events, to brainstorming as a way to open thought processes and prioritize, to comparing the pros and cons of power decision-making and consensus decision-making models, to decision tree models that structure the evaluation of alternate scenarios or consequences.

Is there a recommended sequence for learning these skills? The kind of answer we get probably depends on the view of learning the respondent has rather than the abilities of students. Clearly, the level of abstraction that students can handle on a Piagetian continuum will be a factor when new concepts are presented. One powerful factor for the children of all ages in learning any skill is interest. Is it necessary, for example, to be able to locate all the latitudes in order to understand seasonal changes? Or all the longitudes to relate the effect of sunlight and Earth's spinning on its axis to the causes of day and night and the passage of time? If skills are embedded in a problem that piques their interest, learners are motivated to acquire the skill. If developing the skill consists of answering the question, "At 1:00 p.m. in Honolulu, what time is it in New York?" most students will have no personal motivation to remember how they found the answer or think about the general concept it represents.

In conclusion, the subject of social studies-history appears to be undergoing a change of content emphasis. The emergence of a more historically focused program that emphasizes geography is appearing as a trend in response to one set of curriculum leaders. Another trend is toward focusing on contemporary global issues and/or local social issues without insisting that specific topics be covered and concentrating on problem-solving skills. Proponents of both these tendencies see their versions of this subject as guaranteeing the goal of developing citizenship competence.

Activity 5.2: Relating Social Studies Skills to a Topic

With a partner, choose a social studies topic and brainstorm how you would incorporate practice on one or more of the skills listed below:

- Put events in chronological context
- Find locations on map
- Plot physical location
- Plot seasonal and weather patterns
- Collect data from some kind of sampling
- Portray data in graphic form
- Evaluate reliability and validity of data
- Detect bias or stereotyping
- Prioritize alternatives
- Defend more than one perspective
- Evaluate group work or group project

SCIENCE

By now it is impossible to be shocked by results of the most recent survey that further documents the deplorable state of science learning and instruction in the United States. Apparently students attending American middle level schools have already, for the most part, lost interest in and motivation for studying science. Furthermore, they spend less actual time in science study than their age-mates in most technologically developed countries. The sense of urgency reflected in international and national studies of school achievement in science underscores the connection made by many policy makers between the economic and political well-being of the nation and our national productivity in science and technology. In reading about curriculum ideas for science for the middle grades, we need to begin making our own connections. Do the recommendations of science educators respond to the criticisms of science achievement? What kind of effort would it take for a middle grade school to organize a science program that incorporated these recommendations? Do these recommendations fit what we know about young adolescents and their needs?

Rationale

Our lives are increasingly affected by changes springing from advances in science and technology. To comprehend these changes and to participate in them as citizens requires an understanding of the scientific way of knowing, or process, as well as an understanding of conclusions and applications, or content, emerging from this process. This way of knowing is the scientific method, which seeks to investigate ideas and solve problems by using processes such as objective observation and controlled experimentation that repeat and recheck procedures and results. Often the problems investigated by the scientific method are based on theoretical concerns about, for example, how a gas will respond to pressure or what effect light has on plant cells. Hypotheses are made about the probable interaction of variables; data are collected while controlling the manipulation of the variables; the data are analyzed; and conclusions provide either support or lack of support for the hypotheses.

Conclusions verified by this method become the knowledge or content of science. New experimental evidence, re-examination of the procedures of previous experiments, and different ways of looking at previous conclusions are continuously causing adjustments and even major changes in our knowledge of the universe. Not only is scientific knowledge continually being revised, the actual amount of knowledge grows exponentially. One of the great challenges is to learn how to access the vast amounts of knowledge acquired through the scientific method.

Process and content are equally important aspects of science. Traditionally, content in science for middle grades is a simpler version of high school programs with, in each grade level, strands of earth science, physical science subdivided into chemistry and physics, with further subunits on electricity, sound, and matter, and biology concentrating on humans and the worlds of plants and animals. In their turn, the high school sciences are watered-down versions of college courses. The program has been, with few exceptions, designed for college-bound students.

Content Perspectives

How can the content of this rapidly growing and changing, multifaceted area be addressed by middle level students? What should be included and what is not essential? How much is enough? Or comprehensible? Policy makers want middle level students to study more science. And more technology. An elite commission sponsored by the American Association for the Advancement of Science recommends that the range of content material in science through the high school level be reduced![4] The commission urged that the subfield boundaries be broken down and that a limited set of ideas in science that cuts across disciplinary boundaries be identified and taught to all students. Rather than having programs that try to cover all the knowledge, programs should select a few areas and concentrate on those that are the most powerful and widely applicable. Integration of the fields of science facilitated by a theme approach to instruction is encouraged. Broad and integrated topics or themes such as patterns of change, constancy, models, systems, and scale would each incorporate concepts from many of the fields or disciplines of science. The following list presents areas of study from which integrated themes can be derived.

Science Subfields Recommended as Knowledge Sources for Middle Grades

Earth Science:	Astronomy, Meteorology, Geology and Natural Resources, Oceanography
Biological Science:	Cells, Genetics and Evolution, Plants, Protist, Animals, Human Beings, Ecosystems
Physical Science:	Matter, Mechanics, Energy-Sources and Transformation, Heat, Light, Electricity and Magnetism, Sound[5]

Beyond integration of the sciences, the commission supported integration of science knowledge with knowledge from other subject areas such as math and history. According to the commission, however, science programs should incorporate math but avoid "mathematizing science" since dealing with the mathematical symbols often increases the difficulty for students and removes their concentration on the science concept being studied. Even so, in topics such as human population, students must depend on mathematical skills, for example, in reading graphs and tables, and dealing with large numbers from census reports. Moreover, the role of science in the way we define ourselves and our place in the scheme of things should be addressed. Our urgent problems of population growth, environmental pollution, acid rain, waste disposal, and energy production all require a combination of scientific knowledge and social/ethical effort.

Examples of the kinds of subject area integration recommended by the AAAS commission resonate well with middle school educators. Some educators propose that we should not organize science around knowledge from, for example, earth science or chemistry, but around problems. They suggest problem solving as the most effective approach to the sciences. An example of a program organized around the problem-solving process is the Future Problem Solving Program. This program uses the version of problem solving popularized by Paul Torrance, educational psychologist. Shrinking tropical forests, the arms race, poverty, medical advances, and crime are featured topics on the 1989–1990 list. Long-term investigations of these problems follow these steps:

1. Research and learn as much as possible about the general topic.
2. Brainstorm problems related to the specific situation presented.
3. Identify a major underlying problem from the list of brainstormed problems.
4. Brainstorm solutions to the underlying problem.
5. Develop a list of criteria by which to evaluate the solutions.
6. Evaluate the solutions according to the criteria to select the best solution.

Problems of concern to students are worked on by small groups. A curriculum service for developing materials to engage students in this process, Future Problem Solving Program, now reaches thousands of students. Materials focus on different topics each year.[6] Teachers should note the difference in these steps and those of the scientific method oriented toward experimentation. This problem-solving sequence rather is identified with social or citizenship issues. Problems investigated by this perspective require an interdisciplinary effort between science, social science, and math content and processes.

Many school programs are beginning to attempt some version of narrowing and concentrating the topics they attempt. Other programs are concentrating more on an experimental, hands-on approach to their current definitions of science which divide school years into units on various subfields such as earth science, biology, chemistry, and physics. In both these perspectives, the emphasis is turning more to learning a method of approaching problems and finding out more about them or investigating science concepts through the controlled processes of scientific study.

Skills and Sequence

Science self-consciously focuses on skills. The hallmarks of good science instruction are the posing of problems and the prompting of hypothesis formulation about problem solving by using observation and recording skills interspersed with demonstrations and lectures on basic knowledge. Even though good science instructors attempt to organize content that is sensitive to the canons of scientific procedure while observing students' stages of cognitive development, the mere exercise of the experimental procedure does not guarantee student comprehension. A new group of investigators, known as constructivists, are helping to unravel the connections between student skills and the sequences of instruction necessary for acquiring advanced concept understanding.

The constructivist view of learning skills, sequences, and science knowledge cautions us that student involvement in the active mode of science—measuring, weighing, recording, comparing, making conclusions—might not lead to concept attainment. Just having students actively observe or conduct experiments is not enough. We must build on the student's own reality when introducing content. However, meaning in science does not come from simply adding new knowledge to what students already know, but from relating the new experiences to what they know. In the constructivist view, the sequence of instruction necessarily begins by exploring the misconceptions, or alternate understandings, that students have about the topic, and thus engaging students in activities that help students construct or reconstruct meaning. Such activities do not necessarily follow the logical order of the traditional "science experiment." Science educators Rosalind Driver and Beverly Bell suggest that strategies include: encouraging students to make their own ideas explicit, presenting them with events that challenge their ideas, encouraging the process of hypothesizing and the generation of alternative interpretations of models, giving students opportunities to explore these alternatives in informal and nonthreatening ways—particularly through small group discussion, and providing opportunities for students to use new ideas in a wide range of situations so that they can appreciate their utility.[7]

Sequence, then, becomes the art of exploring topics in an open-ended manner that uses student cues as impetus for extending and elaborating understanding. Skills in observing and arranging data, and using other processes, are essential to the conduct of science and need to be developed when they are pertinent to the problem or content being studied.

In conclusion, the pressures to add on an ever greater load of vocabulary and concepts to science programs are real. Science knowledge continues to grow and change. Test results continue to indicate that American students know less about science than ten years ago and they know less than students from other technologically advanced nations. In the face of these pressures it is important to keep in mind the issue of how to approach science. Merely putting students through the steps of experimental science does not guarantee understanding. Constructivists are discovering more about the interplay between student cognition and concept attainment. It is apparently true that students are more likely to move toward concept attainment by fits and starts that relate to being reflectively engaged with the scientific method. Exploring in depth a few concepts pays greater learning dividends than covering larger amounts of factual material in science.

HOW SUBJECTS CHANGE

The overview of basic subjects points out several issues that will concern you throughout your life as a teacher. First is the realization that even though these subjects are considered to be the basic diet of middle level programs, many experts are calling for different ways of serving them. If you were to scan each subject description for perspectives that suggest some kind of combining or mixing with the others, you could verify that using themes to organize skill development appears in each.

Another strand common to each subject is the continuing attempt by leaders of the area to infuse it with new knowledge and technology. In every subject, the microcomputer and other kinds of high technology have modified the content acquisition and skill-building opportunities accessible to students. Word processing that assumes spelling checks and permits idea reorganization modifies the way writing can be approached. Data bases and laser discs enhance the problem-solving material available to social studies. Tutoring and drill programs individualize remedial work in math. Laser discs permit dissection-like experiences at less expense and with greater acceptability for antivivisectionists.

In every subject, impetus for change comes from a variety of sources. International and longitudinal student achievement comparisons are current indicators used to urge substantive and pedagogical change.[8]

It is interesting to note that not all the recommendations for change go in the same direction. Some, in fact, run counter to each other. For example, most national commissions conclude that more school time should be devoted to science and math, thus increasing the sophistication of the content expectations. Science and math and some social studies leaders, on the other hand, see a different path to improving student achievement in these areas. Urging a greater focus on thinking processes, they are not anxious to increase the conceptual load. Rather, they propose that fewer topics be studied in greater depth.

Typically there is a lag between educational innovation and local school practice. That is, new data from research and/or new program recommendations and materials from national professional groups are not immediately implemented. Knowing about excellent materials or a new direction in a subject area is just the first step of many needed to bring that idea to a school program. Successful program changes at the school level require that teachers work as a team. School staffs are under increasing pressure to make program changes that incorporate new knowledge, that organize student studies in ways that mingle traditionally separate subjects, that take advantage of new materials and technology. In order to respond to changes in the knowledge bases of the subjects, teachers need to find ways to communicate and plan across their specialities. They need to tell each other what they are doing or what they propose in order to keep the program current.

CONCLUSIONS

This chapter surveyed the rationale and content perspectives and skills associated with the most commonly taught subjects of middle level education. Because the survey was necessarily brief, it admittedly commits two kinds of error. One is the perhaps superficial description of the area with which you are most acquainted. The other is perhaps overestimating your level of comprehension for those areas with which you are least acquainted. You might feel that descriptions outside your subject speciality are replete with terms and comments that do not elucidate much.

Why, then, do we dedicate a chapter on this admittedly incomplete survey? We must start somewhere. Through this survey, we hope that you will become aware of what you do not know and take steps to find out more about the whole program of your school. Becoming better versed in every area will prepare you to help students make connections between parts of their day that might not seem connected to them. One of the frequent criticisms of middle level schools is that we put young students into the roles of high school or college students. We separate their learning into 50-minute, unrelated segments where the English teachers do not know that the history teachers have assigned a report and the math teachers do not know that students need to understand frequency tables to complete their science experiment write-ups. Such lack of knowledge and communication is wasteful of student learning time and ignores opportunities to make student learning experiences more holistic. In order to begin grade-level and sequential planning that makes sense for students, every teacher must have an understanding of the whole school program.

EXTENSIONS

1. Borrow a copy of the curriculum or program from a middle level school. Read the outline of topics in only one basic subject. Do you detect an awareness of the issues noted in this chapter for that subject?

2. Find out which subject area professional organizations are represented in your area. What activities do they sponsor for teachers? Make a resource list, including names, meeting dates, phone contact, dues.

3. Make a resource list of subject area periodicals published at national, state, or regional levels. Include the title, audience, address, and subscription cost.

4. Does your state department of education publish subject guidelines or curricula or subject competencies? Gather these and share them with colleagues of different teaching specializations.

NOTES AND REFERENCES

1. National Council of Teachers of Mathematics, *An Agenda for Action: Recommendations for School Mathematics of the 1980s.* Reston, VA: NCTM, 1980.
2. Margaret A. Laughlin, H. Michael Hartoonian, and Norris M. Sanders, eds., *From Information to Decision Making: New Challenges for Effective Citizenship—Bulletin No. 83.* Washington, DC: National Council for the Social Studies, 1989, p. 51.
3. Adapted from *A Guide to Curriculum Planning in Mathematics.* Madison, WI: Wisconsin Department of Public Instruction, 1986.
4. F. James Rutherford and Andrew Ahlgren interpret original American Association for the Advancement of Science Study, *Project 2061: Science for All Americans.* New York: Oxford University Press, 1990.
5. Ibid.
6. Future Problem Solving Program, St. Andrews College, Laurinburg, NC 28352.
7. Rosalind Driver and Beverly Bell, Students' Thinking and the Learning of Science: A Constructivist View. *The School Science Review* (March 1986): 443–456.
8. We note that most recommendations from these sources are in the direction of increasing the time and content load. We may not agree on the validity of comparing American students who represent an attempt at universal education with those from countries that practice ability tracking. However, most of the selection begins in the middle level years, making the comparisons more valid with the American system.

FOR FURTHER READING

American Association for the Advancement of Science. *Project 2061: Science for All Americans.* Washington, DC: AAAS, 1989.

Brandt, R. S. *Content of the Curriculum.* Alexandria, VA: Association for Curriculum Development, 1988.

Hartse, J. C., Short, K. G., and Burke, C. *Creating Classrooms for Authors: The Reading Writing Connection.* Portsmouth, NH: Heinemann, 1988.

Kulleseid, E. R. Whole Language and Library Media Programs. In *School Library Media Annual*, edited by J. B. Smith. Englewood, CO: Libraries Unlimited, 1985.

Laughlin, M. A., Hartoonian, H. M., and Sanders, N. M. *From Information to Decision Making: New Challenges for Effective Citizenship—Bulletin No. 83.* Washington, DC: National Council for the Social Studies, 1989.

National Council of Teachers of Mathematics. *An Agenda for Action: Recommendations for School Mathematics of the 1980s.* Reston, VA: NCTM, 1980.

CHAPTER 6

Basics of Exploratory Curriculum

Did you make a set of bookends in wood shop or bake bread in home economics? Did you have art and music classes where you learned to measure for lettering a poster or experimented with a musical instrument? Did you have a chance to develop your own physical education goals, or did you have six weeks of volleyball followed by six weeks of gymnastics? Did you have opportunities to participate in theater or dance?

You might have appreciated these activities in your years of middle level schooling without knowing why. You might have welcomed these experiences as classes "for fun" and a break from the "routine" without understanding their purpose in your program. Exploration is one of the basic developmental tasks of young adolescents. At all ages we are engaged in finding out who we are and how we want to relate to the world. But for young adolescents, the questions of identity and relating become almost totally engrossing. Research suggests that this age is the optimal time for bonding to occur between students and the larger society. Such bonding occurs when students have opportunities to show competence in diverse areas, are encouraged to pursue individual interests, participate in classroom settings where fairness is modeled, and have opportunities to exert influence.[1] What we organize in their school lives can either assist or ignore these basic agendas of young adolescents.

In this chapter, we:

- Review traditional exploratory subjects in the middle level curriculum and compare them with new trends,
- Consider possible roles for all teachers in the exploratory program, and
- Assess examples of program scheduling and other logistics related to implementing exploratory curriculum.

TWO VERSIONS OF EXPLORATORY CURRICULUM

The exploratory element of middle level education is referred to variously as the extracurricular or exploratory, or the cocurricular or enrichment strand of the program. Let us look at the way two schools have organized this part of the curriculum. These cases are typical of many schools and are presented as a means of prompting your analysis of the issues that must be addressed when formulating this part of the school program.

As you read these descriptions, there are a few guidelines that you may want to use for program comparison. The list in Activity 6.1 is based on guidelines developed in the 1970s by Lounsbury and Vars, leaders in the middle school movement. The seven points are general indicators for thinking about positive and less-than-positive aspects of middle level enrichment programs.

Activity 6.1: Comparing Exploratory Programs

Fill in this checklist as you read descriptions of Fair Meadow and Oak Grove schools. By each item for each school, place a + for *fully met*, a √ for *partially met*, and a − for *not met*.

Checklist for Evaluating Exploratory Programs[2]

School   *Program Indicator*

F.M./O.G.

_____ 1. Exploratory activity is part of regular, daily schedule.
_____ 2. Student participation in activities is open to all.
             a. Sports
             b. Music
_____ 3. Activities and clubs change with student interests.
_____ 4. Teachers involved in exploratory program.
_____ 5. Students involved in organizing and operating exploratory program.
_____ 6. Students gain skills in independent living from program activities.
_____ 7. Students with special interests/talents can specialize and/or enhance them through program activities.

Fair Meadow

Fair Meadow is a suburban school of 1,000 students from grades 5 through 8. Sixty-five percent of the school population is white, 20 percent African-American, 10 percent Asian, and 5 percent Hispanic. Students come from all over the district as part of the open enrollment plan which requires that the racial balance of the school reflect that of district enrollment. As a relatively new school, Fair Meadow is becoming known as a good school that helps every student to develop personal interests.

The exploratory/enrichment curriculum is organized around three strands: traditional exploratory, life skills, enrichment of the present. It remains flexible, changing almost every year to take advantage of teacher and community talents. To implement the changing schedule a combination of mini-courses, schoolwide activity days, and activity periods are devised for each year with the participation of all teachers. (See Table 6.1.)

Fifth grade students have exploratory classes in a modern language. Music, art, and physical education are integrated into their core classes and recreation times. Life skills are pursued through the organization of "home" governance that includes organizing social activities and raising funds for them. Fifth graders sign up for mini-courses that place them in contact with students of all grade levels. They also participate in schoolwide activity days.

Sixth graders have exploratory classes in instrumental music. Every student learns to play an instrument. Art and fitness/dance are integrated into their core classes and recreation times. Life skills are pursued through the home-group activities that are extended to include special components on decision making and health which covers substance abuse and sex education. Schoolwide activity days, interest clubs, and mini-courses provide options for enrichment.

Seventh graders have exploratory classes in independent living. Elective classes in a modern language or instrumental music or allied arts are available. Physical education choices include intramural teams or fitness exercises. Home classes engage students in organizing social activities and exploring careers. Enrichment classes are available through mini-courses, schoolwide activity days, and special option classes of advanced math, word processing, advanced science, work experience, chorus, and drama.

Eighth graders have exploratory classes in technology. Elective classes are the same as in seventh grade as are physical education choices, home class activities, and enrichment classes.

All-school activity days which are almost old enough to be considered traditions include international day, environmental projects day, sports days,

TABLE 6.1. FAIR MEADOW CURRICULUM BY GRADE LEVEL

Period	Fifth Grade	Sixth Grade	Seventh Grade	Eighth Grade
1	Mod. lang.	Inst. music	Indep. liv.	Technology
2	Core	Core	Elective	Elective
3	Core	Core	Core	Core
4	Core	Core	Math/science	Math/science
5	Math/science	Math/science	Mini-course	Mini-course
6	Mini-course	Mini-course	Physical ed.	Spec. option
				Physical ed.

and career days. During career days and environmental projects days, students sign up for off-campus projects that may involve them for more than the initial day away from school. Sports days and international days are organized through home groups where each group organizes a booth or activity for international day and participates as a point-gaining group in sports days.

Mini-courses are offered to all grades on a three-week basis every six weeks. Math and science expand to fill the four weeks between each mini-course segment. Mini-courses change every year. Some popular ones include electronic music, video production, Red Cross babysitting, pottery, karate, Mandarin, vegetarian cooking, photography, gymnastics for girls, gymnastics for boys, auto mechanics, small appliance repair, beginning drums, nature trail, and signing.

Oak Grove

Situated in an urban district, Oak Grove is a magnet school for performing arts with 1,000 students in grades 6 through 8. The student population is racially and economically mixed, with 40 percent Anglo, 35 percent Hispanic, 20 percent Asian, and 5 percent African-American. Seventy percent of the students come to school by bus. The school day begins at 7:30 for some students and lasts until 4:15 for others.

The exploratory/enrichment program includes two components: career and life skills, and performing arts. Scheduling these components involves one required exploratory and one elective class (see Table 6.2.). Sixth graders have one-half-year of either homemaking skills or shop. In addition, they may elect from among the following: beginning band, choir, drama, or dance. For students not interested in the performing arts, classes in art and general music are available. Seventh graders have one-half-year of either word processing or cooking or shop. They may elect one class from band, choir, drama, or dance. For students not interested in performing arts, classes in sewing, Spanish, and art are available. Eighth graders have one-half-year of homemaking skills, career

TABLE 6.2. OAK GROVE CURRICULUM BY GRADE LEVEL

Period	Sixth Grade	Seventh Grade	Eighth Grade
1	Physical ed.	Physical ed.	Physical ed.
2	Language arts	Language arts	Language arts
3	Social studies	Social studies	Social studies
4	Math	Math	Math
5	Science	Science	Science
6	Exploratory	Exploratory	Exploratory
	Elective	Elective	Elective
After Period 6:	Extracurricular activities		

education, or Spanish. They may elect one class from band, choir, drama, or dance. For students not interested in performing arts, classes in advanced word processing, advanced cooking, and art are available. All students have physical education every day. In addition, students may use their elective time to sign up to serve as teacher or office or media assistants.

Extracurricular activities are scheduled before school or during lunch or after school. They include sixth grade intramural fall volleyball, winter basketball, and spring soccer, with separate scheduling for boys and girls. All students signing up are assigned to a team. Seventh and eighth grades have interscholastic football and basketball for boys and volleyball and basketball for girls. Intramural volleyball and basketball for both boys and girls were cancelled due to lack of student interest and teacher willingness to serve as intramural leaders. Spirit squad for girls is limited to 20, with tryouts held each fall.

Student elections are held each fall for student council. Each grade elects three members who serve all year. They are in charge of setting regulations for campus and hall behavior and mediating conflicts that arise between students or groups of students in weekly or on-call sessions.

Student clubs currently include the Science Club, Chess Club, Computer Club, Hiking and Biking Club, and Service Club. Each has a teacher sponsor and meets every other week.

THINKING ABOUT THE CASES

We have intentionally portrayed two very different conceptions of exploratory programming. What are the aspects of each that you feel best meet the needs of younger adolescents? Which is most similar to the experiences you had at that age? We hope you will use the guidelines in the exploratory checklist on p. 112 to think about and discuss these samples with your colleagues.

We would like to give you our perspective on them by looking at what it takes to put together this part of the curriculum. Building the exploratory program for middle level schools requires a fusion of four elements. First is the general vision of what the exploratory program should provide a student. Second is the training and talents of the school staff. Third is the artistry for scheduling the vision and talents into a manageable operation. Fourth is the stamina to keep the program responsive to changing times and interests.

Let us use the descriptions of these two schools to explore the first element. The Oak Grove program is built around a vision of two elements. First it is a top-down orientation. The exploratory program is getting the students ready for high school by imitating its scheduling, activities, and competitiveness. Notice the six-period day is based on semester-long classes divided into equal periods of time. Extracurricular activities do not interrupt the regular schedule. Club activities are also not part of the regular schedule. The second element, the performing arts, is designed as elective, meaning that not every student need participate. The talented students will become more talented in their chosen specializations.

The vision guiding Fair Meadow's exploratory program is different. Year-long traditional exploratory experiences are maintained for all students. Blocks of core classes integrate language arts, social studies, art and music, and even dance. Home groups are engaged in planning and putting together pieces of all-school activities as well as exploring careers and practice in decision making. Mini-courses provide chances for intergrade mixing and experimenting. There is no mention of extracurricular. The competitiveness of sports is limited to intra-murals and home group participation in sports days.

We are biased in favor of the type of program that Fair Meadow has. But we are aware that Oak Grove-type schools offer many excellent possibilities to students. Our conclusion is that good programs do not have any one recipe. Good exploratory programs are those that a school staff, with their various talents, has worked out together in response to their students' needs.

CURRENT TRENDS IN TRADITIONAL EXPLORATORY SUBJECTS

In the past, junior high school exploratory programs typically designated music, art, physical education, shops, and home economics as separate subjects in the exploratory strand of the curriculum. Historically, the argument in favor of including these elements rested on two points: students needed to explore the world of work since many of them would be leaving school when they completed junior high. For boys, an introduction to the man's world of the wood and metal shop would provide experience in working with their hands and getting a sense of the steps involved in planning and working with a variety of materials and tools to produce useful objects. For girls, through home economics an introduction to nutrition, meal planning, cooking, and basic clothes construction would prepare them for their roles as homemakers. Exploration of the worlds of art, music, and physical education were thought to provide the students with exposure to means of expression that would enrich their adult lives. Typically these areas were separated since no one teacher was prepared to integrate the arts into an exploratory initial experience and since performance-oriented training was practiced in the high schools.

Social conditions have changed since the 1920s when junior high schools became a common part of American educational systems. Students stay in school longer. The women's liberation movement has changed expectations about work and home management. Physical activity is considered an essential way to maintain health. The arts have become more popular than ever before.

Changes in our society are reflected by changes in the content and organization of these traditional enrichment subjects. We will survey what leaders in the traditional exploratory areas highlight, interspersing the survey with examples of exemplary projects. But first we need to consider a limitation on these programs.

Many middle level schools include the fifth grade. We have not included the fifth grade in the exploratory discussion that follows, believing that the needs of fifth graders would not best be served by activity periods and mini-course electives. Rather, 10- and 11-year-olds need continued, unstructured activities with their age-mates at recess. They can profit from special activity schedules throughout the year that are theirs alone, such as professional assemblies or special movie assemblies, special sports fields days replete with races, tugs-of-war, physical fitness contests, and other athletic events. They can attend some of the all-school types of activities such as a winter carnival without feeling they are involved in settings that do not match their levels of interests and/or sophistication. Neither are they ready to profit from class elections or competitive science fairs. They appreciate planning and organizing special party times to celebrate holidays or other special events. Once-a-week club activities can be organized as a beginning of their exploratory program. These clubs can be based on academic and recreational student interests such as science club, stamp collectors, outdoor skills, crafts, cooking, and models. The clubs can be scheduled for one session a week at the end of a day as a change of pace and chance to pursue a special interest.

In the next eight sections traditional exploratory areas are described separately as a convenient way of organizing our discussion. This organization is not meant to imply that school days should also be broken into pieces representing each of these areas.

Music

Curriculum experts in music education define music as a basic subject that should be required for every student through grade 7. By the end of middle level schooling students should be able to sing a variety of folk and contemporary songs. They should be able to play classroom instruments such as guitar, ukulele, or recorder. They should be able to read music and do some original composing. Students should be exposed to music from a variety of styles and periods and be able to compare the pieces in terms of musical elements of pitch, rhythm, dynamics, texture, and form. They should be able to identify selected compositions by composer, title, and musical style. Opportunities to perform in instrumental and choral groups should be part of every student's experience.

In many school districts, however, the distance from the ideal to the real music program is growing. Rather than seeing it as a basic part of every student's education, music is a prime target for the budget cutting scalpel. Schools have several options as they attempt to maintain music as part of every student's exploratory experience. Probably none of these satisfies everyone, but each has certain virtues.

The music appreciation approach has been successfully organized by many schools. Usually volunteer parents and/or college music students serve as enrichment teachers. Using a variety of audio- and videotapes, actual instruments, and visits of community instrumentalists, the program explores various forms of classical and contemporary music. Often, attendance at a real orchestra concert or at a school assembly where a small group performs is a culminating experience for this type of program.

Part-time contracted specialists or volunteers organize another form of music exploration when they produce a schoolwide performance such as a musical comedy for the community. Typically this is an annual event and involves only a portion of the student body. Tryouts and rehearsals resemble adult routines for show production. Subgroups for publicity, tickets and sales, ushering, scenery, props, lighting, sound, costumes, makeup, live music, singers and dancers participate and thus increase the number of students who can be involved.

Some districts are forced to resort to keeping a music strand in the program through an after-school program of performance-based small-group lessons that students pay for or that are funded by the parent–school organization. Other schools are fortunate in having nonspecialist teachers who have enough music training to teach beginning music notation and start students on whole-class instruction on instruments such as electronic keyboards or rhythm instruments. Still other schools organize unique versions of a music program as part of an integrated fine arts exploratory program that may involve not only music, but dance and theater as well.

Art

As with music, experts see art as a basic subject that should be part of every student's program. In their experience with art, students should learn to discriminate surface treatments and patterns of light and shadow and explain interrelationships among design elements. They should be able to describe a composition in terms of position, size, motion, and light. Experiences in drawing and painting with wet and dry media to portray ideas, feelings, and moods are essential. Designing useful objects such as fabric, wrapping paper, furniture, signs, posters, murals for varying purposes—to sell products, communicate ideas, decorate—should include practice in processes of weaving, stitchery, batik, jewelry, photography, and filming. Students should relate works of art to cultures, values, and ways of perceiving the world. Comparing and contrasting artworks from various periods and cultural groups as well as identifying uses of the visual arts in business and industry are essential components of the art program.

Art specialists typically combine student exposure to the basic elements of art with projects in various kinds of media that pose different problems. For instance, hue and tone can be explored in tempera or watercolor with a student collage that enlarges a small art print. Balance and movement can be part of a ceramics project that involves students in slab construction or figure modeling.

Commercial art concepts of feeling and tone can be developed in promotional projects for school activities such as posters, fliers, banners, and bumper stickers. Basic cartooning is often used in projects that teach proportion and composition.

Art programs also suffer in times of anemic budgets. To maintain this vital avenue of exploration schools have resorted to some of the same stop-gap measures that are practiced with music programs. In urban areas with art museums, the museum staff often supplements the school programs with visiting docents who bring prints and slides to the school and provide lectures in art appreciation. Where regular docents are in short supply, arrangements are made to train a set of volunteers.

These programs can be coordinated with social studies topics such as Greece or the 1920s or the settling of the West. Another way to incorporate art in the "basic" subjects is to include craft projects as part of units. Carding and spinning and dyeing wool that is then woven or knitted are amazingly effective activites for helping students understand the intricacies of colonial or pioneer self-sufficiency. Needlepoint samplers, papier-mâché dolls and ornaments, whittled wooden whistles, and bamboo flutes are all craft projects that, although not fine art in the more formal tradition, can provide glimpses of artistic experience for students and be successfully carried out by teachers with no art specialization.

Theater

Middle grade students should have experiences in dramatic improvisation that incorporate use of movement, voice, and language to communicate ages, attitudes, feelings, and physical condition of characters. Experiences in working with written drama should promote abilities in delivering memorized lines with appropriate clarity, enunciation, volume, and inflection. Writing scenes for television using existing characters from prose narratives should be accompanied by developing scenic elements, properties, lighting, sound effects, music, costumes, and makeup. Students should analyze stories, plays, films, and television programs for central ideas, character motives, and dramatic elements of rising action, climax, conclusion, and denouement. Using old radio show scripts, or any scripts, helps students diagram and analyze plot and characterization as well as become acquainted with the writing format employed.

Technology offers a resource for drama that can be constantly employed in the classroom. Students who avoid acting on a stage before a live audience are often highly motivated by video production using a hand-held camcorder. A beginning activity of this genre can be a spinoff of the popular television shows, "America's Funniest People" and "America's Funniest Home Videos." Students can replicate the "trick" camera work they see on these shows as a natural lead to the planning phase of shooting known as storyboarding where a shot-by-shot comic strip dissects the action that when speeded up becomes a moving picture.

Making commercial spots is another favorite initial activity for camcorder theatrics. An idea for producing an enrichment resource for primary grades involves using the videocamera with highly illustrated children's trade books. While the prose line is read and recorded on audio, the camera can zoom and fade, suggesting movement and scene change in a book such as *The Ox Cart Man*.[3] The video result, along with the book, can simultaneously be replayed and "read" by younger children in primary room learning centers or in the library media center. Videos based on reading aloud from any text while taping the print and highlighting the illustrations or graphics are highly reinforcing for English language learners as well.

Dance

Dance experiences should assist students to build body strength, flexibility, and endurance. Exposure to dance performance through live performance or film should alert students to the ideas, images, and symbols of dance performance and choreography. Students should know warm-up exercises for various body parts and a vocabulary of body movements and dance steps. Students should be able to create dance steps alone or with a partner. They should relate dances, costumes, and legends to various cultures.[4]

In recent memory, getting boys to participate in dance has been a test of wills. Teachers usually lose when the boys' culture identifies dancing with femininity. Rap music and the dancing that accompanies it has diminished male resistance. Analyzing the moves made by rap groups is a natural interest grabber for middle level students. Breaking down a video of a rap dance-song into "moves" and inserting a demonstration and explanation of them onto another videotape produced on a camcorder that can be used to teach another class is a challenge that entices boys who would never venture into action for a square or aerobic dance routine.

Physical Education

Students in middle grades need opportunities to develop responsibility for their choices and see that their choices go toward forming their identity. Students should assess their interests, abilities, and fitness levels. Fitness instruction should support students in their individual programs. Development of competence should promote students to choose which sport or dance activities they wish to learn and assist them to work on these choices in greater depth rather than introduce students to many activities.[5] Table 6.3 demonstrates content for physical education.

Intramural and team sports continue to have loyal followings in many middle level schools. In other schools they have been replaced by programs that do not emphasize competitiveness or select only a few of the best players to participate. Newer programs repackage physical education as learning lifelong

TABLE 6.3. THE CONTENT OF PHYSICAL EDUCATION

	Performance Skills	Conceptual Knowledge
FITNESS	• Health-related fitness (flexibility, strength, aerobic endurance, body composition) • Skill-related fitness (coordination, agility, power, balance, speed)	• Principles of training • Relationship of exercise and health • Cultural definitions of health and the body
MOTOR SKILLS	• Support: of the body of objects • Suspension • Moving: the body objects • Receiving force: of the body of an object	• Movement qualities (body awareness, effort, space, relationships) • Mechanical principles (balance, force, angles, resistance, buoyancy) • Principles of skill acquisition • Cultural definitions of skillfullness
MOVEMENT FORMS	• Sport • Dance	• Strategy, competition, sportsmanship • Aesthetic principles • Cultural definitions of sport, dance, and leisure

From Ronald S. Brandt (Ed.). Content of the Curricula. *Alexandria, VA: Association for Supervision and Curriculum Development, 1988, p. 137. Reprinted by permission.*

skills and habits of activity. Stretching, relaxing, and aerobic routines taught as optional, free-time activities during breaks and lunch time are becoming more common. Par courses constructed on school grounds also promote individual fitness. Personal training in such activities as running, walking, or biking by keeping records of distances covered and amount of time spent in the activity after school is organized and monitored by some school programs as a way to encourage individual awareness of growth and well-being.

Activities such as obstacle courses that include descending walls with ropes and walking balance beams, falling into a fireman's net held by classmates, and other activities that look like "basic military training" represent an approach to physical education that emphasizes teamwork and personal growth. These activities are designed to require collaboration, as the tasks cannot be performed by individuals without the help of others.

Health

Students should have access to school health services to aid in disease prevention, screening, and detection. Health instruction should integrate factual information while encouraging students to develop attitudes and behaviors leading to healthy lifestyles. However, health programs must expand beyond the "wellness" approach, which focuses primarily on physical fitness, nutrition, and stress management. Programs must help students with models of decision making that address crucial health issues. The crucial issues of substance use and abuse, accident prevention and safety, mental and emotional health, personal health, disease prevention and control, environmental, community and consumer health, and family life need to be included in all health programs. The current AIDS crisis highlights the need for well-developed health programs. How can schools with no strands in sexuality education in their programs suddenly talk about AIDS?[6]

Health is the major problem threatening the youth of today, according to the recent study on young adolescent education, *Turning Points*, published by the Carnegie Council on Adolescent Development. Based on studies of the health situation of young adolescents as interpreted by expert witnesses, *Turning Points* urges schools to move from the study to the action mode by establishing wellness clinics in schools. This report envisions clinics that would combine a variety of community services within the school, such as health counseling of all types and basic medical services and health maintenance care. Indeed, the urgency of this topic, as portrayed in *Turning Points*, would take health out of the exploratory curriculum and place it as the most basic subject![7]

Many health-related topics are central to the affective strand of the curriculum, as we will see in the next chapter.

Home Economics

All students need to learn the basic skills of adult homemaking. Areas that need to be addressed include consumer issues of credit, comparative shopping, and budgeting. Students need instruction in home maintenance and safety involving the use of electricity, gas, toxic substances, and safe water as well as routine skills in preparing foods and keeping clothes and surroundings clean and repaired.

Some programs still meet in classrooms outfitted as kitchens and dining rooms, or in sewing labs. Newer programs set up projects involving students in planning weekly and monthly budgets through simulated situations that prompt them to gather data from varied sources such as newspapers, catalogues, comparative shopping by telephone, banks and savings and loan offices, as well as health insurance and other medical service fee schedules. Cooking and sewing projects tend to focus on learning to plan and prepare diets and keeping clothes clean and mended as a single, young adult. These programs still have kitchen appliances, but they concentrate on the consumer aspect of independent living.

Industrial Arts

According to professionals in industrial arts, "technology education" is the newer identifier for this subject. Students need to use technology to solve problems. They need exposure to the technologies of communications, construction, manufacturing, and transportation. This includes understanding technology career opportunities and the educational backgrounds they require. Experience in the organization and management systems of business and industry is an essential element.[8]

How shall this vision of industrial arts be implemented? Most middle level schools were built with at least one kind of shop. To let it stand unused seems a waste of investment. As a result, shop classes, like home economics, now have both sexes learning to use the equipment and constructing a variety of projects. To equip a high-tech shop would mean spending a lot of money and probably hiring a high-tech-age teacher who understands robotics and computer-aided design. A less ambitious step would be to teach the basics of electronics through study of simple computer control circuits.

Older programs like Junior Achievement are coming back into vogue as a way of modernizing the exploratory areas once separated into home economics and industrial arts. These programs are often known as the allied arts. Though these programs do not necessarily deal with technology, they do engage students in acquiring entrepreneurial skills. Under this approach students learn the rudiments of capitalism through actually forming a company, developing product ideas, doing market studies, and finally, producing and selling their product. Stock is sold, and profits are distributed. Teamwork and decision making, so desired as skills by business leaders, are required at every step of the venture. Versions of career education are also more frequently found as part of the allied arts. Videos, professionals visiting schools, and field trips to work sites are orchestrated to give the young adolescent visions of the kinds of work roles people assume in various industries.

Activity 6.2: Integrating the Exploratory Areas

Within your special area, plan on activity that incorporates one or more of the ideas from the current thinking about the "traditional" exploratory areas. Share your plan with the class.

STRATEGIES FOR EXPANDING
THE EXPLORATORY PROGRAM

Do these descriptions fit your knowledge of what happens in the exploratory strand of middle schooling? Have the school enrichment and exploratory programs for the middle levels changed in recent years? The answer is mixed. There is a gap between the ideals of exploratory content described by curriculum leaders and actual school programs. Certainly, some students have opportunities in all these areas in a few schools. In most, however, the content of the exploratory program rests on the preparation areas of teacher education programs that were developed to supply the historical needs of traditional junior high schools. What can be done about updating and enriching the opportunities for exploration for today's young adolescents? The next section provides some strategies that many schools are adopting.

Criticisms of the traditional enrichment program claim that the programs:

- Are inappropriately competitive
- Do not provide equal access to all students
- Are not part of the regular school experience
- Take too much time
- Do not meet the needs of students
- Are designed to specialize rather than explore and enrich.

School staffs are taking these criticisms into account by organizing exploratory programs that are not limited by the parameters of a semester-long course that meets for 40 minutes for two to five times a week. Let us sample some of these formats.

Activity Periods

Students need time to socialize while being involved in exploring an interest. Activity periods provide an opportunity for both. That is, students pursue an activity in a more naturalistic setting than classroom organizations permit. Activity periods are a newer version of the extracurricular program. Instead of giving students the option of whether to participate, schools are planning activity periods as an integral part of every student's year-long program. They are designed to be recreational and lead to the development of out-of-school and life-long leisure pursuits.

Scheduling activity periods in the middle of the day gives a needed break from the more rigorous, controlled atmosphere of regular studies. Some schools schedule these periods once a week. Schools with highly developed programs have activity periods three times a week. Typical activities for these periods include many of the titles familiar in the extracurricular repertoire: intramural sports, games such as chess or cards or simulations, computers, band, chorus, newspaper, model building, movies or videos, service activities, tutors, teacher assistants, rap room for music listening and conversing, stage band. Activity periods should be organized around student interests, which means that some activities will grow in popularity while others will need to be replaced because they attract fewer students.

Space, equipment, and supervision must be organized for each activity. The objective of the activity and how much time students need to be involved should be clear to the students when they make their choices. For example, learning to play volleyball and then participating in team games can take six weeks in contrast to activities of a drop-in nature such as rap room or movies or card room. Less formal activities such as a card room need to be supervised and organized, teaching the rules of various games or setting up tournaments for students who are avidly interested in one type of card game.

Mini-Courses

Mini-courses are a spinoff from the original electives version of enrichment as practiced in traditional junior and senior high schools. They are different from exploratory classes in that they do not last a full semester and they offer students a larger choice of topics. Mini-courses differ from activity periods because they typically are related to the school's academic rather than recreational goals. Like activity period offerings, however, mini-courses are exploratory in nature. Essentially, a mini-course should provide students with an excursion into a special facet of a topic that takes the student away from required learnings of regular classes. Guest speakers, field trips, special videos, hands-on practice with materials or tools are features of mini-courses. They are concentrated. They can last for a day or two or be given two afternoons a week for two to six weeks.

Topics for mini-courses are as varied as the talent, interests, and recruitment abilities of a school staff. Some course titles might include consumer education, auto mechanics, aviation, first aid, math puzzles, astronomy, Russian, poetry, Greek mythology. Note the active quality of these topics—they bring to mind a variety of activities, including practicing first aid techniques, doing math puzzles, learning to speak or sing in Russian, learning basic car repairs, doing comparative shopping and budgeting, practicing the principles of flight, writing poetry.

In organizing the mini-course, as with the activity period, student interests must be taken into account, and students need to be informed about the choices they have. Some schools organize mini-course handouts that students can study in their homerooms before signing up. These handouts include a description (see sample below) written in marketing language of what will happen, where the course will meet, what grades can attend and how many may sign up, and what kinds of equipment and materials will be used.

Sample Mini-Course Description[9]
Poetry: Its Appreciation and Enjoyment
Poetry can be fun! Sounds corny—think someone is trying to put you on? A look at poetry through the world of art, music, and videotape. Listen to poetry on tapes, tape a poem yourself, write a poem and then have it set to music. Draw or paint a poem and then put it to words, or write a poem and then draw or paint it. Watch poetry on television and then videotape yourself and others doing a poetry reading.

You will have a chance to look at poetry in a variety of ways and, most important, you can pick and choose those poetry activities you wish to pursue.

Room 102   Boys and girls (limit 25)   Grades 5,6,7,8

Resources: Cassette recorders, blank tapes, commercial poetry tapes, videotape outfit, blank videotapes, art supplies.

Schoolwide Activities

The schoolwide activity gives students a chance to participate in special events. Both student-created on-campus and off-campus events make good schoolwide activities. Schoolwide activities differ from the traditional interscholastic competitions or dances that draw participants and observers from across the school. Schoolwide activities also differ from the traditional assemblies that have special programs for the whole student body or that mark special school occasions. All students participate in schoolwide activities because they are scheduled during the day.

The intent is to promote school spirit and ways to practice large-scale cooperative ventures related to the program's learning objectives by involving students in an activity beyond his or her home class or grade. Seasonal carnivals or celebrations such as Spring Fair or Winter Carnival or Fall Follies are typical fun- and fund-raisers that homerooms organize and transport to the multipurpose room or school grounds for a day or evening. Homeroom groups organize different activities and games, including the decorations, equipment, and prizes. Students staff their part of the large event and participate as individuals or groups in the activities of other homerooms. Other organizing themes for all-school events are International Day, Sports Day, or Olympic Day.

Some schools plan schoolwide days that are culminations of coordinated study in various classes. These are typically done by grade level. Often they are organized as living history days. Themes revolve around Renaissance Faires for seventh grade, Roaring Fifties for eighth grades, American Heroes or Colonial Times for fifth grade, and World Cultures for sixth grade. On these days students come to school in costumes. They prepare foods and participate in games, dances, and presentations that re-create their learnings from core studies.

Other schools respond to current events with schoolwide days where each subject organizes activities related to the event. Several schools near San Francisco and Oakland put together Baseball Day in celebration of the Bay Area World Series of 1989. Math classes did problems in figuring batting averages and looked at player and team statistics to predict trends and set probabilities on wagers. Core classes looked at poetry and literature about baseball and researched historical questions about the game. Science looked at the physics of baseball by looking at concepts such as velocity, force, and torque.

Traditional schoolwide days that enrich the goals of the school should be maintained. Career Days and Environment Days are good examples. Before these events, students sign up for several choices which are sorted and sent back to each student as their schedule for the day. During career day, for example, a sixth grade student might spend the morning with a journalist who would describe the kinds of jobs journalists do in print and media, followed by a hands-on activity of writing and producing two-minute segments for the local news channel. During lunch the student attends a brown-bag session with a parent who tells about his work at the post office. The afternoon is spent with a body-building salon owner who discusses how she runs her business and leads a low-impact aerobics session.

For one day students were placed in mixed-grade groups that responded to their individual choices. A committee of teachers solicited outside career representatives, asking them to contribute a day that presented information and involved students actively during a morning and afternoon session. Parents were solicited to donate their lunch hours to lead small group sessions telling about their work. Choosing schoolwide days that enhance the curricular goals of the school requires long-range planning by the staff. Experienced middle school teachers recommend that committee assignments and dates for a school year be set before the end of the previous school year. Experienced staff members also recommend that enough activities be organized so that large numbers of students can be involved. For example, foot races and individual-championship-type activities should be slighted in favor of continuous turn-taking activities that are short, can be repeated, and reward all who participate.

PUTTING TOGETHER AN EXPLORATORY PROGRAM

Implementing a renewed exploratory program in middle level schools cannot be done by building administrators who put together a master schedule for teachers to follow. Whole-staff debate and consensus-building about the goals and teacher participation necessary for the exploratory program are crucial. Putting together a renewed program involves, then, teacher assessment and planning, student involvement, and, finally, scheduling. Let us look briefly at each.

Using Teacher Preparation and Interests

What hobbies and interests do you have? What areas within your subject specialty would you like to have more time to explore? What kinds of organizing roles do you prefer—recruiting outside resources? Organizing student work teams? Doing editorial and clerical work? These are the self-assessment areas every staff member in middle level schools needs to answer in order for the school to build a data base for putting together the exploratory strand of the program. You should anticipate that, as a middle level teacher, a regular and expected part of your teaching assignment includes responsibilities for the exploratory program.

If your university preparation concentrated on a single subject, typically you will need to enrich your subject preparation formally to include the teaching of reading and either a broader version of your subject or a related subject just to handle the academic side of your assignment. Your depth of preparation, however, can have payoffs for the exploratory part of your teaching assignment. For example, if your background is strong in math, you can develop facets of it for mini-courses in statistics, using computers in problem solving or beginning geometry or doing math puzzles with manipulatives. If your special area is English and you love twentieth century American writers, you can develop mini-courses around nearly any juvenile fiction work. If your area is American history, your mini-course ideas could concentrate on local history sleuthing in cemeteries or local newspaper files or the county assessor's office, or you could work on the lives of important local figures or the daily lives of local people in certain periods.

If you are a home economics or shop teacher you probably have adapted your program to include both boys and girls. You can add spice to your program by decanting your semester-long course into the half-bottles of mini-courses. Rather than doing a semester of foods, several shorter topics could be offered such as vegetarian cooking, microwave food preparation, low-calorie desserts, baking bread. Shop courses could be re-packaged into mini-topics such as bicycle repair, basic electronics, painting and wood finishing, cleaning and caring for electronic equipment. Typical units from general music and art classes make great mini-courses—watercolor basics, silk printing, rhythm and blues, electronic music.

If your university preparation prepared you for diversified or multisubject teaching, you might have some specializations you are not using in your regular teaching that would be fine additions to the exploratory program. Did you take a course in storytelling or children's theater or movement and dance? These activities can be linked to, for example, an historical period or culture: Greek drama and chorus, American colonial crafts, songs of slavery and liberation in America.

A general guide to putting together an exploratory program is presented below. It needs to be debated and understood by the entire staff. There are no short-cuts to developing or renewing this program. The steps take time. They require commitment and buy-in from all members of the staff. Extra money and resources may be required for some of the program improvements. However, the principal investment for renewing most exploratory programs comes from the thinking and group effort of a teaching staff.

Steps in Exploratory Program Development

1. Survey current program: What is the content of current offerings? How many students participate? Who participates?
2. Review program goals: Do they meet today's societal and developmental (academic, social, recreational) needs?
3. Survey faculty strengths and interests: What academic facets? What outside resources do they know? What kinds of organizational roles do they prefer?
4. Survey student opinion: What suggestions do they make about the cur-

rent program? What interests do they express? How do these opinions relate to program goals?

5. Decide topics and format(s) to develop for renewed exploratory program: Keep and/or modify current program content and/or schedule? Formats and topics to add to program? Which changes are to be introduced first year, second year, third year?

6. Appoint committees to develop proposals for each agreed upon change: What are the objectives? Who will organize? Which students? Schedule suggestions? How will change be evaluated?

7. Present plan to faculty: Are there amendments? Is there consensus? Are implementation deadlines and duties assigned?

Student Participation in Exploratory Programs

Developing skills for democratic citizenship is one of the most traditional goals for middle level schooling. Most of the "work" of the larger society gets done in teams and committees where goals are debated and defined, tasks developed, and roles of leadership and responsibility for accomplishing parts of a larger task are assigned and carried out. Involving students in the organization and implementation of exploratory program activities can be a rewarding way to develop these skills.

What kinds of tasks can students assume for this part of the program? Let us look at some possibilities. All-school days that are organized by homerooms or particular classes are natural ways to begin. Each group of students works on a part of the whole day. Representatives from each group can form a steering committee that becomes responsible for the overall planning of the event. A staff member works with the steering committee. These representatives carry directions and options to their groups which are responsible, in turn, for putting together their part of the larger event.

After the hoopla of the elections, we are often at some loss about how to give student government some real decision-making responsibility. Frequently they become messengers from the principal or counselors to their homerooms. Why not give these students some real governing responsibilities? Student councils can be given many of the management tasks surrounding activity periods. They can survey student interests for activities, collect and organize student preferences for these activities, write and organize objectives, and gather resources for the activities. They can also inform students about their choices and monitor the activities once they have begun. Students should not be given the ultimate responsibility for supervising activity period sections, but their contributions can lighten the staff workload and bring the enthusiasm of student ownership to the activity periods. Student government representatives can serve similar roles for all-school days that involve preparation by more than one grade level.

Scheduling the Exploratory Program

Discussing the intricacies of building master schedules is beyond the scope of this section. So is the very foundation of successful exploratory programs—team planning and instruction—which is the focus of Chapter 8. Two basic scheduling patterns can be examined as illustrations of where exploratory programs can fit. Of course, any schedule must be based on the number of students and the number of teachers and learning environments. Without becoming burdened with these details, however, let us look as some pattern possibilities. The schedule outlined in Table 6.4 alternates the days of activity periods and electives. Nothing else outside the traditional six- or seven-period school day is changed. In this configuration the traditional elective program can be organized around semester-long courses or divided into shorter mini-courses that include, possibly, some options not in the traditional junior high school exploratory program. All-school days would displace the routine of the schedule. Shorter all-school events could replace the activity period for a day.

Scheduling students in activity periods requires that guidelines about the number of choices and the length of time in each choice be established. A convenient design period is usually the grading period. For example, in a nine-week grading period, students might be able to sign up for no more than four activities with no longer than three weeks in any activity.

Table 6.5 offers a block version of scheduling the exploratory program. Instead of maintaining the traditional scheduling unit of 40- to 50-minute periods, larger blocks of time are allotted to the traditional academic and exploratory components of the curriculum. This allows for greater flexibility in team planning and instruction while maintaining the place of traditional exploratory elements and adding an activity format to the program.

CONCLUSIONS

The current alarmist concern about the academic achievement of our students should not distract us from attending to their needs to explore the worlds of work and play. Exemplary programs provide evidence that the traditional components of the exploratory strand—music, art, physical education, home economics, and shops—have an even more vital role to play in the school program. However, this role should not look the same as it did in the early part of the century when exploratory areas were added to the program. Changing social conditions require that we rethink the content and packaging of the exploratory strand of middle level schooling. Renewal of content needs to take into account newer definitions of gender and family roles and responsibilities as well as the need to expose and enrich rather than to specialize and compete at this age.

Possibilities for reorienting this strand include planning by the entire staff. Reorganization of responsibilities and scheduling of the exploratory strand must

TABLE 6.4. MID-DAY ACTIVITY SCHEDULE

Period	Monday	Tuesday	Wednesday	Thursday	Friday
1					
2					
3					
4		Elective	Elective		
5	Activity Period		Activity Period	Activity Period	
6					
7					
Homeroom					

be evolved. Renewed content can be packaged not only as an elective within the regular daily schedule but also in the formats of mini-courses, activity periods, and all-school days. All teachers at this level need to contribute to the updating and vitality of the exploratory program. Giving the exploratory strand permanent in-school time in the schedule demonstrates that it is a curriculum basic.

TABLE 6.5. EXPLORATORY BLOCKS AND ACTIVITY PERIODS

	Sixth	Seventh	Eighth
8:00	——————— H O M E R O O M ———————		
8:15	Basic Studies (90 min.)	Basic Studies (190 min.)	Related Arts & PE (90 min.)
9:45	Related Arts & PE (80 min.)		Basic Studies (125 min.)
11:05	Lunch (30 min.)		
11:35		Lunch (30 min.)	
11:50			Lunch (30 min.)
11:35	Basic Studies (45 min.)		
11:55		Basic Studies (25 min.)	
12:20	——————— A C T I V I T Y P E R I O D ——————— (45 min.)		
1:05	Basic Studies (90 min.)	Related Arts & PE (90 min.)	Basic Studies (90 min.)
2:35	——————— D I S M I S S A L ———————		

EXTENSIONS

1. Investigate the exploratory strand of a middle school or junior high school in your region with a partner or a small group. Compare your findings with colleagues who have investigated other schools. Do these programs meet the guidelines listed in the beginning of this chapter? What suggestions would you make if you were a teacher in one of these schools?

2. Carry out a personal inventory of the contributions you could make to the exploratory program of a middle school. List your talents in these categories: organizational, supervision of student preferences, special skills and interests, topics you would like to develop for mini-courses.

NOTES AND REFERENCES

1. T. Hirschi, *Causes of Delinquency*. Berkeley: University of California Press, 1969.
2. "Checklist for Evaluating Exploratory Programs" from Curriculum for the Middle Years, by John H. Lounsbury and Gordon F. Vars. Copyright © 1978 by John H. Lounsbury and Gordon F. Vars. Reprinted by permission of HarperCollins Publishers.
3. Donald Hall, *The Ox Cart Man*. New York: Viking, 1979.
4. Source for music, art, theater, and dance trends: Paul R. Lehman in *Content of the Curriculum*, edited by Ronald S. Brandt. Alexandria, VA: Association for Supervision and Curriculum Development, 1988 pp. 112–127.
5. Linda L. Bain in Brandt, *Content of the Curriculum*, pp. 136–144.
6. Richard G. Schlaadt in Brandt, *Content of the Curriculum*, pp. 151–155.
7. Carnegie Council on Adolescent Development, *Turning Points: Preparing American Youth for the 21st Century*. New York: Carnegie Corp., 1989, pp. 60–66.
8. M. James Bensen in Brandt, *Content of the Curriculum*, pp. 167–171.
9. John Frank, Jr., *Complete Guide to Co-Curricular Programs and Activities for the Middle Grades*. West Nyack, NY: Parker, 1976, pp. 160–161. Reprinted by permission of the publisher, Parker Publishing Co., a division of Simon & Schuster, West Nyack, NY.

FOR FURTHER READING

Arnold, John. *Visions of Teaching and Learning: 80 Exemplary Middle Level Projects.* Columbus, OH: National Middle School Association, 1990.

Brandt, Ronald S., ed. *Content of the Curriculum.* Alexandria, VA: Association for Supervision and Curriculum Development, 1988.

Frank, John, Jr. *Complete Guide to Co-Curriculum Programs and Activities for the Middle Grades.* West Nyack, NY: Parker Publishing, 1976.

Lounsbury, John H., and Johnson, J. Howard. *Life in the Three Sixth Grades.* Reston, VA: National Association of Secondary School Principals, 1988.

CHAPTER 7

The Affective Curriculum

Learning to function as a teacher in the affective domain comes naturally to a fortunate few. Some teachers naturally sense their students' moods. They can translate what is happening to how the student interprets it. Most of us, however, do not automatically understand the language of young adolescent feelings. We must learn it. As in any other language, we need to move from a literary perception of the vocabulary and structure of the student's affect to an active comprehension.

In this chapter we begin the process of learning that language through:

- Focus on the critical nature of the affective component of the school program,
- Review of the implementation of the affective curriculum through guidance programs, advisory roles, and infusion into the instructional program,
- Highlight of at-risk students' special needs, and
- Survey of the processes involved in developing the affective component of the curriculum.

TUNING IN TO THE AFFECTIVE DOMAIN

Have you ever had a conversation where the other person seemed to be on a different wavelength and answering completely different questions than the ones you asked? For many students, teacher responses to student acts appear to lack any understanding of the students' situations, as though student and teacher were speaking past each other in two different and mutually incomprehensible languages. In actual fact, students' actions may result from completely different problems and mind-sets than we realize from surface appearances.

Activity 7.1: Messages to Comprehend

To prepare you for what is to come in this chapter, take a moment to study these five sketches of young adolescent behavior. For each, ask yourself: What is the behavior? What does the behavior mean? As a teacher, how should I react to this behavior?

1. The Tardy Student. The school year is into its second week. Antonio has been consistently late to school in the morning. Ms. Reed has sent him to the office each time for a tardy slip, which makes him miss even more school time. Ms. Reed has admonished Antonio that his tardiness will cause him to miss work that she does not intend to spend her time repeating individually for him. When she asked him why he was always late, Antonio said, "My mom does not get home from work until after we must leave for school. I have to get my three younger brothers and sisters to day care and school before I can come here."

Translation and Discussion. Do you agree with Ms. Reed that school rules are to be enforced? What are the positive and negative consequences of enforcing or not enforcing the tardy rule? Is Antonio's tardiness a sign of rebellion? What alternatives does Ms. Reed have?

Our position is that a way needs to be negotiated for Antonio to observe the spirit, if not the letter, of the school schedule. Working out a solution will require extra teacher time. In Ms. Reed's position, we would want to make a family contact to check Antonio's story and to see that all the people involved— the mother, the day-care people, the school attendance office, the siblings—are aware of Antonio's conflict. If a change in the morning routines is impossible, we would negotiate a way for Antonio to enter the class quietly and arrange for a buddy-system to bring him into the activity. Perhaps he could check in with the attendance clerk on his way to class so that he could be counted on the forms already sent to that office. He might need to make up work during the first break.

2. Sixth Graders. This year's new sixth graders came from the same three feeder schools. It is October, and their teachers note that they seem less ready for the new school than previous groups from the same schools. They show little initiative in signing up for intermural sports. During break times they stay in the classrooms and cluster with friends from the previous school. The privileges of this school go unused. For example, students do not venture into free areas such as the media center and the game room. Repeatedly, they lose combinations to lockers or forget and leave materials for class in their lockers.

Translation and Discussion. Are students protesting by inactivity, or is this behavior a sign of slow adjustment to new circumstances? Will the students eventually become more involved or should the staff take positive steps to help them do so? What are some suggestions for integrating students to a new school?

We feel it would be wrong to apply to this situation the old maxim that "you can lead a horse to water, but you can't make him drink." Students need to have articulation opportunities before coming from elementary to middle schools. This staff needs to plan for next year by inviting fifth graders to the new school for tours and participation in activities at the school. The current sixth graders most probably would respond to classroom-based projects that caused them to work together. These projects should be directed toward creating an identity with the new school: for example, creating a core logo or putting on a variety show or an art exhibit that focuses on producing one mural or sculpture or setting to which every member contributed. Contests in the game room that earn points for core or homeroom privileges such as a picnic day or media blitz will promote exploration of the enrichment facilities.

3. Group Research. Mr. Cheer expects seventh graders to work in groups on independent projects for History Day. He prepares a list of possible topics from which groups can choose; he outlines possibilities for projects by describing several projects from last year's class and gives students half a period free to find their group, pick a topic, and choose or assign themselves individual tasks. After a week he asks for progress reports from each group and learns that most have done nothing. He shares this frustration with seventh grade teachers who say they all have had similar experiences. In fact, they have almost stopped assigning group tasks because results are so minimal. The consensus is that kids know less and less about note-taking and organizing their study time in the library, and that today's students need to be spoonfed and cannot assume individual or group self-direction.

Translation and Discussion. What further data do you need to analyze this vignette? Does student behavior indicate lack of interest? Experience? Poor group skills? Poor teacher direction? What teaching steps need to accompany group assignments?

Assuming that skills of collaboration in a research project were learned in the previous year is an excellent prescription for guaranteed failure. One of life's continuing challenges is learning to work as members of new groups. Groups can become productive when teachers carefully structure the group composition and individual roles and tasks within a group. Teaching to evaluate how they performed on the interpersonal level should be part of the coaching teachers do with groups.

4. School's a Waste. Lonnie and Tesha are close. They sit together in class and do each other's hair or chat about boys and the soaps. For these and other acts, they often get sent to the office by their teachers. Often they disappear from campus after lunch. When they are asked why they do not apply themselves and follow the rules, they say things like, "School means nothing to me. I don't want to be here anyway. You can suspend me if you want."

Translation and Discussion. Should we believe the girls' rejection of school? Can this friendship be used to turn around the negative feelings toward school? What can an individual teacher do to reach them? Do they need assistance beyond the individual teacher?

Here's a case when the individual teacher needs to share with colleagues who also have these girls in class. Discovering their patterns and interests in other classes may reveal insights to what could be used to engage them positively in school. Plans to monitor them and involve their families should be evolved as a team. To continue suspension is to condemn these students to leaving school.

5. *Defining Your Turf.* Puerto Ricans gather near the far side of the gym wall during lunch. African-American boys dominate the basketball court while the African-American girls hang around the edges. Other clusters are also more or less ethnic too. The same is true when students are allowed to choose their own seats in class. Teachers hear students using ethnic references in their hallway conversations, but they do not use racial terms in class. Everyone feels a tension related to group identity.

Translation and Discussion. Does the tension exist because of the school, or is it brought into the school? Is this kind of tension better ignored as long as no incidents come to the attention of the staff during school? Do programs that teach about prejudice and racism exacerbate the problem? Do multicultural activities that promote and honor the dances or food of representative groups help group integration?

Keeping the lid on by denying that these problems exist is a solution that will require an authoritarian approach to maintain order and discipline. Racial and ethnic distrust and conflict must be addressed on a variety of fronts in school programs. Individual teachers must learn to help students resolve conflict. Staffs must integrate racial and ethnic representation in the materials studied by students. Activities must promote positive sharing of customs.

Activity Summary

All these situations have implications for the affective curriculum of a school. They seem difficult to resolve. They are not directly related to a specific subject or teacher but involve aspects of the students' lives that are beyond school. We will want you to return to these situations and discuss them later. For now, they help set the stage for asking: What is the individual teacher's role in comprehending and responding to these behaviors? What do these behaviors have to do with teaching and learning? Can the school become responsible for the students' out-of-school lives?

This chapter addresses these questions. First we focus on the critical nature of the affective component of the school program. Then we look at how this component can be woven into the fabric of the school program. Finally, we describe the steps a school and an individual teacher can take to develop the affective component of the curriculum.

WHAT WE KNOW ABOUT YOUNG ADOLESCENT LIFE EVENTS

Recent survey data give educators an updated view of the increasing precariousness of growing up in America. Beyond the difficulties that developmental processes impose on young adolescents, there is the added burden imposed by the conditions of our society. Current predictions forecast that one of every four students entering the fifth grade will drop out before finishing high school. Young adolescents have a 50 percent chance of being involved in the adjustments required by divorce. After accidents, the second leading cause of death among teenagers is suicide. The poorest sector of American society is children. Most of these children are being raised by single mothers. Four of every ten teenaged girls will become pregnant during the teen years; two out of ten will have a child, and most teenage mothers keep their children. Increasingly younger children are at risk from communicable diseases such as AIDS and from substance abuse with alcohol and drugs. The more urban, Hispanic or African-American, and poor the child is, the greater the risk of disease and substance abuse.

Young adolescents are in transition. The nature of this transition is radically different than it was a generation ago. Inundated with media information about drugs and sex and social changes, young adolescents are confronted with choices that their parents did not face until they were much older, if at all. Confirm this with your own life. When did you begin making choices about using controlled substances? Contraception? Body building? Considering your "future"? Protecting the environment by the life style you choose? Thinking about your relationship to the justice system and public services for health and family assistance? Of course, we continue to deal with these issues all our lives. The salient point is that childhood protection from these issues is less of a guarantee for youth.

The middle years of schooling represent the period when students can grow into full adolescence with excitement and discovery or lapse into self-limiting patterns. Schools tend to trigger and confirm patterns of success or failure in the ways students are organized for instruction, the kinds of instruction offered, and the methods used to apprise students of their progress in learning. Child development experts as well as social analysts see the middle school years as the last, best chance to identify and alter these patterns toward life-enhancing directions. Arguing that educational aspiration and attainment are nested in young people's beliefs about themselves, their view of the world, and their sense of the future, policy makers charge middle level educators with the responsibility for keeping alive a full range of educational options for young adolescents. Let us explore the affective strand of the middle level school program to learn how teachers and schools can make a difference in the kind of future a middle adolescent has.

THE AFFECTIVE VIEW OF THE CURRICULUM

Traditionally, teacher education requirements direct us to prepare ourselves for the profession by learning more about the content of our chosen subjects and honing our skills for organization and presentation of that content. Typically, we, as teachers, lack specific study and planning for the affective curriculum; we often become defensive when the need arises for us to perform in this realm. We often reject any responsibility for interpersonal learning by explaining that we are not trained as therapists and, therefore, should not venture into potentially explosive topics. Other traditional defenses are expressed as: "I barely have time to cover the mandated content in my classes; how can I take time out for all these additional demands to teach group work and problem solving and relate to individual students on a daily basis?" Or, "I'm a teacher. I cannot make myself responsible for handling all the problems that a student brings from home. School is an academic place. We cannot assume the roles of parents." At the same time that we fall back on these defenses, we hastily admit that how a young person—or a person of any age—feels, affects that person's ability to concentrate and learn.

Social policy runs counter to our feelings and traditional training. Our society has made schools increasingly responsible for orchestrating the welfare of children. Entitlement programs legislated to offer additional assistance to children of low-income families or children with special needs reach targeted audiences through the school. Family protection services depend on the school for the identification and reporting of child abuse and antisocial behavior. State legislatures mandate that information and prevention programs for a variety of societal concerns—sex education, substance abuse—be delivered through the schools. Whether teachers like it or not, schools are being asked to organize programs that respond to these social needs. The issue of whether to assume this responsibility has been decided in the affirmative by the larger society. The professional issue, then, becomes how to prepare for this critical part of the curriculum.

In the next sections we attempt to lay the foundation for preparation in the affective curriculum. First we consider the various strands of the affective curriculum. Then we examine the needs of at-risk students and possible school responses to them. Finally, we consider both school and individual recommendations for integrating "the fourth R of relating" with the school program.

Affect as a Learning Dimension

Recall the sketches we used as springboards for this chapter. In each there was some reason related to feelings or clashes between two sets of needs that provoked unacceptable or negative student behavior at school. In each of these instances students are derailed from learning for reasons related to feelings and values. Antonio tries to meet the demands of his family role even though these demands cast him in a negative situation at school. The sixth graders feel insecure in a new setting and are, at least initially, not able to take advantage of the wider opportunities offered there. Without specific and gradual development of individual and group study skills, the seventh graders feel inadequate to the tasks assigned them. Lonnie and Tesha have not been motivated to relate to what is going on at school. The Puerto Ricans and other racial or ethnic groups bring their turf battles into school since no other mode for relating to each other is in place in the school. Every school day is filled with interpersonal events that have the effect of liberating or limiting a student's self-image and motivation to achieve.

A well-balanced school curriculum aims to develop the character of students by addressing their social and emotional as well as their cognitive needs. The affective aspect focuses on beliefs and appreciations and feelings and traits through specific programs for development of each individual while keeping in mind the importance of the individual's social integration. Affective components may be integrated with academic subjects or taught separately. One tool that can lend understanding to the developmental approach of how affect operates is the representation of Taxonomy of the Affective Domain as a kind of umbrella, shown in Figure 7.1.

This taxonomy is as important to the design of curriculum and delivery of instruction as Bloom's taxonomy of cognitive behaviors. Bloom assisted Krathwoll in conceptualizing this hierarchy and viewed it as parallel and necessary to a fuller map of learning. Thus, in correlating the cognitive with the affective, we see that the basic cognitive level of knowledge is equivalent to receiving or attending affectively. Cognitive comprehension correlates to responding; application of knowledge parallels valuing; analysis and synthesis of knowledge correspond to organizing a set of values; while evaluating equates to characterizing or employing a value complex.

The levels of the affective hierarchy are arranged from simple to difficult. *Receiving* is the most basic level of the hierarchy. It entails being aware or observing. Doing something because it is expected, or complying, is the *responding* level. *Valuing* implies choice or making a belief statement. Putting beliefs or choices together is the *organizational* stage. Putting values and principles into action as guides to living is the most complex stage of this hierarchy. For example, the sense of fairness is sharply recognized as an issue by students in upper primary grades. They expect to take turns in games and not take cuts in lines because that's the fair thing to do. They recognize and follow the rules

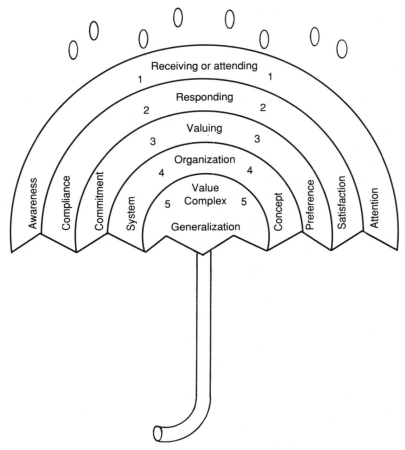

Figure 7.1. The Affective Umbrella. (Based on D. Krathwohl, B. Bloom & B. Masia, *Taxonomy of Educational Objectives, Book 2: Affective Domain.* New York: Longman, 1964.)

of fairness. When they begin to leave games because kids aren't playing fair, or vote for a classroom procedure because it gives everyone a better chance, they are at the valuing level.

Middle level students are deeply engaged in exploring the valuing level. They are ready to question authority at home and in school and society, to examine character traits in literature and history, to explore various points of view in making choices. As with the cognitive domain, movement from the initial levels to valuing can happen quickly. The intent of the affective program should be to provide experiences that assist students in internalizing, or acting consistently according to positive values.

Like the umbrella image in Figure 7.1, attention to the affective domain in program planning acts as a shield for the cognitive side of learning. Images like this and epigrams such as "If the student doesn't know you care, he won't care if you know" are shorthand ways, perhaps misleading in their simplicity, of underscoring the threshold nature of the affective aspect of learning. Affect is a pervasive, precondition to cognition. Emotional reactions to circumstances can help or block a learner. Unless middle level schools are responsive to this aspect of learning, many students will not be able to attend to the cognitive side of learning.

Components of the Affective Curriculum

Middle level schools organize the affective curriculum in different ways. Although the titles and configurations may vary, there are three basic components in the fully developed affective curriculum. They are the professional guidance and counseling, the advisory program led by teachers, and the infusion of the affective perspectives in the academic program.

1. Guidance and Counseling. Guidance counselors perform a specialized role in schools. In many instances, what guidance counselors do represents the sum of the consciously affective curriculum of a school program. The general responsibility of providing individual attention to students who are not getting along in school and overseeing the academic well-being of the whole student body allows room for interpretation in each school of how best to use the guidance counselors' expertise. Some schools use them as counselors. As such, they function as therapists and advisors. Students who act out and cause difficulties in classes are often sent to counselors as are students who evidence dysfunctional behavior—truancy, low motivation, abuse with peers, aggression with teachers—that teachers connect with poor academic achievement. Still other schools use counselors as liaisons between home and school to contact parents and keep them involved with their child's school life.

Most teachers complain that there are not enough counselors to serve all the students. They say that by the time the counselor gets around to attending to their referrals, the crucial moment when the student needed help has passed. Tight budgets do not allow the luxury of adding more specialized people to most school staffs. In fact, guidance positions have traditionally been some of the first to be cut from budgets when monies for schools are frozen or cut.

Recently, several studies and reform initiatives have urged the reconceptualizing of the middle school guidance program. Instead of seeing the counselor as a lone professional, serving difficult cases and being responsible for keeping the parents linked to their difficult son's or daughter's school progress, the counselor becomes a coordinator of an overall guidance plan for the school. Relating directly to students would continue to be part of the task, but instead of being the sole responsibility of the counselor, students would be monitored using a team approach. Under this recommendation the counselor becomes a "promoter of student potential and an advocate and orchestrator" of the school plan.

Teachers, parents, administrators, and community agencies become part of the guidance network. New avenues for guidance programs are emerging. In an 1986 middle grade improvement program,[1] sponsored by the Lilly Endowment in Indiana, suggestions for designing these new avenues included:

- Changing the traditional way(s) in which the school day and/or school week are organized to provide more varied and sustained opportunities for learning through hands-on laboratory experiences . . . in teaching and learning activities outside of school
- Recasting remedial work for youngsters-in-struggle and expanding the range of basic skills offerings for students at the "bottom"
- Rethinking and reworking the entire testing and grouping philosophy and process by which students are, in essence, given their role and place within the school
- Developing outside-of-school field and service experiences for students that are part of the regular school program and for which full credit is accorded
- Changing teaching assignments to encourage more varied and stimulating challenges for what we call "regular classroom teachers"
- Developing with youth-serving agencies an experimental school day in which youngsters spend some of their 9:00 a.m.–3:00 p.m. day at a "Y," a Boys or Girls Club, or some of their "after-school" time inside the school building
- Thoroughly assessing and redefining guidance functions within the school and collaborating with adults who give informal guidance to youngsters in the out-of-school hours.

These suggestions involve the guidance professional with the teachers and the community. Development of any one of them would entail wide-ranging plans for change. The sections of this chapter that discuss developing the affective curriculum will address how this planning process could be developed. For any of these suggestions to become translated into action would require the collaborative effort of the school staff, parents, and community who are examining the specific needs of students of a given school.

2. Advisory Program. Advisory programs are the organized and daily part of the affective curriculum in a growing number of middle level schools. Most have adopted the goal of middle school philosophy as their own: every student has an adult with whom close, daily contact is maintained. Under this program teachers become advisors, or special advocates for the individuals—and their group of advisees. The teacher advisor serves as a "homebase" teacher who assists students with their studies as well as their emotional concerns.

Typically, the advisory component of the affective curriculum will have a planned program that is flexible enough to attend to the emerging needs and interests of the advisory group. Advisory programs explore a broad range of social, emotional, physical, and thinking skills. Table 7.1 provides an overview of content possibilities for the advisory program. Topics respond to the transitional stage in which young adolescents find themselves. School begins with sessions that help students get acquainted with their group and the school as well as the kinds of academic expectations the school has of them. As the school year progresses, issues of self-concept, peer and family relations, decision making, leadership, wellness, conflict resolution, and group development are woven into the daily session's activities. Frequently these sessions involve group discussion and individuals sharing with each other. Sometimes activities are physical, taking place outdoors. Culminating moments take groups into the school or the community to carry out action projects.

The tone of the advisory program is personal and exploratory. The intent of the program is, at the same time, deeper and broader than the previous teacher-

TABLE 7.1. ADVISORY PROGRAM CONTENT

Topic	Sample Skills/Activities
Academic effectiveness	Conducting study habit survey, following directions, knowing how to get help, solving problems alone, knowing key words on tests, preparing for tests
Self-exploration and self-definition	Knowing strengths, likes, and dislikes; describing oneself; dealing with anger; being alone; having physical and mental health; becoming independent
Decision making and problem solving	Knowing how to analyze a problem, asserting oneself, being aware of conflict styles, thinking for self, taking steps to solve problems
Physical, emotional, social, and academic growth	Being involved in family roles, recognizing behavior patterns, making friends, having good grooming habits, sensing mistreatment, making classroom/career connections, setting goals, expressing love
Meaningful participation in school and community	Understanding the disabled; knowing and being involved with campus issues, community workers, school projects, community projects
Positive communication and interaction	Listening actively, expressing body language, participating in group discussion and problem solving, solving communication roadblocks, having positive feedback, giving compliments
Competence and achievement	Taking responsibility, keeping promises, striving for success, doing assignments and self-monitoring, taking risks and facing the consequences
Self-esteem	Having personal goals, climbing the self-control ladder, connecting values and goals, stereotyping, adjusting attitudes, striving for sucess

led "guidance" efforts known as "homeroom." The reality of homeroom amounted to an attendance-taking-announcement-making-settling-down administrative moment outside the real work of the school day. For the advisory sessions to avoid the homeroom syndrome, several conditions must be present. There must be adequate time in the schedule for building and maintaining the teacher-student and teacher-advisory group intimacy. Programs must be developed in response to needs felt, or evidenced, by students. Teachers must be given appropriate training and materials to support their efforts.

The issue of acquiring or developing support materials for advisory sessions is crucial. One option is to investigate the commercial materials available. These range from individual videos that focus on one or another of the advisory topics, to units on teaching thinking skills, to packages that encompass a year's worth (or more) of teacher-ready readings and activities for students. Table 7.2 lists sources of materials that can be examined for advisory programs.

These materials are illustrative of a growing list of advisory resources. Many are available only through a training workshop in the effort to guarantee that, as they are used, they will be placed within the broader framework of affective education. Each needs to be examined in the light of the specific circumstances of the individual school.

3. Infusion with Subjects. Beyond the specialized guidance and personalized advisory program, there is a third way that affective goals can become part of the school program. By re-examining the content and strategies for instruction in every class, we can ascertain if and how each integrates, or infuses, concern for the affective. Let us look first at some possibilities for infusing subject content with affective goals.

Choosing novels and nonfiction selections with an eye for the affective may simply require that the exemplars currently being used be analyzed in terms of affective content. Key elements to look for are role models, differing perspectives, and problem solving. We should look for role models that overcome obstacles, risk failure, make mistakes and learn from them, do the right thing in the face of pressure to the contrary. We should highlight circumstances that can be seen from different points of view. Differences due to age, social status, region, religion, race or ethnicity, family role, sexual orientation, and physical attributes are all fertile sources for different ways of being in and observing the world that students need to see reflected in their reading. Looking at the advantages and disadvantages, or the consequences of problem-solving options in people's lives, both fictional and real, helps to reinforce the adolescent's bridge from school to real life. Focus on a value or principle is an additional avenue to examining the affective elements. Core values included in most social studies programs include: responsibility, justice, equality, independence, competition, freedom, tolerance, honesty, respect, loyalty, cooperation, compromise, and individualism. These elements, which abound in historical as well as contemporary topics, fuel an imaginative search for solutions to problems through reading.

TABLE 7.2. SAMPLER OF MATERIALS FOR ADVISORY PROGRAMS

Title/Source	Description
Skills for Adolescence Lions-Quest Program 537 Jones Rd. P.O. Box 566 Granville, OH 43023	Course develops skills in responsibility, decision making, communication, building self-confidence, and goal setting; available to educators via paid workshops. Materials include a student book, and a teacher/group facilitator guide that defines session objectives, suggests activities sequence and timing.
Tribes Center for Human Development 301 Taylor Blvd. Suite 120 Pleasant Hill, CA 94523	Program that structures groups with low peer acceptance so that processes for social development and cooperative learning can be learned. Available via training program for teachers and/or parents and supported with teacher manual by Jeanne Gibbs.
R.A.P. Mary Young Williams Dale Seymour Publications P.O. Box 10888 Palo Alto, CA 94303	Binder of resources for an advisory program developed in Franklin–McKinley School District for grades 6 through 9. Contains month-by-month reproducible activity sheets focused on getting acquainted, study skills, interpersonal communication, community involvement, school spirit, career planning/goal setting, self-esteem, problem solving/conflict resolution, relationships, accepting responsibilities, and positive attitudes; accompanied by teacher plans for each.
Adviser-Advisee Programs: Why, Why and How James Michael National Middle School Association Columbus, OH 43229	Pamphlet that advocates advisory programs directed to administrators with suggestions about how to develop programs that start with survey of student needs and include community involvement. Useful for process of program development.
Everybody Gets an "A" in Affective Education Sandra L. Schurr, Kathy Callahan-Hunt, Kathy Shewey The National Center for Middle Grades Education Tampa, FL 33620	Workshop with accompanying materials directed to administrators and teachers charged with program development initially sponsored by PRIME Legislation in Florida. Materials available via workshop.

Activity 7.2: Building a Book File

Correlating literature with social studies and science and the popularity of whole-language approaches to language arts make building a file of novels and nonfiction books an important part of preparing for teaching. Divide a bibliography of recommended juvenile fiction and nonfiction with your colleagues, or reread one of your favorite works. As sketched in the preceding section, look for affective approaches. Write an affectively infused plan for group study of the book. Assign yourselves a sharing date. On that date bring enough copies for everyone in the class. Each teacher should then spend two minutes giving a highlight of his or her plan.

Here's a sample to get started. The novel *Hatchet*[2] explores the theme of early adolescent physical survival from a plane crash in the Canadian wilderness while struggling with the emotional trauma of parental divorce. During the course of the plot, Brian must use his life skills of responsibility, common sense, initiative, problem solving, effort, motivation, perserverance, confidence, caring, and teamwork. These are called "megaskills" by Dorothy Rich.[3] Indeed, discussing them as a result of classroom sharing of the adventures in *Hatchet* can lead early adolescents to connect these vital skills to their own lives.

Relevance was a popular concept for curriculum developers of the 1970s. We feel that asking questions of relevance, though doing so might not be in vogue, can increase the affective alignment of the content curriculum. For every subject or class, we need to look at textbooks and activities through the lens of relevance. Do students of the 1990s have a need for the topic? Can we justify to ourselves, and the students, why a topic must be studied? What value does it have to their future? Their present? Their goals? Does it help them learn to learn? If most of our justifications are based on "because you need it in order to get into college," or because the topic is on a best-selling cultural literacy list, we either need to see if the material truly responds to student needs and/or interests, or we need to consider deleting it from the program.

It is also true that affect permeates the way we teach. Whatever the class or topic, motivation of students is a prerequisite for student learning. The checklist below allows you to gauge how motivational the instructional, often reproducible, materials are that we give classes to organize their exploration of a text or their research of a theme. Even if one project handout could never meet all these criteria, the list serves as a prompt to what teachers need to evaluate. Young adolescents need projects and materials that encourage their independence from the teacher. Activities that allow students to construct their own meanings and feel successful when they share their results are necessary for students to see themselves as reaching goals and gaining greater control over their environment and being capable of social interaction.

Checklist for Evaluating Guided Practice Materials

Place a check by each statement that applies to your assignment.

Materials used as assignments should:

_____ Give clear sequential directions

_____ Engage the affect and/or challenge students to think

_____ Deal with content worth learning

_____ Use stimuli that vary from the main mode of presentation

_____ Help students relate content to their own learning goals

If you are using a reproducible worksheet, it is designed to:

_____ Give direction and purpose

_____ Promote a positive attitude

_____ Offer choices that promote perseverance

_____ Provide for critical thinking about the topic

_____ Try to meet learning needs of students of this age

_____ Fit into a larger premise or generalization

_____ Leave students with a sense of accomplishment

Materials should meet at least some of these criteria for good teaching:

_____ Stop misconduct indirectly by suggesting a positive activity

_____ Orient students to the assignment by telling what is expected

_____ Explain what the student is going to accomplish

_____ Involve students in recalling the content of prior lessons

_____ Alert each student to material that deserves special attention

_____ Engender enthusiasm nonverbally

_____ Encourage students to use time productively

_____ Engage students in analyzing both cause and effect

_____ Require justification, evidence, or comparisons

_____ Appeal to different sensory modes of learning

_____ Maintain instructional momentum by providing alternatives

_____ Initiate student to student interchange related to lesson content

_____ Acknowledge specific instances of academic progress

Infusing affective content into the curriculum brings up issues related to content organization and scheduling as well. We call topics like substance abuse, sex education, and AIDS part of the affective curriculum since students' feelings and behaviors bring them into contact with these topics. Many states mandate that these topics be addressed during the middle years. State-originated materials may even be part of the mandate. In organizing a curricular response to these needs, many schools negotiate a balance between finding time in the schedule and space in the existing curriculum as well as training teachers to become knowledgeable about these topics. Too often when schools respond to mandated programs, the vital issue of how the information and skills can be presented to have the most effect on students is not given adequate consideration.

The evolution of school response to substance abuse can serve to illustrate this point. The first generation of drug education programs typically consisted of guest lectures and scare tactics. Often uniformed police officers unveiled a briefcase full of drugs and paraphernalia. Students were told "no." For many students, seeing exotic items exhibited by a rejected authority figure further challenged their spirit of rebellion against the law. Personal knowledge they had about drugs often ran counter to the messages contained in these presentations about the effects of drugs. Second-generation drug programs featured a more sophisticated approach involving testimonials from ex-abusers and group discussions that analyzed peer pressure and role-played decision making with the object of getting students to say "no." Still the efforts tended to be focused on a campaign week or a separate, add-on part of the school program. More recently, what we might call a third generation of curricula addressing abuse and health-threatening disease from an even broader, yet more personal, perspective of individual growth and decision making has become more common. Middle grade educators are recognizing the priority that wellness topics have in student lives. Drugs and AIDS information is still included as information in the program, with the more consistent and sustained efforts devoted to learning to handle peer pressure, building positive friendships, and valuing wellness.

The planning stage for organizing health and wellness topics must be broad-based and schoolwide. Some questions that must be addressed are: Should all the health and wellness topics become part of the science, or do they more easily fit with advisory, or should some of this content be in both classes? Is having campaign weeks about AIDS or substance abuse the most effective way to reach students? And what about sex education? Does it belong as a unit in a science or health class, or should it also be part of advisory? Each school must find the best way for that school to infuse these topics into its program. Part of the answer, we feel, should include scheduling initial exposure to a topic by specific information-giving and question-asking sessions. Advisory, or other groups, need to keep the topic open by using it in problem-solving sessions. Ongoing individual assistance on these issues needs to be made available as well.

IDENTIFYING AND RESPONDING TO AT-RISK STUDENTS

We have just explored three components of the affective curriculum. During normal times, each has an integral part to play in a carefully considered school program. But, as we have seen, social indicators tell us that these are not normal times. We are in danger of losing significant percentages of young adolescents to further schooling and healthy development patterns. We are somewhat cognizant that growing up in decaying urban centers is like crossing a minefield. For many middle level students, growing up in a suburb or small town or the countryside can be almost as dangerous. Increasingly, the cards seem to be stacked against poorer students who come from single-parent homes or homes where parents have little education and students from African-American or Hispanic backgrounds. Of course, not all students with these social characteristics have difficulty in school. But they are more likely to.

Some of these students are known to be at risk. *At-risk* is a term for denoting high probability that a student will not complete high school. How are these students identified? In a recent study, principals identified them as the students who are frequently sent to the office, or who come to school infrequently or due to intervention of the court, or who move frequently, or who live with boyfriends, or who have total responsibility for younger siblings, or who get into trouble with the justice system. Girls in this category appeared to be unkempt and physically undernourished.[4] Experts generally agree on which school factors are present in at-risk students. Students who have low self-esteem, feelings of alienation, deficits in basic literacy and numeracy skills, emotional or physical problems, financial need and/or heavy family responsibilities, precocious sexual activity, pregnancy, and lack of bonding with school are at risk. Students at risk may evidence one or a cluster of these factors.

Learning At-Risk Vocabulary and Symptoms

Teachers are not expected to become therapists, but increasingly they need to acquaint themselves with physical and emotional problems relevant to young adolescents. Learning the vocabulary of some risk categories as well as the symptoms that accompany some of these categories is a necessary part of professional preparation. Our intent here is suggestive, not exhaustive. You will need to read about and discuss these categories in greater depth. Use these descriptions as prompts, or suggestions for pointing out significant at-risk categories.

1. Drugs/Alcohol. Factual information about these substances is important but not related to reducing student drug abuse significantly. More effective prevention programs stress concepts related to the development of individual standards, critical thinking, decision making, interpersonal relations, stress reduction, communication, and self-esteem. In essence, the kinds of topics that fit in a typical advisory program are also correlated with the most effective drug abuse prevention strategies. Terms you should know include the latest ones used on the street to refer to drugs and activities of the substance abuse culture. You should also learn about co-dependency behaviors and early warning signs of abuse such as sudden changes in behavior or mood, listlessness or sleeping in school, loss of weight or appetite, loss of interest in physical activity, poor academic performance, inability to get along with peers, expressions of not belonging at school.

2. Suicide. Prevention of this second-most-frequent cause of death among American teens is related to watching for signals a student typically sends. Many of the same symptoms are similar to drug/alcohol-related ones. Girls are more prone to suicide attempts than boys. Students contemplating the idea that not living will solve their problems with life will also do things like distribute their possessions, write goodbye messages, make statements about using a gun or other weapon. Teachers picking up on any of these signals need to report them immediately to their principals. Schools must organize a system to protect the safety of the student.

3. AIDS. Do young adolescents need information about this sexually transmitted disease? You decide after reading this incident. In a health class Ms. Rose wondered if her fifth graders should be given information about sexually transmitted diseases as part of the regular family life unit. She decided to survey her class informally. She began by asking, "How many of you know what a condom is?" Several hands shot up.

"Sure, we know what they are," one boy answered, "but you have to use rubber bands to keep them on."

Graphic information about self-protection may not be enough. Students need to know where to get condoms. Recent findings indicate that even when students have AIDS information they do not believe they are vulnerable, or are unwilling to negotiate their own safety in the heat of the moment. Making condoms an essential erotic accoutrement is a solution for the mass media. But school programs must provide basic protective information. Furthermore, schools need to anticipate how to handle students who are HIV positive by developing a policy and action plan.

4. Anorexia and Bulimia. Anorexia is the loss of 25 percent of appropriate body weight. Bulimia is the pattern of eating and self-induced vomiting or using laxatives and diuretics to flush the body of food. Girls entering adolescence are more prone than boys to this obsession with body image. They often come from middle-class or upper-class homes and are seen as perfect children, very attached to their parents. A key symptom is an excessive interest in appearance. As with substance abuse, students will deny they have any problems. Also, as with substance abuse, prevention efforts in the forms of health or advisory programs that discuss the ways media and society promote the idea of a perfect body and that instruct about ways to deal with anxiety are potentially effective.

5. Teen Pregnancy. One million teens become pregnant each year in the United States. The average age of these girls is becoming lower. Studies show that information about the reproductive process is an inadequate preventative for teen pregnancy. Newer sex education approaches include content on personal growth, the effects of pregnancy on education, career and earning power, and resume writing.[5] Teachers need to be sensitive to community feelings about abortion.

However, schools are ethically responsible, in the broad sense, for making knowledge available. Community sentiment must not be allowed to work to the detriment of the young pregnant teen. On the student's behalf, schools must use student advisory teams to detect and intervene, to provide information and guidance.

6. Divorce and Family Instability. Half of the children of the United States are affected by divorce or family instability during their youth. Changes in family often mean that parents move away, family income drops, supervision at home declines, and children have more responsibilities. Some middle school students cross these changes without losing their own sense of security. Others react with anger or guilt. Stress may provoke all kinds of acting out. Warring parents may see school as the only place they can get to their children. Parents in trouble with the justice system or losing their homes may feel ashamed to respond to school contacts. Teachers and schools should attempt to maintain communication about school activities and student progress with all parents. Students should be monitored for signs of stress and given opportunities to participate in peer groups of students going through divorce and family change. Schools need to keep contact with family courts and inform police in case of custody trouble. Advisory sessions can provide information about the legal and emotional bonds of marriage and divorce as well as recommend juvenile fiction selections to read as a springbord for understanding how children can handle these changes.

7. Child Abuse and Neglect. Most states have specific reporting procedures that make teachers legally responsible to report suspected cases of abuse. Schools typically develop their own procedures for initiating an investigation of these cases. Some of the possible symptoms of abuse resemble those of other at-risk circumstances: changes of behavior, loss of self-esteem, initiation of sexual innuendo or advances with other students, unexplained bruises or bodily injuries, and unexplained absences. Students often feel they are at fault for the abuse they suffer. They fear loss of parental love, and only rarely will they voluntarily ask for help. Teachers should not attempt to intervene alone when they suspect abuse.

Planning for At-Risk Students

Designing programs that are responsive to at-risk youth requires action research. The National Association for Secondary School Principals[6] recommends that principals keep a log of the students sent to their office by teachers, and then interview multiple offenders using these directives:

1. Tell me about your school.
2. What do you like to do in your spare time?
3. Tell me about the kind of teacher that you learn best from.
4. Have you ever been sent to the principal's or assistant principal's office?

5. Why were you sent?
6. What was your teacher doing when you were asked to leave class?
7. How did you feel about being asked to leave?
8. What is the easiest subject for you to learn and why?
9. What is the hardest subject for you to learn and why?
10. What do you think should happen to students who act out in class or break other school rules?
11. What message would you like to give teachers and principals about how to make school a terrific place to be?

Information gathered in interviews should be tabulated and taken to the staff and shared. These data are even more provocative if they are compared to data from a random sample of students who are never sent to the office. Teachers need to look for patterns and think of positive, not punitive, measures that could be taken to improve the contacts they have with behaviorally at-risk students. The responses below are the suggestions of at-risk students for making school a better place.[7]

- "Listen to kids."
- "Make the school day shorter."
- "Everything is ok the way it is."
- "Be easier on us."
- "Don't be so strict."
- "Don't give so much homework."
- "Go easy on kids for minor offenses."
- "Don't make kids wear a gymsuit or be sent to office if they forget it."
- "Let us go outside for lunch."
- "Give us a chance to succeed."
- "Give us more choices."
- "Give equal treatment."

Teachers should begin to identify students they feel are behaviorally at risk and tell why they think these students are having problems. Many schools set up a structure that formalizes attention to at-risk cases. In Figure 7.2 we see that the student assistance team can be initiated upon a request for assistance or referral by anyone in contact with the student. The object of this team is to identify at-risk cases and organize an intervention plan for them. Teams assemble data on the student by looking at health, academic, and family records, and by interviewing the student's teachers and asking that they document behaviors that support initial concerns. With the assembled data the team meets to review the information. If the data suggest intervention, parents of the student are then asked to meet with the team. During this meeting a plan is discussed that sets out specific recommendations for the student, the parents, and the school. Timelines for ongoing feedback are established. Based on the practices of child

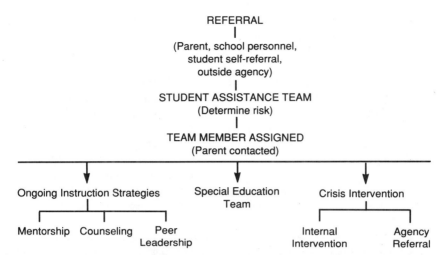

Figure 7.2. Organization of a Student Assistance Program. (Evelyn Hunt Ogden and Vito Germinario, *The At-Risk Student: Answers for Educators.* Lancaster, Pa.: Technomic Publishing Co., 1988, p. 29. Reprinted by permission.)

study teams, this group forms as needed and stops meeting when no longer necessary. The strengths of this approach are many. School and community resources collaborate. Students become involved with a group that sees their situation from the home and school perspectives. Accountability to a group rather than one teacher is more powerful for the student and less stressful for individual teachers.

Allied to the discipline plan and the formal advisory sessions is the day-to-day, period-to-period approach of each teacher. Teachers who watch for early warning signs from students and take steps to investigate them are acting in the guidance mode rather than waiting for the student to behave in a way that will activate the discipline mode. Frequently the investigation takes the form of asking a student how it's going today, and then being sure to listen to the answer and act on it either by making adjustments for that student related to expectations or meeting basic needs. Teachers who share at-risk students should communicate with each other to keep abreast of what is happening with a particular student and share activities or arrangements to which students respond positively and show signs of success.

Saving future opportunities for young adolescents by keeping them in school requires coordinated and timely action. Educators have always recognized that the problems of students cannot be solved by schools alone. Innovative programs for at-risk populations extend beyond the school to engage parents, community groups, and community agencies. The traditional isolation of low-income, minority parents is overcome by including them in the process of determining the guidance needs of students. Aspects of this effort as envisioned by one program[8] include:

- Give parents new roles and status in helping their children make critical transitions between elementary, middle, and high school, including greater say in their children's course selection, group placement, educational stream, and so on.
- Align parents, community organizations, and schools in reconceptualizing ways in which families and parents relate to the schools, including reworking home-school communications and creating homework and other curriculum-related opportunities for parents to help their children learn at home—all with an eye to increasing parent involvement and energizing the guidance process.
- Provide parents with peer support and information to promote positive parent-child relationships, which become the cornerstone for parental guidance, especially as children enter the critical preteen and teenage years.
- Place families more nearly at the center of existing access to postsecondary education programs and better equip parents to enhance their children's opportunity to go to college or vocational school.
- Create a community-based network of parents whose common focus is to play a stronger and more intentional guidance role in their children's lives—the intent being to build their children's sense of aspiration and striving to continue education beyond high school.

Community groups are urged to place *providing a better environment for youth* at the top of their agendas; they are challenged to move toward the vision they develop. Youth-serving agencies and schools attempt to close the gap between their efforts by designing a set of opportunities and services that reaches students beyond the school day while still collaborating with the school program.

DEVELOPING THE AFFECTIVE CURRICULUM

We have described the vital nature of the affective curriculum for a school program. Furthermore, we have explored the components of a program and briefly defined special-need students and a broader concept of a community-based guidance program. In this section we review the phases of program development including considerations of district- or school-level planning responsibilities, as well as planning for classroom management.

District and School Planning Responsibilities

Program development for the affective curriculum follows same process discussed in Chapter 3. The process of solid curriculum development cannot be accomplished without study and development beginning at the district level that explores advisory program goals, models, and materials. After establishing a set of goals and objectives like those in the outline below, the district must then provide staff development at the school level so that each can develop an implementation plan and program that meets its special circumstances.

Sample: Philosophy, Goals, and/or Objectives
of a Model Advisory Program[9]

Three general goals have been selected to describe what it is we hope to accomplish through the Advisory Program. They are as follows:

   I. To help middle school students develop their maximum physical, emotional, social, and academic potential
 II. To foster a positive school environment for students and staff
III. To enhance communication among students, peers, home, and school.

The 12 objectives designed to accompany the goals are likewise general in nature. They are not intended to be highly specific and measurable, nor are they intended to be assigned to a particular goal. Each objective can easily accompany any goal. They should serve as a guide to the advisor in designing a program for his or her advisory group. They are as follows:

  1. To help students learn about the school
  2. To help students learn how to make friends
  3. To help students learn how to get along with others
  4. To let students have a different relationship with teachers—other than teacher-student
  5. To provide advisors with an opportunity to know students one-to-one
  6. To provide all students with an understanding listener
  7. To help students cope with academic concerns
  8. To help students solve everyday problems
  9. To make appropriate school personnel aware of children with special needs
10. To help students know themselves
11. To help students develop feelings of self-worth
12. To provide another link for home/school communication.

Once the staff arrives at a set of goals and objectives for the advisory program, the alternatives for scheduling must be explored. There are advantages and disadvantages in each. If the advisory is scheduled to begin every day, the advantages are that advisory sets the tone for the day and provides a continuity for students. On the other hand, if program activities are not strong, the tendency will be for the sessions to degenerate into a homeroom atmosphere where administrative tasks of organizing the day absorb the period. One way to prevent this is to set up a weekly routine that varies activities. The activity schedule presented here illustrates such a possibility; each week takes on a rhythm that can be fit onto most advisory topics.

Sample Daily Activities for Advisory Periods[10]

Monday   Socialization Day
              a. Free conversation to being the week
              b. Weekly plans are solidified
              c. Friday activity is planned

Tuesday   Content Day
              Topical activities from manual are completed

Wednesday   Content Day
              Topical activities from manual are completed

Thursday   Reading/Journal/Conference Day
              a. Students write in journals or read silently while teacher
                 holds conferences with individuals
              b. Teacher reads aloud to students

Friday   Activity Day
              a. Activity is decided on by students on Monday
              b. Activities could be trivia bowl with next-door advisory,
                 outside or gym activity, breakfast together, or "show and
                 tell."

Other methods of scheduling include keeping a beginning-of-the-day home-room while reducing all periods by five minutes two days a week, or a schoolwide dropping of a period in two different classes so that special advisory sessions can be held. Advantages to these plans include separating "administri-via" from advisory content while maintaining daily contact between advisors and students. Keeping students and teachers aware that "today is advisory" requires more sophisticated scheduling and possibly more class and teacher switching for students, which we know is one of the sources of students' not bonding to their middle level schools.

Classroom management is intimately tied to the affective curriculum. The management of each teacher and the discipline plan for the entire school is involved. If some teachers seem to send more students to the office, they need special assistance from either the principal or other teachers. More and more, however, peer coaching is one of the most effective tools for helping teachers improve their classroom management. In this mode, colleagues assist each other by sitting in on each other's instruction and critiquing each other. The most positive approach here is for the teacher being observed to define for the observer what the problem under consideration is. Sometimes the problems relate to presentation of content. Most often, they relate to management issues. Typical instructional difficulties include too much lecture, too little attention to physical needs of students, too much time spent getting ready for or being distracted from learning, poor transitions between activities, lack of proximity of the teacher to students who are causing disturbances, unrealistic teacher behavior standards, students in groups that encourage negative behavior, and content expectations that cannot be met. Helping teachers see these problems concretely and brainstorming ways to solve them need an ongoing strategy to improve instruction that will, consequently, improve the school's affective curriculum.

Devising a discipline plan is part of the classroom management system that must be hammered out at the school level. Good plans have few rules. They are simple and explicit about what will happen to students who break them. Rules should be based on the need to respect other people, schedules, and the school environment. Students must learn them at the beginning of a school year. They may choose to refine or elaborate them in individual classes as an exercise in self-governance, but they must not be allowed to ignore or violate the basic rules.

PREPARING FOR THE AFFECTIVE CURRICULUM

Teachers can never get enough preparation for this aspect of their profession. Learning continues throughout their careers with each new group and with those memorable individual students. Beginning teachers always complain that they were not adequately prepared for this part of teaching. Perhaps that is inevitable. "Learning to be with students" does come through experience, but that experience can mean more, at any stage of a teaching career, if the teacher-learner will seek outside resources to assist in that learning.

Activity 7.3: Investigating School-Community Youth Programs

What kinds of programs exist for the youth in your community? What services do they offer? What connections are there between the school and community or youth services? Teachers need to know what resources are available in their communities. In small groups they should investigate these resources and share results with the class to form a youth resource file. They should find out the agency or program name, location, contact person, phone, services available, fees or registration, ages covered; they should also present their impressions from observing the service.

Classroom Management

All teachers must evolve their own system of classroom management and keep evolving it throughout their careers. Management means devising your system of organizing the way your classroom works and making sure that students understand it. The attention you give to thinking through the details of how your classroom will function will be important to your teaching success. Below we list some of the elements that should be considered as you plan a management system.

Elements of a Classroom Management Plan

- Furniture arrangement: group work, traffic flow, individual space for movement, light
- Equipment and supplies: kind of student access, individual possession or classroom set, frequency of need, care and cleaning
- Classroom routines: student movement, signals for attention, attendance, bathroom permission, leaving and entering for pull-out activities, student-student communication, daily and weekly schedule, emergency procedures for group and individuals, classroom jobs for students
- Record-keeping-grading system: student participation in evaluation and record keeping, cumulative folders and permanent records, standardized testing and scoring, attendance record responsibility, book and supply responsibility
- Dynamics between teacher and students: setting tone for school year, getting acquainted games, reward or relax or free time possibilities, consequences for not doing work or handing in late work, group problem-solving techniques, individual problem-solving techniques.

Your management system should evolve and change according to the students and your needs. It must take the schoolwide management system into consideration. Teachers who permit, for example, gum chewing when the school expressly forbids it are creating confusion about rules for students. If you feel that such a rule is not necessary and too picayune to be included at the school level, a better way to proceed would be to work with the school staff to change the rule.

Courses in classroom management or discipline or educational psychology, professional reading, and workshops are excellent ways to collect ideas you will need to think through for continuing to revise your classroom management. The way you organize your work with students is vital to the informal affective curriculum of your school.

CONCLUSIONS

Learning is enveloped in affect. Charting a course in a school program that challenges students while, at the same time, giving them the structure and security to help them grow is as important as deciding what to teach and how to sequence it. In reality, the affective curriculum is present whether we plan it or not. Becoming aware of what impact our feelings about ourselves and others have on learning is the consciousness-raising step toward developing the affective curriculum. This chapter outlined some of the areas to work on when taking the step of addressing the affective curriculum in a proactive manner. We have seen that to develop the affective curriculum, specialized guidance, formal advisory programs, and affective infusion into school subjects should be addressed. Further, at-risk students must be identified and assisted. Teacher "child-study" teams can best monitor and guide at-risk students and parents and teachers. Just as importantly, individual teachers need to keep abreast of classroom management issues for their own teaching and participate with colleagues in the formulation of schoolwide discipline policies.

EXTENSIONS

1. Find out about current concerns in education related to student self-image and motivation to succeed in school. Review curriculum materials designed to build self-esteem. Interview students to find out what activities, characteristics of teachers, or facets of school life motivate them to come to school and to do their best work.

2. For TV homework assign students to watch programs on the public broadcasting or commercial networks that feature early adolescents and their interactions with their worlds. Discuss reactions, feelings, and "How real is it?", as well as "What if. . .?" and "How would you . . . .?" situations.

NOTES AND REFERENCES

1. Middle Grade Improvement Program Prospectus. Indianapolis, IN: Lilly Endowment, Inc., 1986, p. 6.
2. Gary Paulsen, *Hatchet*. New York: Puffin Books of Penguin Group, Viking Penguin, 1987.
3. D. Rich, *Megaskills*. Boston: Houghton Mifflin, 1988.
4. Sherrel Bergmann, *Discipline and Guidance: A Thin Line in the Middle Level School: What At-Risk Students Say About Middle Level School Discipline and Teaching*. Reston, VA: National Association of Secondary School Principals, 1989.
5. See *Life Planning Education*. Washington, DC: Center for Population Options, 1983.
6. Bergmann, *Discipline and Guidance*, p. 2.
7. Bergmann, *Discipline and Guidance*, pp. 13–14.
8. *Program for Developing a Broader and More Dynamic Range of Guidance Experiences for Young People*. Indianapolis, IN: Lilly Endowment, Inc., 1990, pp. 11–12.
9. Prime Time Program, Sarasota County School District, Sarasota, FL.
10. Broomfield Heights Middle School, Boulder Valley Public Schools, Boulder, CO.

FOR FURTHER READING

Beane, J. A., and Lipka, R. P. *When Kids Come First: Enhancing Self Esteem*. Columbus, OH: National Middle School Association, 1987.

Curwin, R., and Mendler, A. N. *Discipline with Dignity*. Washington, DC: Association for Supervision and Curriculum Development, 1988.

Hamburg, D. A. *Early Adolescence: A Critical Time for Intervention in Education and Health*. New York: Carnegie Corporation of New York, 1989.

Ogden, E. H., and Germinario, V. *The At-Risk Student*. Lancaster, PA: Technomic Publishing Company, Inc., 1988.

Rich, D. *Megaskills*. Boston: Houghton Mifflin, 1988.

CHAPTER 8

Core Curriculum
Implementation

A casual glance and you might think that Jaime and Lucy are seventh graders at Jefferson School. But this week Jaime and Lucy are hydraulic engineers. They and their teammates have allocated most of the morning preparing a proposal on how to efficiently and effectively deliver water from a limited supply stored in containers to all nonhuman living things in their homeroom class for a two-week period. First the team researched what the needs of the organisms in the class "ecosystem" are and now they wrestle with how to avoid wasting what they realize is a very precious resource. Their team of consulting engineers is just one of several student teams solving problems within a theme designed around "Water as Opportunity and Limitation." During the course of this unit, these middle level students, working with a team of teachers, are learning specific concepts that are included in the school district's core curriculum, a program that includes expectations for mathematics, science, social studies, language arts, and other subject areas.

In this chapter we:

- Review how a core curriculum is delineated at three levels in a decision-making hierarchy,
- Explore how curriculum expectations can be met through combining core and interdisciplinary instruction, and
- Consider ways the core curriculum can be implemented at the middle level.

Several of the main ideas in this chapter are addressed from different perspectives in other chapters.

DEFINING THE CORE CURRICULUM

The middle level core curriculum refers to the learning that all early adolescents are expected to acquire and, therefore, what all middle level programs should provide. There are three levels of decision making involved in defining the parameters of the core curriculum and in determining its effective delivery to middle level students. First, at the national or state level, or both, the essence, or broad set of goals, of the curriculum is established. Second, at the intermediate level involving the state, county, or district, the subject content that supports the goals is described in terms of learning expectations so that instruction can be planned. Third, at the local level, instruction is organized including actual planning carried out at the school level to identify ways to teach specific concepts, integrate subject areas, and incorporate the curriculum components into real-life or close-to-real-life experiences.

The *first level* involves a consensus among experts in diverse fields or disciplines about the nature of common knowledge that should be assimilated by every middle level student. In *Turning Points, Preparing Youth for the 21st Century,*[1] middle level curriculum developers are urged to ensure that young adolescents are taught to (1) think critically, (2) develop healthful lifestyles, (3) be active citizens, and (4) learn as well as test successfully, and to do so in an environment that integrates subject matter across disciplines. Broad goals like these for the core curriculum serve as a screening device for separating concepts that are basic and transferrable from those that are less general, less durable, and less relevant. General frameworks described at this first level are often accompanied by specific examples of expectations in order to provide guidance for curriculum developers at the second level.

The *second level* involves constructing contextual frameworks for addressing the overall goals like those listed above. The process of describing instructional components or concepts to be learned incorporates the input of expert educators and subject area specialists who recommend what specific knowledge is worth learning at the middle level as we saw in Chapter 5. This task is often carried out at the state, county, and/or school district level. These frameworks are usually organized as learning expectations in mathematics, social studies, language arts, and science, as well as in other traditional subject areas. Content, such as topics and subject-specific procedures is easy to identify, describe, and categorize using traditional subject-based schemes, while thinking processes and generalizable skills are appropriately treated in interdisciplinary contexts and are more challenging to organize. Current efforts include thematic approaches in organizing expectations and integrating content, thinking processes, and affective components in interdisciplinary coverage.

The *third level* involves instructional planning. In order to meet the integrative goals, teacher teams must work together designing activities that involve higher level thinking processes.[2] This is not an easy task as teachers are typically educated to think in terms of one subject rather than across the curriculum.

Although the core curriculum, by definition, should be built around the most generalizable themes and processes, or skills, typically core gets translated into learning expectations in the major subject areas. In part, this avoidance of the integrative program may be due to a lack of knowledge, or conviction, about the arguments favoring this approach. Themes such as change, patterns, time, and evidence must be derived from the subjects and are developed most effectively by teams of cooperating teachers.

ARGUMENTS FAVORING CORE CURRICULUM AND INTERDISCIPLINARY INSTRUCTION

Reasons to adopt interdisciplinary instructional approaches in core subjects are both pedagogical and practical in nature. As you read the arguments presented in the following pages, take mental notes. Are these points logical? Have you heard them before? What might cause teachers to resist them?

1. The knowledge explosion in every subject area has increased the necessity to select content to be learned based on transferrable concepts and multidisciplinary generalizations. The emphasis now placed on learning concepts or structures in which to organize facts, and on using resources to find information as needed, has priority over memorizing details.

> **TALKING WITH TEACHERS: REFLECTIONS ON DEPTH OVER BREADTH** We decided to have students do an in-depth unit on energy. They spent a lot of time investigating, discussing, doing projects, and designing action plans for conserving resources here at school as well as in the community, really getting involved in their own learning. We were criticized because we didn't spend much time on some other science topics, but when the state standardized test results came out, our students did as well or better in the areas we hadn't covered as anyone else. I think the attention to process and long-term understanding paid off.
> —Eighth-grade science teacher

2. Instructional time must be responsive to learning expectations. The fragmented school day that segregates subjects into uniform time periods does not allow time to think in depth or make long-lasting connections between related areas of knowledge. The frequently used expression of frustration, "There aren't enough minutes in the day," reflects our preoccupation with apportionment of subjects into specific and discrete units of time as a check-off device, and reveals the misconception that time on task is a cause of success rather than a correlation to success. Simultaneous scheduling of students for blocks of time in the care of cooperating teachers allows flexible use of both space and time for extended instruction and projects. In addition, cooperation among teachers can

eliminate repetition or redundancy resulting from concepts being repeated in several subject areas with no plan for how students would gain from the multiple exposure.

3. Relevance is increased when students can, first, apply knowledge to real-life situations that by nature are themselves interdisciplinary, and, second, carry out problem solving that requires addressing content from different perspectives. Lack of relevance directly correlates with school dropout rate. Attitudes about school and its worth are often solidified at the middle level. Attitudes about individual abilities and aspirations, including career choices, often gel at this time as well.

Life does not consist of 15- to 50-minute experiences sequentially arranged and in discrete units insulated from other ideas. Life requires us to address issues from synthesized perspectives and make decisions based on multifaceted knowledge bases. It is helpful to select components of a field for the purpose of study, but students should not be left thinking about concepts only in isolation. Learning that units of knowledge relate to each other, and can be transferred to new situations that fit into real life, is part of the educational process. We must help students make connections, synthesize, and summarize, so that they can integrate learning into the mainstream of thinking and problem solving in society.

4. Integration in the curriculum has public approval. When properly communicated, interdisciplinary programs are viewed by society as closely aligned with what schools should do to prepare young adults for life. The communication effort can itself be integrated into the curriculum. Open house; science fairs; academic competitions; newsletters and newsvideos sent home; sports programs; displays in museums, government buildings, and shopping centers; coverage of school programs and events in the newspaper and on TV; and other evidence of achievement, productivity, and innovation—all contribute to a more positive public image of middle level schools, and all can involve student participation in the communication process.

TALKING WITH TEACHERS: COMMUNITY CONNECTION AND THE INTEGRATION PROCESS Our core group calls itself KOMO Core using an acronym based on the core teachers' names. They maintain a communications station, Audio-Video Station KOMO, and present triweekly updates on audio- and videocassette covering school news, announcements, upcoming events, and special reports. Special reports and summaries of school events are placed on audio tape, videotape, or both, to be checked out for home use for parents to see. Closer school community ties result from this exchange of information. Special reports include videotaped interviews and demonstrations by community experts: Geraldo's mother demonstrates cooking for a holiday. Tamn Vu's father is a mechanic who provides tips on bicycle repair and safety. Sam's special friend the grocer gives nutrition tips. The activity is founded on the idea that every kid has a special adult who has something important that can be shared on tape, and that during the course of a year, all kids can be featured.

—Eighth-grade advisor to a student team of reporters

5. Individualization is optimized. When the emphasis is on thinking processes and generalizable concepts, the specific topics, serving as the media through which the processes and concepts are learned, may be chosen more at the discretion of the teacher rather than dictated by a higher authority. Opportunity is therefore increased to match students with preferred learning styles and topics of interest while encouraging peer cooperation, acceptance of responsibility for personal progress, development of independent investigative skills, and productivity.

6. Assessment and evaluation opportunities are abundant, especially when checking for transfer of concept learning to new situations. Beyond the traditional paper- and pencil-demonstration of retention of facts, students can be rated on performance in oral communication and problem-oriented tasks as well as knowledge reflected in reports, models, videotapes, displays, creative writing, and other media. In addition, students can be credited with achievement demonstrated in group work as well as individual effort.

TALKING WITH TEACHERS: A REAL FIELD TEST Mr. Petris was teaching a unit on the settlement of the West in Social Studies. He wanted the students to better understand the struggles involved in traveling by wagon train to California. Mrs. Hirata was teaching a unit on Simple Machines in Science. She provided experience in using levers, pulleys, inclined planes, screws, and the wheel and axle to make work easier. Mr. Petris decided to provide a simulation of some of the hardships encountered during a wagon train journey. He took the students to a sandy beach and assigned each pair of pioneers a four-wheeled hand wagon laden with "supplies." The task was to get across the sandy area (it could have been a muddy field or snow bank to provide similar challenges in physics). Safety was a priority, of course. One pioneer of the pair was required to ride in the wagon at all times. The concepts used in problem solving by applying knowledge of simple machines were shared by both subject areas. Transfer from one subject area to another was concrete and interactive. The activity also resulted in looking at the tools the pioneers used and categorizing them by type of simple machine employed. Assessment of student knowledge, problem-solving approaches, and cooperative effort could be carried out at the same time students were in the process of learning and reinforcing concepts. Mr. Petris and Mrs. Hirata prepared a checklist to assist them

in recording observations that would help them give students credit for knowledge demonstrated during this test in the field.
—Principal of a middle school

7. Several strategies can be used to carry out integration processes, including long-term or short-term instruction, instructional components that are simultaneous or staggered, and variations in the degree and nature of integration. Strategies should match the instructional intents and should vary to provide numerous avenues toward learning. In addition, integration should not represent the sole curriculum implementation approach. Each discipline has distinct characteristics that must be considered in isolation to be appreciated.

8. The school structure at the middle level supports the implementation of the core curriculum in several ways, including the establishment of (1) an intermediate stage between elementary and secondary levels of schooling, (2) flexible daily schedules in control of teacher teams, and (3) teacher hiring practices and team composition.

9. Hiring practices seek to place at the middle level those teachers with a student-centered orientation and expertise in at least two core subjects. An ideal team would consist of teachers who work well together, are competent in at least two core areas, and have some overlapping areas of expertise, including shared interests in the electives and special topics. These middle school teachers typically have greater in-depth subject area preparation than elementary teachers and broader, more general, knowledge and expertise than high school teachers. In addition, their understanding of the early adolescent in terms of cognitive, social, and physical growth patterns contributes to making effective curriculum decisions, particularly at the school site level. Notice how these hiring practices are reflected in the teaching assignments of the teachers featured in the examples shown in Tables 8.2, 8.3, and 8.4 later in this chapter.

INTEGRATION POSSIBILITIES AND LIMITATIONS

The rationale in favor of interdisciplinary instruction is strong but does not automatically ensure productive results. Success of interdisciplinary efforts is dependent on critical elements in the school program including (1) the commitment of the teacher, (2) choice among several options for interdisciplinary plans or kinds of integration, (3) quality of communication among team members, (4) logistical support from school administration, and (5) careful development of instructional units. It is worthwhile at this time to consider integration possibilities and limitations as well as certain obstacles to implementation.

Kinds of Integration

Integration of knowledge, occurring across fields within a discipline or across disciplines, can take many forms. Here are some variations, followed by examples, that emphasize integration of knowledge across the disciplines that make up the main subject areas at the middle level:

1. *Students learn about the same topic or concept in different contexts or subject areas and thereby acquire additional details about the topic or concept.* For example, students can learn about the elephant by finding out about (1) its role as a working animal in a social studies unit on India, (2) its status as an endangered species in a science and social studies unit on conservation of wildlife, and (3) its size in relation to other animals in a math unit on comparative measurements. Students can learn about magnetism by (1) experimenting with the properties of attracting and repelling in a science activity, (2) using a magnetic compass in a geography exercise, (3) constructing a stereo speaker in industrial arts class, and (4) incorporating magnets in a product manufactured and sold by the school business club.

2. *Students learn about a concept or process in different contexts and thus they can confirm or restructure their understanding of the concept.* For example, in a variety of lessons taught within various subject areas, students manipulate the center of gravity in (1) packing a backpack, (2) designing earthquake-safe storage, (3) loading a boat, and (4) jumping hurdles. In another example, students practice listening, reading, and writing skills associated with following and giving directions. They then consider the consequences of clarity in communication in a variety of settings involving the operation of equipment and safe handling of substances. In a final example, students find out about the economics of conservation in a math and social studies unit that allows them to calculate the savings in dollars in a variety of situations including repairing a dripping faucet, using recycled notepaper in the classroom, turning off lights at school and at home, and planting trees to alleviate the need for air conditioning.

3. *Students learn a concept or skill in one subject area and apply it directly in another.* For example, they learn how to collect and organize data on major agricultural production in the United States into a chart for a social studies report and then use the same skill during a science investigation on the rate of seed germination in different soil conditions. In another example, students learn about global weather patterns and transfer this knowledge to a problem-solving situation involving sources and effects of air pollution. Students learn about democratic practices in our country and apply the principles when conducting cooperative group activities or carrying out responsibilities in class governance. Skills learned in language arts related to organizing ideas and communicating them through audiovisual media can be used when presenting the history of a local family business as part of a social studies project.

4. Students learn a concept or skill, or detailed factual knowledge, and extend, transform, or adapt the knowledge to fit new contexts. For example, a study of the properties of water enriches the way students interpret or write poems that refer to water metaphorically. In another example, students learn about how parts of a bicycle work together in various relations and as a system. For art class, the students videotape specific movements and shapes found in the bicycle and combine the imaging with a sound track.

Processes of Integration: Developing Interdisciplinary Units

The following steps in designing integrated units are recommended to ensure success in both learning and accountability.[3]

1. Select a focus such as a theme, problem, issue, event, or area of interest.
2. Brainstorm details related to the focus and identify associations.
3. Establish guiding questions to serve as a scope and sequence and to reinforce congruence of purpose among teacher team members. Decide which concepts should be taught in isolation and which should be integrated.
4. Write activities for instruction that reflect a model of cognition, are coordinated in terms of prerequisite knowledge development, use a variety of modes of instruction, and describe performance outcomes for evaluation purposes.

Drafting a Unit Framework: One Example. The four core teachers of Shenandoah Community in the eighth grade at Jefferson School decided to plan a three-week unit around the theme of water with emphases on water as a resource and on issues related to water quality and conservation. They began by individually brainstorming in each of their subject areas and then, together, constructed a concept map that identified important discipline-specific and interdisciplinary concepts, skills, and thinking processes. In order to broaden the transferability of learning and provide a structure for students to think about other resources, the teachers decided to embed an awareness of opportunities provided by and limitations resulting from the presence or absence of water—sort of a ying-yang approach, based on the idea that for every perspective there is an interesting alternate and opposite perspective to consider. The teachers produced the working model shown in Figure 8.1 to serve as a framework from which to develop discrete lessons. Ideas for some of them are outlined in an example in Chapter 10.

Processes of Integration: Recognizing Limitations

Integration efforts weaken instruction when distinctions between subjects that should be made apparent are instead camouflaged, or when integration is superficial or trivial, represents a forced fit, or results in distracting students from the

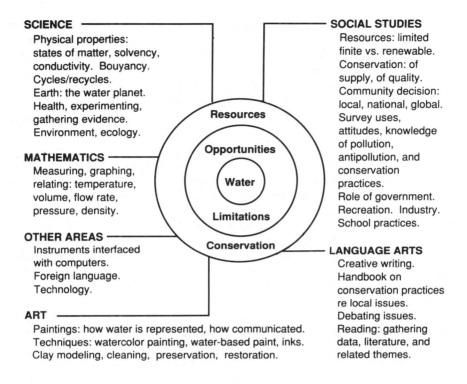

SCIENCE
Physical properties:
states of matter, solvency,
conductivity. Bouyancy.
Cycles/recycles.
Earth: the water planet.
Health, experimenting,
gathering evidence.
Environment, ecology.

MATHEMATICS
Measuring, graphing,
relating: temperature,
volume, flow rate,
pressure, density.

OTHER AREAS
Instruments interfaced
with computers.
Foreign language.
Technology.

ART
Paintings: how water is represented, how communicated.
Techniques: watercolor painting, water-based paint, inks.
Clay modeling, cleaning, preservation, restoration.

Resources
Opportunities
Water
Limitations
Conservation

SOCIAL STUDIES
Resources: limited
finite vs. renewable.
Conservation: of
supply, of quality.
Community decision:
local, national, global.
Survey uses,
attitudes, knowledge
of pollution,
antipollution, and
conservation
practices.
Role of government.
Recreation. Industry.
School practices.

LANGUAGE ARTS
Creative writing.
Handbook on
conservation practices
re local issues.
Debating issues.
Reading: gathering
data, literature, and
related themes.

Figure 8.1. Draft Framework for Developing an Interdisciplinary Unit on the Opportunities and Limitations of Water.

main purposes of the lessons. Subjects differ in special characteristics, details, and approaches to learning associated knowledge. When to fuse and when to correlate in the process of integration are decisions that need to be made. The pairs of examples that follow describe traps that await the unwary integrator and strategies for overcoming them.

A Case of Fusing or Losing the Purpose. There is usually more than one approach to providing special assistance within an activity. The challenge is to avoid obscuring the main goals by overemphasizing details. The following examples present two approaches to integrating technical rules into an activity meant to promote creativity.

1. Mrs. Kaye gave a writing assignment about living in a fantasy world of geometric shapes as part of a math activity. As the students word processed their first story drafts, she interrupted several times to review basic rules on punctua-

tion and subject-verb agreement. When she realized that the students were not being very creative, she took one day to review the process of brainstorming, writing selected ideas, reviewing them, and rewriting for clarity. When the stories were complete, the students read each other's products in small groups, made editing suggestions, rewrote the stories with corrections, and bound them into small booklets with illustrations. When asked to describe the assignment, they reported learning about some rules for English and drawing geometric shapes.

2. Mr. Perrit gave a writing assignment identical to Mrs. Kaye's. He began by brainstorming with the whole class and leaving students to make their own choices and write their first drafts. He noticed numerous errors in punctuation and subject-verb agreement, but said nothing. When the story drafts were complete, he had students form three-member "eddy" (for editing) groups to circulate the drafts for peer review and for trading suggestions. Students then rewrote their stories for clarity, illustrated them, and, after a final check by the teacher, bound them into small booklets. Mr. Perrit noticed that the final drafts had significantly fewer technical errors as a result of the peer review process and selected only two or three corrections to make during the final check. When asked about the assignment, his students reported learning about geometric shapes and becoming authors of math adventure stories.

The students in Mrs. Kaye's and Mr. Perrit's classes were challenged with a writing assignment. It was distracting and counterproductive, in terms of reinforcing math concepts and encouraging creative communication, when Mrs. Kaye chose to dwell on certain technical details during the story development stages. The interruption served to disrupt the flow of effort addressing the creative-writing task. In Mr. Perrit's class the processes of writing ideas, reviewing them, and rewriting for clarification were allowed to occur naturally as students discussed their stories with each other. In Mr. Perrit's case the writing mechanics were allowed to remain fused within the story development effort. The outcomes in terms of students' perceptions of learning and value of the experience present a striking contrast.

A Case of Isolating Instruction Before Integrating. Possessing prerequisite skills or concepts needed to learn new ideas can make the difference between experiencing success or failure. We often have students learn skills in a familiar context for mastery and then transfer the skills to new areas. For example, when finding out about time zones, the annual change in daylight hours at different locations, hurricane patterns, circulation of air and ocean currents, and other global phenomena, it is useful—even essential—to understand that the earth rotates on its axis, revolves around the sun at a tilt, and can be sectioned by references known as latitude and longitude.

The following example involves a health unit on substance abuse taught two consecutive years; but, in the second year, it integrated with science instruction on the physiological effects of substances on the human body.

1. First year: Ms. Hannah presented an alcohol and drug abuse unit in her health class. Activities involved discussing problems of substance abuse, viewing informational films, writing individual reports on specific drugs, and drawing decision maps that plotted ways to say "no." The results were rather flat with basic facts regurgitated during class discussions and with assignments completed more as a duty than through inspired purpose toward self-enlightenment.

2. Second year: Prior to the unit on substance abuse taught in health class by Ms. Hannah, the science teacher Mr. Grodin introduced students to ways the body reacts to a variety of substances. Students experimented using computer-interfaced instruments to measure heartbeat, breathing rate, and temperature to see how the body responded to drinking a soda containing caffeine, eating a candy bar, and ingesting a variety of other common, and legal, substances. Students viewed videotapes that demonstrated the effects of substances commonly abused by adolescents today, and carried out research using books, interviews, and other resources to report on the history, chemistry, and physiology of tobacco, alcohol, and specific drugs. In the meantime Ms. Hannah had students involved in reflecting peer relationships with emphasis on how to communicate ideas and opinions without closing the door on friendships. When students had (1) a background understanding of basic science concepts and enough factual knowledge to make decisions and (2) a skill structure for communicating personal stands without threatening friendships, the class was divided into groups to prepare and present simulated situations about handling peer pressure and drinking alcoholic beverages. This year some groups prepared skits based on their own ideas about current life on the street in addition to addressing assigned challenges. Three of the skits were videotaped for presentation to the fifth grade classes. Ms. Hannah noted that planning instruction to provide background knowledge and skills made a significant difference in the depth of discussion of drug- and alcohol-related issues, in the attention span during research safaris to the library, and in the instances when students voluntarily brought in newspaper articles and other related items to share.

In the example above, Ms. Hannah tried two variations in her teaching of the unit on substance abuse. During the second year, she provided for instruction in isolated areas and then facilitated an instructional unit that utilized the newly acquired knowledge and skills in an integrated context. Her second plan ensured success among a greater number of students, and the results, both affective and academic, gave positive testimony to the value of cooperative teacher teamwork.

Making Distinctions between Disciplines. The nature of specific subject areas and of fields within a discipline should not be obscured by subscribing to interdisciplinary approaches on a full-time basis or by consistently fusing the disciplines to such a degree that students cannot identify when they are operating from one discipline base and when from another. Critical thinking or decision making, for example, can have different orientations and purposes in science and social studies. In science, we gather data to determine the amount of support or lack of support for an hypothesis.[4] We weigh evidence for and against statements of accepted fact to determine the stability of what we consider to be true. We change our acceptance of what is true or factual as new evidence indicates. In social studies, many of the same activities are carried out, gathering data and weighing evidence in order to make interpretations.[5] However, when social issues are under consideration, additional steps are included to determine relative values and to select choices or stands in relation to consequences or other value-laden criteria. Often group opinion is taken into account. When science and social studies are combined in an interdisciplinary unit, it is often important to distinguish when we are doing science and when we are doing social studies. Table 8.1 outlines an example of shifting between disciplines during the instruction of an integrated unit.

Students benefit when they learn to identify these subject area perspectives. Many societal debates and miscommunications are precipitated when people do not make such distinctions, particularly when attempting to draw objective conclusions or make subjective judgments. Evolution vs. creationism represents

TABLE 8.1. DISTINGUISHING SUBJECT AREAS IN AN INTEGRATED TOPIC: HUMANS AND THE MARSHLANDS

Instructional Processes	Subject Area
Brainstorm the impact of human activity in the marsh. Identify problems.	All
Find out about the natural inhabitants and ecological effects of seasonal changes, water supply, and interaction with humans. Describe the effects of human activity on the marsh.	Science
Evaluate the effects of human activity. Identify positive and negative aspects of the interactions, what is detrimental, and what is constructive.	Social studies
Project the condition of the marsh in the future.	Science
Evaluate the importance of the marsh's condition. Decide that the marsh should be preserved.	Social studies
Determine how the marsh can be preserved and what methods are likely to succeed.	Science
Determine cost factors for preserving the marsh and sources of revenue.	Social studies
Vote on the methods, to find student preference.	Social studies

a debate that becomes heated when a distinction is not made between the role of science in gathering data and describing *how* things work in nature and the role of the social studies areas of philosophy and religion in placing value on events and projecting *why* things work as they do or what purpose is served. Engaging in the debate, and placing value on whether it is important to establish a distinction between the two views, is itself an activity in the social studies domain. Arbitrators, who are hired to bring resolution to volatile or stagnated situations in which two sides cannot agree, need to be highly skilled in identifying the perspectives of information, interpretations, and personal arguments with which they must work.

Activity 8.1: Identifying the Trees in the Woods

Plan an interdisciplinary unit involving concepts from two or more subject areas, or choose one from Chapter 10. Organize the activities and/or procedures in a chart that associates each with its respective discipline.

WAYS TO IMPLEMENT THE CORE CURRICULUM

It is difficult to envision an interdisciplinary core curriculum in action without looking at the school organization and daily schedule. Not all middle level schools employ the same degree of cooperative teacher team involvement. Let us compare three examples, representing composites from typical schools, that illustrate variation in school structure and instructional environment for core curriculum implementation. All three schools have certain characteristics in common: (1) students attend for three years in grades 6, 7, and 8; (2) students move together as a class except for exploratory courses that allow individual choices; (3) designated teachers serve as advisors for students assigned to them throughout their three years at the school, and are accessible during homeroom and by arrangement during other parts of the day; (4) the day is divided into six instructional periods; and (5) the core subject teachers who work together in teams within each grade level have a prep period at the same time of day.

Example 1: Core Classes

Washington School uses a system in which each regular teacher has a core class of 30 students for homeroom and three main subjects. The school day is evenly divided into six instructional periods with the same subjects taught daily. Electives are provided in six-week sessions and are taken on a rotating basis. Teachers within the same grade level pair up to trade classes for specific core subjects based on the expertise and preferences of the two teachers. For example, Mr. Jones and Ms. Smith form a partnership in which Mr. Jones teaches language arts to each of their classes while Ms. Smith teaches science. Both of these teachers have their own base classes for mathematics and social studies. Mr. Jones is assigned to the all-school student council and student affairs for one period of the day and Ms. Smith teaches an elective class in dance for another grade level. Specialty teachers provide instruction in other subjects such as technical arts, fine arts, and physical education. Students at Washington School keep their belongings in assigned desks in their homerooms where they also have half of their instruction. A sample daily schedule is shown in Table 8.2.

Strengths and opportunities embedded in this example of Washington School include several logistical elements. Teachers who share classes have a common preparation period that facilitates cooperative planning. There is flexibility in arranging instruction for a teacher who has several subjects with the same students, or who shares students with another teacher. It is not necessary to follow in lock-step fashion the division of the day into designated periods. Thus, an individual teacher can plan units that integrate several subject areas

TABLE 8.2. SAMPLE DAILY SCHEDULE FOR FOUR CLASSES AT THE SAME GRADE LEVEL AT WASHINGTON SCHOOL

Teachers: Mr. Jones teaches language arts, math, and social studies to his base class and serves as advisor to the student council and student affairs.

Ms. Smith teaches science, math, and social studies to her base class and dance as an exploratory course at another grade level.

Mrs. Gomez teaches science, math, and language arts to her base class and exploratory foreign language (Spanish).

Mr. Brown teaches social studies, language arts, and science as well as exploratory subjects in music (not shown on this schedule).

Other teachers who teach exploratory courses to these classes include Ms. Yuen (art) and Mr. Reilly (computers).

Class	Jones	Smith	Gomez	Brown
Homeroom	Jones	Smith	Gomez	Brown
Period 1	Lang. arts (Jones)	Science (Smith)	Math (Gomez)	Soc. studies (Brown)
Period 2	Science (Smith)	Lang. arts (Jones)	Soc. studies (Brown)	Math (Gomez)
Period 3	P.E. (prep period for Jones and Smith)	P.E.	Science (Gomez)	Lang. arts (Brown)
Period 4	Soc. studies (Jones)	Math (Smith)	P.E. (prep period for Gomez and Brown)	P.E.
Period 5	Exploratory Spanish (Gomez)	Exploratory Music (Brown)	Exploratory Computers (Reilly)	Exploratory Art (Yuen)
Period 6	Math (Jones)	Soc. studies (Smith)	Lang. arts (Gomez)	Science (Brown)

and schedule activities in time blocks as appropriate for the concepts being learned. Note that students receive instruction from one teacher for more than half of each day. This intermediate level of stability or consistency provides a transition for the student from the self-contained classroom of upper elementary grades to the segmented schedule of the high school setting. The minimal expectation for teacher team work is welcome for teachers who prefer to work independently from other faculty members.

Limitations or obstacles to overcome revealed in the Washington School example include a fairly demanding teacher load of up to four preparations each day with expectations for instruction at significantly greater depth than for elementary grades, and a schedule lacking shared preparation time that does not allow base teachers to meet easily with teachers of other specialties or exploratory courses. Teachers often tend to think of classes as "my students" and "your students."

Example 2: Core Teachers

Adams School assigns students to core teachers who teach two main subjects, usually language arts and social studies. Students move to the classrooms of other teachers for the remainder of their six-period schedule. Science is taught in a science lab by a specialist. A few teachers teach both science and mathematics as well as an elective. One teacher specializes in mathematics and teaches several of the electives on a rotational basis. Other specialty areas with single-subject teachers serving the whole school are industrial arts, physical education, and computer technology. Core teachers have common prep periods by grade level. Students are assigned to designated teachers who serve as advisors to the same students throughout their three years at Adams School. Student have assigned "mailboxes" in their homerooms and individual lockers in a commons area. A sample daily schedule for four classes is shown in Table 8.3.

Strengths and opportunities at Adams School seem more numerous than for the previous example. Each class of students has a base (homeroom) teacher and several subject-specialty teachers providing exposure for students to a variety of subject areas. Teachers have about three preparations per day with at least two with their homeroom class. This allows blocks of time within which to manipulate activities as appropriate for concepts being taught by subject area or in integrated fashion. A common prep period for most of the teachers having contact time with these classes facilitates cooperative efforts and sharing of information on individual student progress. Teacher teams, which are, to a large extent, personality dependent, can form on a volunteer basis and disband as interdisciplinary projects are planned and completed. There is more of a sense of "our students" than at Washington School.

Limitations or obstacles to overcome at Adams School include the necessity for professional and personality complements on each teacher team in order to carry out integrated instruction effectively.

TABLE 8.3. SAMPLE DAILY SCHEDULE FOR FOUR CLASSES AT THE SAME GRADE LEVEL AT ADAMS SCHOOL

Teachers: Mr. Thomas teaches language arts and social studies and exploratory courses in life skills (to classes not shown on this schedule).
Ms. Richie teaches language arts and social studies as well as exploratory courses in dance and other electives (not shown on this schedule).
Mrs. Lopez teaches science and exploratory foreign language (Spanish).
Ms. Keith teaches math, language arts, and social studies as well as exploratory subjects in music (including classes not shown on this schedule).
Mr. Neuton teaches social studies and science and exploratory subjects in art (including classes not shown on this schedule).
Mrs. Kato teaches math and science (not shown on this schedule).

Class	Thomas	Richie	Keith	Neuton
Homeroom	Thomas	Richie	Keith	Neuton
Period 1	Lang. arts (Thomas)	Science (Lopez)	Math (Kato)	Soc. studies (Neuton)
Period 2	Science (Lopez)	Lang. arts (Richie)	Soc. studies (Keith)	Math (Kato)
Period 3	P.E.	P.E. (prep period for teachers Thomas, Richie, Keith, Kato, Lopez, and Neuton)	P.E.	P.E.
Period 4	Soc. studies (Thomas)	Math (Kato)	Science (Lopez)	Lang. arts (Neuton)
Period 5	Exploratory Spanish (Lopez)	Exploratory Music (Keith)	Exploratory Computers (Jones)	Exploratory Art (Neuton)
Period 6	Math (Kato)	Soc. studies (Richie)	Lang. arts (Keith)	Science (Lopez)

Example 3: Grade Level Communities

Jefferson School is organized into grade level communities, two for each of the sixth, seventh, and eighth grades, with each community consisting of 120 students in the charge of four core teachers. Each core teacher has a base class that meets daily during a homeroom period.[6] The core teachers together, as members of a team, are responsible for scheduling instructional time blocks for their students, for teaching mathematics, social studies, language arts, and science, and for working with other teachers and support personnel in the school. Teachers of physical education, fine arts, home arts and life skills, and foreign language are adjunct team members at the time students are taking those classes. Jefferson School uses this structure to implement the middle level core curriculum developed by the school district in response to state guidelines. In addition to the basic subjects, three cycles of exploratory courses are offered each year. Students take two exploratory subjects at a time and can take advanced sessions in some, such as foreign language and music. Spanish is required for at least one cycle. Students can choose between computers and music. Students at Jefferson School have small, open, stowage areas in their homerooms and assigned lockers near a community assembly area. A sample daily schedule for four classes shown in Table 8.4. The daily schedule has two variations to accommodate elective classes that do not meet daily. These "A" and "B" days alternate independent of the day of the week throughout the year. Note that nearly all instruction, except physical education, is carried out by a team of four teachers who have diverse and somewhat overlapping interests and represent a broad range of expertise.

Strengths and opportunities provided by the Jefferson School structure include a flexible schedule that accommodates a variety of configurations for basic subjects, electives, and exploratory courses, and one that facilitates optimal collaboration between teachers who have different as well as similar areas of expertise. Teachers have fewer preparations than in the other schools, with some classes meeting only two or three times each week. Because so much decision making, including student schedules, lies with the teacher teams, the

TABLE 8.4. SAMPLE DAILY SCHEDULE OF A COMMUNITY AT JEFFERSON SCHOOL

Teachers: Mr. Kelly teaches language arts and social studies.
          Mrs. Garcia teaches math and science and exploratory subjects foreign language (Spanish) and dance.
          Ms. Wall teaches math and exploratory subjects in computers and music.
          Mr. Tien teaches social studies and science and exploratory subjects in art.

Class	Kelly	Garcia	Wall	Tien
Homeroom	Kelly	Garcia	Wall	Tien
Period 1	Lang. arts (Kelly)	Science (Garcia)	Math (Wall)	Soc. studies (Tien)
Period 2	Science (Garcia)	Lang. arts (Kelly)	Soc. studies (Tien)	Math (Wall)
Period 3	P.E.	P.E. (prep period for teachers Kelly, Garcia, Wall, and Tien)	P.E.	P.E.
Period 4	Soc. studies (Kelly)	Math (Garcia)	Exploratory A. Music (Wall) B. Art (Tien)	Exploratory A. Art (Tien) B. Computers (Wall)
Period 5	Exploratory A. Spanish (Garcia) B. Computers (Wall)	Exploratory A. Music (Wall) B. Spanish (Garcia)	Science (Tien)	Lang. arts (Kelly)
Period 6	Math (Garcia)	Soc. studies (Tien)	Lang. arts (Kelly)	Science (Tien)

sense of community—the mind set of "our students" rather than "my students"—is generated internally rather than externally as is probably the case in the other school examples.

Limitations or obstacles to overcome at Jefferson School include the challenge of meeting individualized student needs with an increased student-to-teacher ratio. Teachers contact many more individual students each week and must still maintain a personalized plan of instruction and monitor the individual student's socialization patterns. In addition, the expectation that the four main teachers can and do indeed work together in harmony could present professional and personal challenges that some teachers might find difficult to meet.

The school structures and schedules exemplified by Washington, Adams, and Jefferson schools present a variation in (1) expectation and facilitation for teacher teaming, (2) number of different teachers that work with each student, and (3) teacher preparation load. All three configurations represent an intermediate stage between the elementary school environment and high school. It is possible to have different scheduling structures at different grade levels in one middle level school and thus have elements from all three of the examples presented in this section.

Activity 8.2: Comparing School Schedules

With a colleague, compare in more detail the three school schedules outlined above. What are strengths and limitations of each? In which would you feel comfortable working? No school schedule designed to implement a core curriculum needs to remain set forever. What variations might you suggest, and how would you suggest precipitating changes?

> **TALKING WITH TEACHERS: A FINAL WORD ON INTEGRATION** Racial, ethnic, and multicultural integration in the schools does not work simply by putting kids together. The students from different groups must work together, interact, depend on each other, and be embedded in the same processes. Integration involves interaction. The same goes for integrating topics and subjects. Side-by-side treatment achieves limited results and doesn't really work in the long run. Knowledge interacting with knowledge does.
>
> —Seventh grade teacher

CONCLUSIONS

The core curriculum, the knowledge base that all students at the middle level should acquire, can be implemented effectively and with greater efficiency (1) through strategic scheduling of instructional periods, (2) by assigning instructional responsibilities to teachers based on background expertise and interest, and (3) by facilitating team interaction among teachers. Interdisciplinary approaches to core instruction, while not intended to be used to carry out the total school program, have important pedagogical, psychological, and organizational benefits and are natural extensions to a core program. Subjects can differ in special characteristics, details, and approaches to learning the associated knowledge. Subjects also share certain concepts and processes. The distinctiveness justifies separate treatment as discrete areas of study. However, to accommodate growing amounts of material to be learned and to assist students in constructing understanding and using knowledge in an integrated fashion, as in real life, integrated approaches to teaching and learning are recommended.

While flexible block scheduling and theme teaching contribute significantly to successful implementation of the core curriculum, cooperation among teachers is a key factor and involves cohesive instruction, sharing feedback about students in common, and coordinating time periods, topics, and use of resources.

EXTENSIONS

1. Study the topic map begun for the theme on water. Discuss it with one or more colleagues and add details. Check it for balance of subject area content, thinking processes, and skills that empower students to organize their own learning. Propose a tentative schedule of activities for the unit.

2. Students in Monroe School can take any of the following subjects: mathematics, social studies, language arts, science, first aid, art, drama, music, interpretive dance, folk dance, gymnastics, swimming, team sports, crafts, shop, French, Spanish, German, Japanese, Russian, technology arts, homemaking, health, life skills, and calligraphy. The first four are the traditional core subjects in the United States. With your colleagues, brainstorm a list of interdisciplinary possibilities between the core and exploratory subjects.

3. Interview core subject teachers for their views on interdisciplinary instruction. Compare their experiences with those discussed in this chapter. How do you account for the differences?

NOTES AND REFERENCES

1. *The Report of the Task Force on Education of Young Adolescents.* New York: Carnegie Council on Adolescent Development, Carnegie Corp. of New York, 1989.
2. Refer to Chapter 3 for characteristics of higher-level thinking.
3. Adapted from H. H. Jacobs, *Interdisciplinary Curriculum: Design and Implementation* Ch. 5. Washington, DC: Association of Supervision and Curriculum Development, 1989.

4. Note that we do not prove that a hypothesis is true in science. Proofs are reserved for mathematicians and logicians.
5. These strategies patterned after the procedures of science and applied to areas in social studies have precipitated the discipline cluster known as the social sciences.
6. The function of homeroom is addressed in Chapter 7.

FOR FURTHER READING

Ambron, S., and Hooper, K. *Learning with Interactive Multimedia: Developing and Using Multimedia Tools in Education.* Redmond, WA: Microsoft Press, 1990.

Jacobs, H. H. *Interdisciplinary Curriculum: Design and Implementation.* Washington, DC: Association of Supervision and Curriculum Development, 1989.

Lewbel, S. R. *Interdisciplinary Units in New England's Middle Schools, A How-to Guide.* Rowley, MA: New England League of Middle Schools (NELMS), 1988.

CHAPTER 9

Instruction at the Middle Level

Once the decisions about the national agenda, state goals and objectives, district curriculum guidelines, and school program are made, teachers can set about implementing, through instruction, the middle level curriculum as it relates to their own students and classes. Weaving together all the parts that contribute to effective instruction is what teachers do best. Experienced teachers make it look easy. Theories, strategies, background knowledge, sensitivity to student responses, interpretation of nonverbal behaviors, logistics, and many other components of instruction—all are brought into play, simultaneously and often invisibly, as teachers facilitate learning. It is useful to look at many of the parts separately, however, so that they can be more effectively integrated when planning and carrying out instruction.

In this chapter, we:

- Relate learning theory to practice,
- Compare a variety of teaching approaches and lesson types,
- Examine the learning environment from the learner's perspective, and
- Describe ways to plan effective instructional units and lessons.

CONNECTING LEARNING THEORY TO INSTRUCTIONAL PRACTICE

Theory seeks to explain why certain practices work and why some do not. It is based on patterns of observed behavior, such as what children do and how they think in certain circumstances. Knowing theoretical principles helps us devise

181

practices that have greater probability of succeeding. Although psychosocial and cognitive characteristics of early adolescents have been reviewed in Chapter 3, it is beneficial to discuss the related theoretical bases that influence decision making in actual instruction at the middle level. Of particular importance are practices designed for (1) fostering a student's sense of success, (2) adapting to individual learning styles, (3) self-structuring of understanding, and (4) learning to learn.

Student Sense of Success

Developing self-esteem and self-sufficiency are critical at the middle level, a time when students are gaining foundational knowledge and skills, establishing patterns of interaction with ideas and other people, and setting personal life goals. A major goal of the middle level school is to help students keep their options open for future decision making. Even though society maintains and improves the spectrum of opportunities, a student without confidence will not even identify with the many and varied possibilities for his or her own future.

> **TALKING WITH TEACHERS: ABOUT ROLE MODELS** After showing a film on science careers featuring a variety of technicians and professionals, I asked one of my students if he thought he'd like to become a scientist like any of those we saw. He said that he could only be a mechanic. When I probed further, I found he really thought that was the only job he liked that was available to him because all the mechanics in his part of town belonged to his ethnic group and none of those in any pictures or films, or among people he met, looked like him. I was shocked by the power of role models and really scurried to find better representation among my posters and "professional propaganda."
> —Seventh grade science/social studies teacher

Central to our efforts at the middle level is the development of positive self-esteem and the acquisition of intrinsic or internal reward systems. As early adolescents move from dependence on adults for direction toward independent decision making, there is more importance placed on how they evaluate themselves and their own achievements. A sense of success is the essential ingredient for building positive self-esteem and maintaining the motivation to learn. The feeling of success derived from self-evaluation is more powerful and long-lasting than that resulting from external judgment. In order to ensure the kind of success that leads to the desired results, teachers can:

1. Facilitate interaction with problems and concepts within the appropriate range of cognitive development, both in terms of vertical growth and in level of abstraction (horizontal growth);

2. Provide opportunities for students to choose from a variety of instructional tasks and to function in their preferred learning styles;
3. Facilitate students having ownership in carrying out instructional activities and in establishing and maintaining classroom climate;
4. Provide nontrivial criteria for judging success in any given task, including criteria selected by the students and checked by them; and
5. Promote a shift from a dependency on extrinsic reward systems for determining self-worth to intrinsic systems.

Society conditions us, in many ways, to respond to extrinsic rewards. It is difficult to purge them completely from schools and from the classroom, and doing so might erase certain positive communications that are basic to psychological support and valued personal relationships. Many teachers think students with very low self-esteem need to gain more through external reinforcement before they can ever hope to develop internal strategies for positive self-evaluation. The lists below compare practices related to external and internal reward systems. Your challenge, as a teacher, is to be aware of the direct and subtle effects of your actions, sort trivial and superficial interactions from those that are sincere and meaningful, find a balance that works for you, and help your students move in the desired direction in their development of self-esteem.

A Comparison of Practices That Affect Self-Esteem

The following practices reinforce the association of superlatives with success and foster a dependence on an external reward system for a sense of self-worth:

1. Teacher praises routine tasks as they are completed with "Great job," "You're wonderful," "Fantastic," and comments that are so overly positive that they seem insincere.
2. Teacher grades assignments with letter grades and puts stars and stamps on papers. Grades are posted on the wall with student code numbers.
3. Teacher posts essays on the bulletin board entitled Famous Authors.
4. During discussions the teacher accepts all responses with a "good," "yes," "that's right," or "excellent."
5. All entries in the school Desktop Publishing Fair are displayed. Ribbons for first, second, and third place are awarded to the best entries.

The following practices reinforce a sense of self-satisfaction and encourage social contributions as well as growth of an internal reward system.

1. Teacher reacts to completed tasks as they are turned in with "Thank you for finishing it on time," "This looks interesting," "Did you learn something important?" and other reflective comments.

2. Teacher checks criteria established for the assignment and adds one or two comments or questions that recognize an important relationship or idea and encourage further thinking. Grades, based on established criteria, are available for individual student review.

3. Teacher asks students to post their essays on the bulletin board entitled Author Forum.

4. During discussions the teacher accepts all responses with "Ah!," "That's a thought we haven't heard yet," "I'll have to think about that," "Mmm," or just a nod of recognition. The teacher incorporates specific responses in summaries or lead-ins to new portions of the discussion.

5. All entries in the school Desktop Publishing Fair are displayed. Many are incorporated in school publications during the remainder of the year.

Sequencing instruction can affect student success and subsequent feelings about self and the topic, skill, or subject. If initial activities are frustrating and uninteresting, students might not be motivated even to try those that would provide successful experiences. At the same time, activities that are too easy also will fail to generate a sense of success. Tasks need to contain respectable challenges that are within students' abilities and, when overcome, precipitate a sense of pride. Learning experiences that build on one another can reveal the payoff for learning, the potential for applying knowledge. Discovering the empowerment of being able to use what one has learned is more likely to generate long-term self-confidence than immediate right answers that have only temporary value.

Activity 9.1: Thinking about Confidence Levels

Shifts in self-confidence about how well one understands the concepts being taught occur during an individual lesson or a unit. Figure 9.1 shows a confidence profile during a lesson on inertia and momentum at the eighth grade level.[1] Students were asked to rate themselves in terms of confidence in understanding the concepts and in being able to teach someone else. When is confidence the lowest? The highest? How often does instruction end with a unit test? What effect do you think this has? What alternative could you propose? Evaluation is covered in greater depth in Chapter 10.

Adapting to Individual Learning Styles

The students in any given class will exhibit variation in interests, talents, and intelligences, all of which translate into corresponding variations in learning styles, or preferred modes of learning. Gardner's multiple intelligences, Jung's personality types, and the characteristics of right brain and left brain activity were presented in Chapter 3. In responding to this variation, teachers provide ways for students to succeed in ways that are comfortable. It is also important

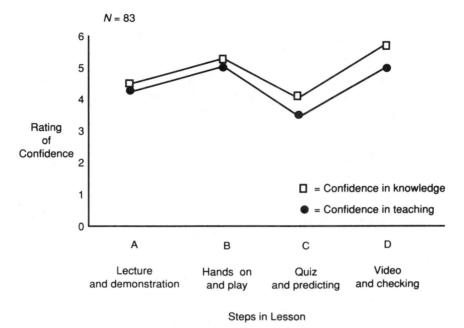

Figure 9.1. Change in Confidence Levels During a Lesson on Gravity and Inertia.

to give students experience in adapting to other modes of learning. Therefore, different instructional approaches are used, and students are given a certain amount of choice in the kinds of activities they may carry out.

Activity 9.2: Matching Instruction to Learning Styles

Below is a list of activities for possible inclusion in a unit on gears. First, select the activities you might use for this unit, which might consist of three to five lessons, and number the activities in the order you think students should carry them out. Second, relate those you selected to one or more learning styles described or implied by the ideas of multiple intelligences, personality types, and/or right/left brain function. Do you have an appropriate balance and logical order? Discuss your results with a colleague.

Possible Activities for an Instructional Unit on Gears:

_____ View videotape of how gears work in familiar objects.

_____ Build working models that utilize gears from a Technic Lego kit.

_____ Repair a toy that uses gears. Listen carefully to the moving parts to help determine the cause of the problem.

_____ Draw and label a Rube Goldberg–type invention that incorporates gears.

_____ Listen to music for which clocks are the theme.

_____ Choose a machine, large or small, that relies on gears. Select a time in history when that machine was important. Write a story from the perspective of the gear and the role it played.

_____ Find information about gears in an encyclopedia.

_____ Collect pictures from magazines that relate to the use of gears in daily life or in industry.

_____ Analyze the working parts of a bicycle.

_____ Compose or learn a song or rap that explains how gears are used to control direction and speed of movement.

_____ Take a test that requires you to construct a gear system that has a 3:1 ratio.

_____ Take apart a broken watch or clock and make jewelry or a small statue from the parts.

_____ Write a report on the role of gears in the kitchen.

Helping Students Construct Their Own Knowledge

Students do not begin middle school or any school year or any topic or subject with a blank slate. Students come with a personal and complex understanding of all aspects of their world based on prior exposure to their surroundings and on prior active experience. Their understanding changes with cognitive growth and experience. Research, both formal and informal, has demonstrated that it is self-regulated experience that leads to long-term learning.

Variations on Wisdom
I hear and I forget.
I see and I remember.
I do and I understand.
            —*Confucius*

I hear and I forget
(unless I'm an auditory learner).
I see and I remember
(assuming I'm a visual learner).
I do and I get the idea.
I teach and I understand.
            —*Confucius' wisdom reconstructed*
            by a psychology professor

I hear and I forget.
I see and I remember.
I do and I become confused.[2]
I then compare to what I know
And adjust my understanding.
—Confucius' wisdom reconstructed
  by constructivist theorists

Ideas about learning that recognize that each student builds knowledge and constructs understanding individually from personal experience are associated with constructivism. The constructivist environment is one that allows students to identify and test personal understanding and thereby reinforce or alter this understanding according to new internalized perceptions. In this approach new knowledge is incorporated into individualized mental schemes and, since mental schemes are unique to individuals, acquisition of new knowledge must be under the student's own control. The constructivist environment is student-centered and is rich in problem-solving, manipulative, and communication activities. It encourages learning from different perspectives and in different modes. The constructivist environment is, therefore, well suited to the middle level where students vary considerably in personal experience and cognitive developmental level. A distinction is made between a "discovery" environment, which tends to be more exploratory and less formal, and a "constructivist" environment, which carries with it the responsibility to monitor the quality of conceptual understanding and provide experiences as needed to optimize progress. Discovery, in fact, represents a portion of, and is subsumed by, constructivism.

In the constructivist setting the teacher assumes the role of facilitator rather than authority. Facilitating, although not obvious to an observer, requires extensive preparation and a strong enough content background to respond spontaneously to student questions and lines of thinking. Teachers must be sensitive to group and individual progress and know when it is time for new knowledge and the challenging of old ideas. Facilitating requires "prepared flexibility" and is riskier in that it requires a higher level of teacher self-confidence than does conventional direct teaching in which a preset amount of information is presented. Methods based on constructivism can exist in varying degrees in any lesson or unit. The list below presents examples of constructivist teaching practices. Activity 9.3 allows you to compare instructional strategies and their support of a constructivist environment.

Constructivist Teaching Practices[3]

Related to lesson design:

1. When designing curriculum, organize information around conceptual clusters—of problems, questions, discrepant situations.
2. Look for students' alternative conceptions, and design subsequent lessons to address any misconceptions.

3. Both before and during class, adapt curricula so that their cognitive demands match the cognitive schemes of students.
4. For selected tasks, group students according to their demonstrated cognitive complexity.

Related to student involvement:

1. Encourage and accept student autonomy, initiation, and leadership.
2. Whenever possible, use raw data and primary sources, along with manipulative, interactive, and physical materials.
3. When framing tasks, use cognitive terminology like *classify, analyze, predict,* and so on.
4. Allow student thinking to drive lessons. Shift instructional strategies or alter content based on student responses.
5. Encourage students to reflect on experiences and actions and then predict future outcomes.
6. Ask students for their theories about concepts before sharing your understanding of their concepts.
7. Encourage students to engage in dialogue, both with the teacher and with one another.

Related to questioning strategies:

1. Encourage student inquiry by asking thoughtful, open-ended questions, and encouraging students to ask questions of others.
2. Allow wait-time after posing questions.
3. Seek elaboration of students' initial responses.
4. Pose contradictions to students' initial hypotheses and then encourage a response. (This process requires considerable diplomacy—an idea must be contradicted without attacking an individual's whole perspective.)
5. Provide time for students to discover relationships and create metaphors.

Activity 9.3: Comparing Instructional Strategies

A unit on the World of Rice was taught by three different teachers. Read each of the descriptions below. Look for similarities and differences. In each, identify the opportunity for students to compare prior understanding to new knowledge in such a way that their ideas might be reconstructed or adjusted. Discuss with a colleague what from each lesson might result in long-term learning, and list the reasons for your choices.

1. **Mrs. A** presents a lecture on how rice is planted and cultivated in various parts of the world. She then shows rice growing in dry soil and in flooded conditions to demonstrate that flooded rice fields have weed control value, and do not represent required conditions for growth of the

rice. She then gives her students a written quiz to see if they can identify areas of the world where rice is a staple.

2. **Mr. B** gives each team of students a list of ten statements about rice, its cultivation, and agricultural importance in the world. The student teams are to read the statements and decide to what extent each statement is true. The teams then are to use appropriate resources to find information to adjust the statements as necessary to be valid. After allowing four days for teams to work, Mr. B gives a quiz based on the statements.

3. **Ms. C** presents the class with a problem: Suppose a virus was discovered that destroyed rice in its growth stages just prior to harvesting. This specific plant virus can attach to pollen grains and was discovered in California in June of last year. What needs to be done, if anything? After brainstorming possible impacts, student teams volunteer to assume specific perspectives such as Grain Growers of the Orient, U.S. agricultural inspectors, the World Health Organization, and Meteorologists International, and they prepare reports to present to the class.

INSTRUCTIONAL PRACTICES

A middle level teacher carries out instruction by presenting lessons, assuming a facilitator role, maintaining an interactive and instructive physical environment, using feedback constructively, counseling on an individual and group basis, and modeling desirable behaviors and attitudes—all almost simultaneously. A separate look at teaching strategies, classroom organization, discipline, and evaluation will help us understand how all of these aspects of instruction fit together into the "act of teaching."

Activity 9.4: Flashback

Think about your own middle level school experiences. Describe something you learned very successfully. How did you learn it? Why were you so successful? Describe a not-so-successful experience. Compare notes with colleagues. Do you see any patterns related to what were the successes and the non-successes?

TALKING WITH TEACHERS: HOW WE TEACH You know that old saying, "You teach as you were taught"? I think we tend to teach the way we were successful in learning. I think we forget the lessons we were taught that didn't make sense or from which we got no long-term benefit. Otherwise, why would I naturally choose my own teaching style, which is effective for my students, but very different from the teaching I was exposed to when I went to school? My favorite teaching style happens to correlate with my favorite learning style and I have to be

careful to use a few other, less favorite styles to be sure all my students
have a chance to learn in their favorite ways.

—A seventh grade teacher

Teaching Strategies

The nature of instruction can be described in many ways. One dichotomy to
note is teacher-centered instruction compared to student-centered instruction,
with gradations in between. With direct instruction, lectures, teacher-led discussion, and guided activity, the locus of control lies primarily with the teacher, and
student-teacher interaction predominates. When the student makes choices, plans
the use of time, decides individually or collectively on resources to use, the
locus of control is with the student, and student-student interaction is the rule.
Ideally there is a balance in terms of locus of control. Middle level students
experience the greatest success when allowed to make decisions within guidelines set by the teacher.

Questioning Strategies

A great deal of class time is spent in teacher-directed questions. Questions that
precipitate thinking, clarification, articulation, and problem solving are powerful
in terms of their instructional value. Here are a few reminders in cultivating
effective questioning techniques:

1. To improve thoughtfulness and depth of response, allow a wait time of
   three to ten seconds between the question you ask and the next thing
   that is said. Benefits of allowing students time to think before respond-
   ing to questions include[4]:
   • Student utterances increased in length
   • Unsolicited but appropriate responses increased in number
   • Failure to respond decreased
   • Confidence in answers increased
   • Speculative thinking increased
   • Teacher-centered discussion decreased, and student–student dialogue
     increased
   • The incidence of evidence/inference statements increased
   • The number of child-asked questions increased
   • Contributions by children regarded as "slow" increased
   • Disruptive behavior decreased.
2. Follow a response with an additional question of the same student that
   will help the student clarify, expand, or explain the thinking behind the
   answer.
3. Accept and comment on answers without being judgmental of the person
   responding. A reaction to a wrong answer could be "Hmm, is there

another possibility?" or "That answer doesn't quite fit what I had in mind." An inappropriate reaction is "You're wrong." Remember that early adolescents are particularly sensitive to criticism and easily feel ridiculed in front of peers.

4. Do not echo responses. Echoing reinforces a reliance on the teacher rather than a reliance on listening to each other.

5. Use selective and positive rephrasing to steer discussions in desired directions.

6. Avoid inflated, insincere praise. Being recognized for providing answers that are valued for the contribution to the discussion, including posing interesting or challenging problems, is more important than being right on trivial matters. "That's an interesting idea" or "Good answer" is preferable to "You are fantastic!"

7. Call on everyone, not just the students in the front and center.

8. Avoid asking certain groups of students—for example, boys or Asians— more challenging questions while reserving trivial or recall questions for other groups of students, say, girls or African-Americans. The embedded message from such stereotype-prone patterns of questioning is that boys and Asians are more capable of complex thinking than girls and African-Americans.

Additional skills to nurture in students related to questioning are the ability to look at new things or pictures, reading, and asking questions that will lead to a better self-understanding of the topic or concept involved. Some students can pore over a map, photograph, or painting and maintain a fascination for the details they observe and the relationships they discover because they have learned to ask their own questions and set up their own interaction with an investigation of the material.

Cooperative Learning

The middle level student benefits greatly from a cooperative learning approach in which each member of a team accepts specific responsibilities to accomplish a learning task including the responsibility of making sure every member of the team understands his or her portion. Teamwork can be manifested in various forms, such as (1) study group for content coverage using a jigsaw activity; (2) problem solving, as in a social studies or science investigation, with designated roles for each team member; and (3) creativity, productivity involving brain-storming, decision making, and collaboration.

Cooperative learning has the elements that match characteristic needs of the early adolescent: (1) it provides guidelines, (2) students make decisions and have personal investment in the results, (3) students communicate with each other, articulating and defending ideas, discussing and debating, (4) it accommo-dates a variety of cognitive levels, learning preferences, and individual talents that exist within a class, thus ensuring success for everyone. Cooperative learning complements a constructivist environment and can be incorporated into most types of lessons.

Group work is a common organizational strategy for instruction. It is important to distinguish cooperative learning from cooperative effort. In the former, group members are responsible for the success of the other members of the group and highly dependent on intercommunication. In cooperative effort, group members are responsible for doing their share to accomplish the task or produce the product, and in many cases could do this without much real interaction between themselves.

Cooperative learning, like any instructional approach, should not be employed 100 percent of the time. Research indicates that 60 percent is optimal.[5] Other approaches such as direct teaching and independent study are still important and should not be eliminated if every student is to be reached through a preferred learning style. All students also should be exposed to a variety of skills for learning that are transferable to other situations in later years.

Cooperative learning addresses the needs of various learning styles. Activities typically allow students to work together and alone, and to carry out a variety of tasks that engage diverse talents such as logic, intuition, verbal communications, and artistic presentations.

Addressing the Needs of At-Risk Students

Although we have addressed At-Risk students in previous chapters, a review in the context of instruction is appropriate. Our students represent many different orientations and backgrounds shaped by home environments, life experiences, and interaction with local and mainstream cultures. Their personal expectations might not parallel those set by a school's educational program. Lack of congruence between the student's and school's expectations reduces the benefits to the student of even the most carefully planned curriculum. Who is at risk? Students who have limited English proficiency; members of single-parent families; children of families with special problems—for example, alcoholism, hard drugs, poverty; the physically handicapped; the gifted and talented; and often the average student who doesn't demand special attention—all of these students are at risk. In fact, it sometimes seems that nearly everyone is at risk in one way or another.

For at-risk students, middle level schooling can represent the pivotal experience that sets the stage for the rest of life. Awareness of student diversity is paramount. Adaptive strategies are essential. Most of what we do to accommodate at-risk students is good for all students: knowing students as individuals, demonstrating respect and expecting excellence, providing success-based opportunities to learn, measuring progress against personal growth, and embedding objectives within instruction that are related to developing self-esteem, independent competence, and decision-making abilities. However, it is particularly important to monitor how these students are thinking and working and what strategies they need to employ for success. In general, focus on process has greater benefit for maintaining flexibility than focus on products. The bottom line is that instruction must reach all students and, therefore, must take as many forms as is necessary to accomplish this imperative. This responsibility is shared by all the players in the school program. As teachers, we cannot solve all the problems of the universe, but we can make a distinct difference between whether the problems are solvable by contributing positively to the development of the next generations that face these problems.

Organization and Classroom Climate

There is more to facilitating learning than planning the progression of instruction. Organizing the learning environment includes designing how students can learn in ways other than when interacting with you, the teacher, or with fellow students. Students should be given opportunities to learn how to learn from pictures, posters, displays, discovery stations, long-term demonstrations, models, practice areas, inventor's corners, and other teacher-independent activities. No classroom space need be wasted. The use of ceilings, walls, windows, doors, and floors can assist in the effort. Consider the following questions as you prepare your classroom environment:

- What natural traffic patterns occur? Can students move about without disturbing others?
- Can you have group work, whole class presentations, and other configurations?
- Where is the classroom multimedia station? Who can use it? Are computers set up for individual productivity as well as guided interaction with programs?
- How are materials organized, stored, and made available to students?
- Are there bulletin boards, posters, models, and other items on the walls? Are they interactive? To what extent do they help teach, motivate, and/or decorate?
- How are the windows made to facilitate instruction? What is happening on or from the ceilings?
- Is there at least one station for inventors and designers, with junk, spare parts, and materials for constructing, tinkering, and experimenting?
- What resources are available for your students? How are they maintained?
- Have you taken care of security and safety?
- Are students actively involved in decision making and in maintaining materials, displays, schedules, and the variety of uses of classroom space? Do they feel ownership?

Time and scheduling are important to make things work. To ensure success, students need:

- Wait time (uninterrupted time to think after questions and challenges are presented. *Uninterrupted* means silence between when the question is asked and the *next thing said* by anyone, including the teacher. This becomes important when a teacher feels the need to rephrase or continue to talk while students are trying to think.)
- Time to sleep on it (extended thinking time, in hours or days)
- Time to interact with materials and peers (time to meet and plan and mess around and design and carry out)
- Study time (with assistance in developing good concentration habits, discipline, and awareness of effective use of time).

Instructing in a High-Technology Environment

The popularization of computers, camcorders, television, videodisc technology, sensors that detect heat, sound, and light, and other data-gathering instruments, means that touch screens, voice synthesizers, video and audio digitizers, and many other high technology devices are becoming more commonplace in middle level schools. When making educators' decisions about their appropriate use, the guiding rules are to (1) analyze what thinking processes students are engaged in when interacting with the technology in specific ways, and (2) plan the use in such a way that the technology itself becomes invisible and the student is absorbed in the instructional or assessment problem or task at hand. Activities can be teacher-centered and student-centered, and range from one-way tutorials, like TV documentaries, to self-initiated productions such as an animated videotape designed, organized, and carried out by students. As a teacher, you should feel comfortable using technology for your own purposes such as word processing, record keeping, and generating materials, and you should be familiar with a variety of instructional uses. You also should be knowledgeable enough to facilitate trouble shooting, but need not know everything about electronics or even all the details about every piece of software in the school. Students respect equipment and handle it carefully when properly trained in operating and maintenance procedures. Middle level students especially enjoy becoming resident "techie" experts and are delighted to take on responsible roles in facilitating the variety of uses you will want to encourage in carrying out the curriculum in your school.

Avoiding Behavior Problems

Organizing student behavior and avoiding related problems, or "discipline problems," is often a major concern for new teachers. Student behavior is tied closely to instruction and the classroom climate. Problems are prevented when students understand what is expected of them, feel successful in their efforts, and can rely on consistent relations with their teacher and fellow students. Mutual agreement on classroom rules, usually not more than five, that are carried out on a consistent basis and involvement in various kinds of decision making contribute to a sense of stability and self-esteem. Confident students who are not frustrated by ambivalence in expectations or a mismatch of task to ability, demonstrate positive classroom conduct, naturally and without coercion. Students who regularly exhibit exceptional behavior can be referred to specialists such as a school psychologist, nurse, or counselor. Isolated cases of outrageous behavior needing immediate resolution can be referred to higher authorities such as the principal, assistant principal, or dean, according to school policy. The stable environment essential for students to develop the needed confidence is brought about through a consistency of expectations and of reinforcing follow-through, in addition to the maintenance of a high standard of respect and an assumption of the goodness in all individuals demonstrated by teachers toward students.

PLANNING INSTRUCTIONAL UNITS AND LESSONS

First let us distinguish between planning a unit and a unit plan. Planning a unit is a process. It is what you do when you are deciding what and how you will teach a cluster of lessons. A unit plan is a product. It is an organized description of procedures, materials, and support, usually listed in order of expected execution. The unit plan is usually divided into a cluster of related lesson plans. A similar distinction is made between lesson planning and a lesson plan. Lesson planning is a process, often involving opportunity in search of objectives rather than objectives in search of opportunity. A lesson plan is a product, a formalized and structured outline of expectations and procedures for instruction and evaluation that serves as a checklist for completeness.

A unit may have as few as two or three lessons or as many as 20 or more. It is important to emphasize that a lesson is a segment of instruction, not a segment of time. Fitting a lesson into a class period is often very neat but might not be appropriate for meeting objectives. Often overnight thinking time is important for students to grasp main ideas or solve problems, and some assignments within the lesson might take several days. At the other extreme, some lessons might last only a few minutes. They serve to review, reinforce, introduce, or master specific skills or concepts between other lessons in the unit. Here are some steps that you, as an individual teacher or as part of a team of teachers, can take in the planning process.

1. Select themes for integrating subject areas or topics, or decide on a distinct topic for instruction.
2. Brainstorm by using techniques of concept mapping or idea listing.

3. Identify places on the concept map or in the list where opportunities exist for incorporating specific teaching processes or thinking skills. Note areas that have prerequisite knowledge.
4. Select main concepts and identify supporting examples and factual content.
5. Determine a time line, teaching responsibilities, and specific learning outcomes. Draft matching evaluation strategies.
6. Delineate specific teaching strategies, sequences, materials, and assignments. Recheck for emphasis on main concepts, avoiding an overloading of facts. Also check for higher order thinking skills, keeping in mind that higher order thinking:
   • Is nonalgorithmic (the path of action is not fully specified in advance)
   • Tends to be complex, involving multiple perspectives
   • Often yields multiple rather than unique solutions
   • Involves dealing with uncertainty and gaps in information
   • Involves the application of multiple, sometimes conflicting criteria
   • Is self-regulating
   • Involves considerable mental effort.
7. Make adequate plans for organization of time, space, materials, and movement in order to ensure success and reduce chances for management or discipline problems.
8. Include planning ways to assess your own teaching techniques including self-check lists, videotaping, and collegial observation.

Balancing the Content of a Lesson

What will be taught? Knowledge in the form of facts? Processes? A guiding rule for making decisions, one that becomes more important as the information age explodes with more and more "factoids" or specific facts and information bits, is to make choices based on the transferability of a concept; that is, if what is being taught can be used in other contexts, the rationale for keeping it in the curriculum is strengthened.

Strategies for thinking and problem solving (thinking processes consciously applied—for example, decision making) are obviously valuable and, when studied in context, through real examples, can be effectively assimilated and used broadly by the student in many subject areas. Choosing concepts is somewhat more difficult. Studying the life cycle of the whale is worthwhile as an example of an endangered species and the factors that affect its well-being. Whales serve as a model of interaction of living things in their ecological setting, a concept that transfers to other animals in other environments. Selecting whales as a topic for the purpose of studying large mammals is arbitrary, however, as many animals could serve the purpose and might even be more relevant in a given school community. There are many cases in which it is the underlying concepts that will be transferred, while the particular topic that serves as the vehicle for the concept is not critical. Any curriculum topic needs to be designed with that in mind—that is, leaving flexibility to choose according to student interest or need. Sometimes, because students already know a lot about local conditions, you choose to cover something else and use their knowledge base to identify similarities that lead to generalities. The important thing is that you don't get lost in the factoids at the expense of the real reason for teaching the given topic. Planning evaluation as part of planning instruction helps to ensure this.

Experienced teachers have lesson plans in their heads, and write decisions about what to teach in short lists or in the small squares of a plan book. When they design new instructional units, or lesson clusters, they often write out details. Using computer-based word processing and outlining programs makes writing out long, original lesson plans rather painless and streamlines the refining process. Copy machines allow rapid and easy sharing of ideas with fellow teachers. A lesson plan itself usually has several main parts: objectives or purpose, a procedure, and a way of assessing success in meeting the objectives. Terms such as *anticipatory set, motivation, introduction, materials, presentation, review, reinforcement, assessment, evaluation, summary, extension*, and others are all used to describe the lesson parts in more professional detail. The section that follows describes five different lesson types. In practice, teachers often combine two or more of these basic plans.

Contrasting Types of Lessons

Different types of lessons can be compared based on how students acquire knowledge and the nature of feedback. In many lessons there is transfer from an authority to the student with checking for mastery against a standard. These include information acquisition, skill development, and some concept development lessons. In others knowledge is gained through investigation and inquiry,

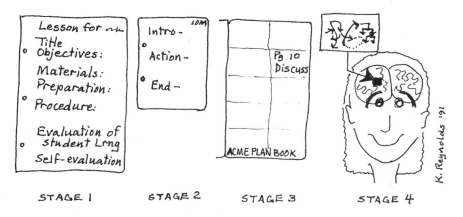

Miniaturization of the Lesson Plan.

and evaluation involves a comparison of growth in understanding. Examples include certain concept development and all inquiry lessons. In some, such as values awareness lessons, the process is important but there is no direct evaluation of results. The following section provides a description with examples of five contrasting lesson types. Table 9.1 summarizes their characteristics.

Teachers plan a variety of lesson types in order to meet different instructional goals and objectives and to appeal to different student learning preferences. When carrying out different types of lessons, teachers can employ a variety of teacher-centered and student-centered strategies, separately or in combination. Five contrasting lesson types are described here.

Lesson for Information Acquisition. In this type of lesson, the students are told what they are to learn and how they will be evaluated. The teacher gives specific information and checks for understanding. The students are given practice with feedback. The students' ability to recall the specific information is evaluated as initially described.

TABLE 9.1. COMPARISON OF FIVE CONTRASTING LESSONS

Characteristics	Lesson Type				
	Information	Skill	Concept	Inquiry	Values
Tell students what will be learned and how evaluated	Yes	Yes	Maybe	No	No
Give specific information or demonstration and monitor understanding	Yes	Yes	Yes	No	No
Provide practice and continual feedback	Yes	Yes	Yes	No	No
Pose problem for investigation	No	No	Maybe	Yes	Maybe
Maintain nonjudgmental climate	No	No	No	Yes	Yes
Ask question or use activity for discussion which allows students to form own decisions	No	No	No	Maybe	Yes
Facilitate growth in using thinking processes and evaluating results	No	No	No	Yes	No
Do not directly or indirectly influence responses or explanations	No	No	No	Yes	Yes
Evaluate ability to recall information	Yes	No	Yes	No	No
Evaluate ability to perform skill	No	Yes	No	No	No
Evaluate transfer of learning to new situation different from that practiced	No	No	Yes	Maybe	No
Assess growth rather than mastery	Maybe	Maybe	Maybe	Yes	No

Example for Language Arts. Students are given a spelling list of ten words to learn for a test. The teacher reviews them orally, checking for correct pronunciation. Students write the words several times and complete a fill-in-the-blanks worksheet. The teacher gives a trial test and allows the students to check their own answers. The students make up sentences using the words they missed. A final test is given to evaluate the learning.

Example for Mathematics. Students are told they are to be able to distinguish between several geometric shapes and be able to recognize and name them on sight. Worksheets allow students to name the shapes as the teacher describes them and gives additional examples. Students, working in groups, then go on a treasure hunt, finding and identifying shapes located all over the classroom. Evaluation of learning is through a written test containing items involving shape recognition, identification, and comparison.

Example for Social Studies. Students are given a list of countries and capitals which they must memorize, be able to locate, and spell. Each student receives a blank map of the United States and an atlas. The teacher monitors pairs of students working together and checks for accuracy as students label their maps. Students form small quiz groups and use the computer station for drilling purposes. At the end of the week students are given another blank map to fill in individually from memory.

Lesson for Skill Development. For this lesson type, the students are told what skill is to be learned and how it will be evaluated. The teacher provides a demonstration and necessary explanation of the skill, including appropriate steps required to do it successfully. Students are monitored for understanding. Both guided and independent practice are provided with feedback. Students' performance is evaluated as previously described.

Example for Language Arts. Students are provided dictionaries and told they will be learning how to find appropriate word meanings with this reference and how this skill will be evaluated. After the teacher presents a paragraph containing a new term, he or she leads the class through the procedures for finding the word in the dictionary and selecting the most reasonable definition. Using an interactive questioning technique to monitor understanding, the teacher takes the class through two more examples. The students are then given an additional set of sentences with terms having multiple meanings and worksheets for recording selected definitions. The teacher observes progress and assists those who need extra help. Finally, to evaluate competence in this reference skill and the ability to utilize it in a contrasting situation, students are given a reading passage with five underlined words and the task of rewriting the paragraph with appropriate synonyms.

Example for Science. Students are told they are to learn safe procedures for lighting a Bunsen burner and would have to demonstrate it to the teacher's satisfaction before being allowed to use it in the laboratory. The teacher demonstrates the steps in lighting the burner safely. The teacher also cites some of the consequences of not following safe procedures and demonstrates first-aid steps should accidents occur. The students are questioned for understanding and asked to evaluate additional demonstrations by the teacher. Students are then allowed to practice in pairs and be checked off by the teacher.

Lesson for Concept Attainment. The teacher provides the concept definition or allows students to discover it. Students are provided with practice in recalling the concept definition and in using the concept to make something, explain observations, organize, or predict. The teacher monitors and provides appropriate feedback. Students' understanding of the concept is evaluated both for ability to recall the definition and to use the concept appropriately in a different setting.

Example for Science. The teacher demonstrates the difference in behavior of a toy truck allowed to coast down a ramp and across the floor when loaded with a heavy weight and with a light weight. The teacher introduces the concept of momentum and defines it. Students are given toy vehicles and materials to make ramps in order to practice controlling momentum. The teacher monitors progress among the groups and gives feedback. The teacher also provides examples using other wheeled vehicles to discuss effects of momentum in daily life and ways it is controlled, changed, or accommodated. Student responses provide opportunity to evaluate understanding of and ability to recall the concept definition. The teacher provides a set of problem situations involving boats in water to evaluate use of the concept in a different setting.

Example for Music. The teacher plays a scale on a portable keyboard and then plays a given pitch. The teacher then hums a note and asks the class to hum the same note, then in a higher note, in a lower note, and then the same note again. The teacher introduces the concept of pitch. Several students are then asked to play a note on the instrument in their possession and indicate if it is the same, higher, or lower. The students play more notes and describe the results in terms of pitch. Finally, the students make rubber band instruments that can be used to produce at least five different pitches.

Inquiry Lesson to Develop Problem-Solving and Thinking Strategies. The teacher presents a problem for which student investigation will result in finding relationships and explanations, building theories, or engaging in other logical processes. A nonjudgmental environment is maintained, and students are responsible for their own investigative designs and data gathering. The teacher facilitates students' growth in determining appropriate problem-solving strategies and evaluating results but does not directly or indirectly influence or judge students' explanations and theories.

Example for Science. The teacher provides a variety of small objects, clear containers, and several large bottles of clear soda pop, and asks the students to find out what kinds of things make the soda pop bubble a lot and only a little. Students are allowed to explore and are encouraged to look for patterns that lead to generalizations. The teacher provides magnifying lenses and other instruments so that students can compare objects in greater detail and adjust their hypotheses and predictions.

Example for Art. Students are provided brushes, water, paper, and a set of four watercolor paints (red, blue, yellow, and white) and are challenged to mix colors to match a sample of brown.

Example for Physical Education. The teacher gives a group of students a ball and directs them to play the new game that he or she has in mind. The teacher referees, blowing the whistle on violations and announcing scored points. Students must figure out the rules. They may ask yes-and-no questions during designated breaks in play to verify their conclusions or understanding of game rules and strategy.

Lesson on Values Awareness. In this type of lesson, the teacher presents a question for discussion or provides an activity that allows students to make judgments or suggest courses of action and to give reasons for them. Students' reasons and proposed actions are identified as values. A nonjudgmental environment is maintained, encouraging open discussion. The teacher encourages responsible attitudes but does not directly or indirectly influence or judge students' responses or present his or her own opinion.

Example for Science. The teacher distributes copies of a newspaper article chronicling the demise of local salt marshes. He or she reads a letter appealing for funds to support a preservation project and asks for student reaction. Student responses and reasoning are accepted for discussion, and values are established. A nonjudgmental environment is maintained, and the existence of differing sets of values on the issue is recognized.

Example for Social Science. After lunch the students are shown the collection of garbage cans with food thrown away during the lunch period. An estimate of the amount is made and the question posed as to whether this represents serious waste. Students are allowed to respond with reasons and identify their values in terms of wasting of resources—in this case, food. If

INFORMATION ACQUISITION LESSON PLAN OUTLINE
Instructional objectives
Materials, organization requirements
Introduction/motivation/expectations
Presentation of information
Practice and reinforcement
Assessment and feedback
Evaluation information mastery

SKILL DEVELOPMENT LESSON PLAN OUTLINE
Instructional objectives
Materials, organization requirements
Introduction/motivation/informing of skill to be learned
Demonstration of skill, steps, information
Monitoring understanding
Practice and reinforcement
Assessment of competence and/or skill mastery

CONCEPT ATTAINMENT LESSON PLAN OUTLINE
Instructional objectives
Materials, organization requirements
Introduction/motivation
Presentation of concept or discovery activity
Monitoring understanding
Opportunity to use concept
Feedback
Evaluation of ability to transfer to new setting

INQUIRY OR PROBLEM SOLVING LESSON PLAN OUTLINE
Instructional objectives
Materials, organization requirements
Problem posed
Investigative environment
Facilitation of problem-solving strategies
Assessment of learning demonstrated

VALUES AWARENESS LESSON PLAN OUTLINE
Instructional objectives
Materials, organization requirements
Presentation of situation or problem
Facilitation of discussion leading to independent decision making

Figure 9.2. Examples of Lesson Plan Outlines

there is a consensus that food is being wasted unduly, students are allowed to work in groups to propose courses of action. Plans are posted on butcher paper for comparison and discussion.

Example for Music. Students are allowed to listen to a variety of audiotapes to determine which music should be considered happy and which sad. Students give reasons for their responses and sort which judgments are made based on values. Students are allowed to survey other people's opinions of the tapes. They summarize results and look for patterns related to respondents' age, musical training, or other characteristics that might affect individual values.

Activity 9.5: A Closer Look at Lesson Types

Of the five types of lessons we have reviewed, which two or three do you think you would feel most comfortable teaching? Do you also feel most comfortable learning from lessons like the types you chose? For two of the types, can you think of another example in a subject area not represented for that type? In general, beginning teachers can be expected to be proficient in teaching two or three of these lesson types and to add the others to their repertoires by their third year of teaching. In reality, teachers often plan lessons that are combinations of these types. Can you think of a lesson that integrates characteristics of two or more of these types?

Lesson Plans That Reflect Lesson Types

The components of lesson plans have been discussed in an earlier section. Adapting a generic plan to specific lesson types allows you, as a teacher, to refine your planning. Figure 9.2 provides a variety of outlines that match the five lesson types described in this chapter. Notice in what ways they are alike and in what ways they differ.

CONCLUSIONS

Instruction, the primary means of implementing the middle level curriculum, is a multi-faceted endeavor. It involves facilitating learning through both teacher-centered and student-centered activities; organizing materials, time, space, and other components of the physical environment; maintaining positive emotional and social surroundings; and gathering and responding to feedback related to achievement, feelings, and interests. When deciding on how instruction should be carried out at the middle level, we look at the characteristics of the student to make student-centered decisions; we look to learning theory for a grounding on which to build approaches; we look at successful practices, analyze why they work, and seek to incorporate those aspects into our own strategies. We consider all these things when going about the process of planning and formally describing plans, each of us combining, adjusting, and fine-tuning the elements of instruction to fit our own philosophies and personal "best ways" that we can carry them out.

EXTENSIONS

1. Observe instruction being carried out in a classroom. Fold or mark a sheet of paper into quarter sections and label each section *Teacher-directed activities, Student-centered activities, Organization techniques*, and *Classroom environment*. Fill the quadrants with notes on features and practices that you observe.

2. Observe students during a cooperative learning situation. Draw a map of the classroom. Locate resources and trace student movement on your map.

3. Follow one student during an instructional activity period. Make a time line to plot the student's activities. Review the data and categorize your observations by their nature: for example, social and recreational, social and instructional, independent, interaction with teacher, use of special areas, level of activity.

4. Select two or three activities that involve computer-based materials, including multimedia and/or computers interfaced with other technologies such as videocameras or videodiscs. Indicate how you would adapt these activities to fit your teaching specialties. Describe how you would render the technology "invisible."

5. Diagram and label a classroom arrangement that supports your ideal instructional program and learning environment.

6. Consider this statement: "Schooling takes place during certain hours of the day and during certain years in one's life. Learning, however, is a lifelong endeavor. Students who can learn independently can progress at their own levels and in their own ways while in school, and can continue to learn after formal schooling. This is the ultimate goal of education." Discuss to what extent you agree and, if so, how we can foster this behavior.

NOTES AND REFERENCES

1. Part of a multifaceted study in progress since 1987 by author Karen Reynolds.
2. Adjusted by Rosalind Driver. Conference on Constructivism. San Jose State University, San Jose, CA, April 1989.
3. Adapted from Jacquelin G. Brooks, "Teachers and Students: Constructivists Forging New Connections." *Educational Leadership* 47 (Feb. 1990): 68–71. (Items renumbered and grouped into three categories by authors.)
4. "Rakow on Research," reporting on research by Mary Budd Rowe. *Science Scope.* National Science Teachers Association. (Nov./Dec. 1987): 24.
5. Conference on Cooperative Learning. Presentation by David Johnson and Roger Johnson. San Jose State University School of Education. San Jose, California, January 18–19, 1988.

FOR FURTHER READING

Collins, Cathy. *Time Management for Teachers*. West Nyack, NY: Parker Publishing Co., 1987.

"Connections," an issue dedicated to the teaching of thinking. *Educational Leadership*, Journal of the Association for Supervision and curriculum Development (Feb. 1990).

"Cooperative Learning," an issue dedicated to cooperative learning. *Educational Leadership*, Journal of the Association for Supervision and Curriculum Development (Jan. 1990).

Costa, A. *Developing Minds, A Resource Book for Teaching Thinking*. Alexandria, VA: Association for Supervision and Curriculum Development, 1985.

Johnson, D. W., Johnson, R., and Holubec, E. J. *Circles of Learning: Cooperation in the Classroom* (rev. ed.) Edina, MN: Interaction Book Co., 1986.

Schurr, Sandra L. *Dynamite in the Classroom. A How-to Handbook for Teachers*. Columbus, OH: National Middle School Association, 1989.

Warger, Cynthia, ed. *Technology in Today's Schools*. Alexandria, VA: Association for Supervision and Curriculum Development, 1990.

CHAPTER 10

Evaluating Student Progress

Grading is the hardest part of teaching. You are never sure if the mark you put in the book really represents what the student knows.

Wouldn't it be nice if we could just teach and not have to give grades? I know that many of my students have learned a lot. But they flunk all their tests and then I have to fail them. It doesn't seem fair.

We waste a lot of valuable time preparing for these annual standardized tests. I'd like to ignore them, but if we don't get good scores, our district looks bad, our school looks bad, our kids look bad, and I look bad.

How can I give a grade to a student who doesn't even speak or read English?—at least not well enough to take a test.

These are the voices of teachers who feel that they are victims of common testing practices. These teachers view testing as a necessary evil and probably transfer their resentment and frustration in some form to their students. Evaluation doesn't have to be like that.

In this chapter we

- Look at purposes of assessment and evaluation at the middle level,
- Consider effects of evaluation practices and address current issues, and
- Review strategies for evaluation and reporting results.

The terms *assessment* and *evaluation* are used interchangeably in this chapter.

WHAT TO EVALUATE AND HOW TO USE THE RESULTS

Evaluation and assessment can be formative (in progress) or summative (end result) and should address such expectations for student learning and development as:

1. Understanding of facts, concepts, and generalizations;
2. Ability to perform and transfer certain skills;
3. Ability to transfer concept understanding to new situations;
4. Ability to use thinking processes;
5. In the affective domain, success in terms of motivation, interests, self-worth, and perception of self in relation to other people, the community, and the world at large.

In addition, evaluation is designed to provide information about teaching effectiveness and success of the curricular program at the class, school, and/or district levels.

Evaluation is carried out in the course of daily instruction and through district, state, and national testing programs. The results are used to:

1. Judge success in completing specific assignments;
2. Assess student progress in learning and level of achievement;
3. Determine a student's pass–fail or letter grade for a subject;
4. Advise students and report to parents;
5. Determine subsequent instruction;
6. Assist in revising old instructional units and planning new ones;
7. Compare two or more different teaching approaches, instructional programs, schools or school districts; and
8. Determine the need to reform current instructional practices and curriculum.

In order to make decisions based on evaluation results, it is prudent to be aware of strengths and weaknesses of the evaluation instrument (test, task) or procedure, the background students must have to succeed, individual abilities or styles for communicating knowledge, and other contexts that render the evaluation fair or not fair.

FORMING EVALUATION POLICY

Guidelines used when establishing evaluation policy at the middle level reflect a sensitivity to characteristics of early adolescents. The following are particularly important.

1. Evaluation should reflect instruction, and in the cognitive domain should involve not only assessment of content knowledge but also concept application, problem solving, and critical thinking.

2. A distinction between cognitive, affective, and physical-physiological domains must be made both in formulating objectives and assessing student success in meeting them. Although success in one domain often correlates with success in another, such relationships are not reliable for predictive purposes. A student who enjoys an assignment, for example, has not necessarily learned the major concepts involved. A student who makes significant progress in mastering ball-handling skills does not automatically become a cooperative team player. Although the domains are addressed in integrated fashion when planning and carrying out instruction, they must be considered separately when evaluation is taking place. It is important, since students are expected to develop in all domains, that they be evaluated in all of them.

3. Evaluation that addresses individual progress rather than emphasizes achievement on a peer comparison basis recognizes that students at the middle level are at different stages of development and that it is both unrealistic and inappropriate to expect all students to function or pro-duce results at the same level. It is unrealistic to expect to obtain a basis for fair judgment, for example, when cognitive demands of the evalua-tion items or tasks are beyond the abilities of some students or far below that of others. It is inappropriate because students can so easily perceive themselves, or be perceived by others, as failures, at an age and in an environment that needs to focus on individual success. Experiencing inflated success resulting from always being at the top of the class testing scale also can lead to an unrealistic self-image, particularly in later years when peers "catch up," or when success depends on a broader spectrum of skills than is measured by tests traditionally given in schools.

CURRENT ISSUES

Most records of evaluation, whether for classwork or on standardized tests, are scores from paper-and-pencil tests. In the case of standardized tests, the scores receive considerable publicity and affect school reputations, local real estate values, state legislation, and national status in the eyes of the world. Unfortu-nately, these results are generally interpreted as indicators of success or failure rather than as information that is useful for making changes. We say "unfortu-nately" because this emphasis results in test anxiety for students and adverse pressure on teachers to "teach to the test." In the past, standardized tests, as well as teacher-made tests, have emphasized skills in isolation and recall of factual information. The result was the design of curricula that reinforced the teaching of skills in separation and the coverage of broad ranges of content. A facts-fat model was particularly inappropriate for evaluation at the middle level for several reasons:

1. The recent information explosion challenges old standards of what constitutes an adequate factual knowledge base. Curriculum reform now places emphasis on generalizations and transferrable concepts within and across subject areas, thinking skills, and problem-solving and decision-making abilities.

2. The middle level period is the time for exploring subject areas and developing interests and potential. Students who take advantage of opportunities to pursue divergent interests, even within core subjects, will develop divergent areas of factual expertise, not all of which are likely to be addressed in a standardized test of content-specific knowledge. This is especially true of the less linear subject curricula such as science and social studies in comparison to mathematics and reading and writing. The middle level years are not a time for labeling students—who are very much in transition in both interests and academic abilities—as successes or failures in any given subject area.

3. Students who are at various cognitive stages cannot be expected to perform at the same level. Comparisons with peers are not appropriate, even though early adolescents, because of concomitant psychosocial transitions, compare self with peers extensively. Evaluation reinforces individual perceptions of self-worth.

Reform efforts currently under way in several states call for an increased assessment of thinking skills, a focus on measuring the learning of basic and transferrable concepts within and across academic disciplines, and evaluation through a variety of avenues including alternatives to multiple-choice, objective tests. Assessment that includes writing samples has allowed students to demonstrate ability to combine communication skills. Problem solving, using examples relevant to the life of early adolescents, provides more reliable indicators of concept understanding than lack of ability to memorize algorithms. Although testing traditionally favors those who excel in reading and analytic thinking, assessment can be devised to utilize pictorial, multimedia, and practical modes for interacting with assessment items on tests.

CHALLENGES IN EVALUATION

Matching Evaluation to Objectives

Jane Stoneberg's first-draft attempt at planning a sixth grade unit on "Moving More Than You Weigh," which featured pulleys and other simple machines, had some very general objectives. For the pulley part, the students were to know (1) about pulleys, and (2) how they lift things. Those objectives, however, besides not matching the inspired instruction Jane had planned, did not clearly suggest a way to evaluate student learning. When Jane refined her plans for the pulley lessons, she also refined her objectives and designed matching evaluation strategies shown in Table 10.1.

In addition, Jane wanted her students to appreciate the pulley as a basic machine that makes work easier, one that can be included in improvised mechanical systems as well as in complex, sophisticated designs, and one that contributes to the esthetics inherent in efficient and balanced systems. Appreciation, like so many affective objectives, is difficult to score with a test but easy to check off from anecdotal information. For this, Jane noted evidence from student comments, behaviors, and ideas as they arose during the year. She also collaborated with other teachers who shared the same students. For example, during a social studies discussion involving how to transport goods in the 1600s, students identified mechanical devices in use at that time and compared them to ones used today. In a language-arts creative-writing activity, students were shown an adventure movie up to the point where the main characters and their heavy gear were stuck in a high-walled dry creek bed with a flash flood imminent. The students were then to continue the story on their own. Proposed

TABLE 10.1. JANE'S REFINED PLAN TO MATCH EVALUATION TO OBJECTIVES

Student Learning Objectives for the Pulley Lessons	Evaluation Strategy
1. Identify a variety of uses for pulley systems. Show knowledge of how the parts of a pulley system work together.	View a videotape of machinery in action; list five examples seen of pulleys. Explain in detail how two work, and give an additional use for each of the two besides that shown on the tape. Whole class or small group viewing of tape with no discussion; individual answers reported in writing, by drawing, or on audiotape.
2. Demonstrate how to assemble a working pulley system with two or more pulleys.	Given a box containing a variety of pulleys, cords, stands, and weights, assemble a two- (or more) pulley system that works. Individual demonstration checked by a student assistant.
3. Compare the mechanical advantages of two different pulley systems.	Given two systems already set up, hypothesize which has the greatest mechanical advantage. Give reasons. Measure the resistance and effort forces to confirm. Explain discrepancy if there is one. Individual student task using a prepared report sheet.

problem-solving strategies that utilized knowledge of pulleys and other simple machines were noted.

Jane Stoneberg's pulley lessons reinforce several effective practices in the evaluation process. Learning objectives and evaluation processes should be aligned. Students can be given credit for learning in many ways, including written and oral examinations, practical demonstrations, situation analysis and problem solving, and anecdotal evidence. Although direct assessment by the teacher is valuable, it is not the only strategy used in deriving a profile of achievement. Keeping colleagues apprised of instructional plans and objectives makes it possible for teachers of other subjects to provide additional feedback.

Addressing Multiple Expectations

Evaluating progress and/or achievement often involves problem-solving, critical thinking, and transferring knowledge in new combinations. Tests involving open-ended essay items, although time consuming to review, are valuable in assessing thinking and ability to apply content knowledge. However, it is often difficult to assign one grade to such a written test, particularly if more than one kind of knowledge or skill is utilized in the student's response. Here is one teacher's experience.

Bob Nolan's students were completing a three-week interdisciplinary unit on the Panama Canal that covered topics in geography, politics, history, engineering, health, geology, oceanography, Spanish, biology, culture, and society, as well as other subjects. To see how they would organize information learned from different areas in a situation with a new focus, he asked his students to respond in writing to several open-ended questions, including: "What happens when a boat passes through the Panama Canal?"

Answers to this question varied considerably. Here are three he chose at random to share with colleagues. What information did the responses give him? How do you think Bob graded these three answers?

> 1. The Panama Canal is a series of locks that allows ships to pass from the Pacific Ocean to the Atlantic Ocean without having to go around the continent of South America. This saves time and money for shipping. —Alan D.

> 2. A boat go through the canal and when they hit the lakes snails and stuff fall off the hull. This is a short cut thru the land. Anyway it makes it real fast and cheap and the tourists like the trip too. They meet boats from alot of countrys. —Bobbie M.

> 3. Boats going east go uphill and downhill if they go west. That's because the sea level is different on the two sides. I'm not sure why. That's all I remember. —Carl F.

Bob's first reaction was surprise at how little each student wrote considering the number of concepts and amount of information the students had explored and reviewed during the unit. A follow-up class discussion revealed that the students actually knew a great deal. It was clear that they needed help in identifying relevant ideas and organizing them into written paragraphs. He also realized that the question he asked was so broad that it was probably overwhelming for students at this level. That is, they would have to generate categories of possible answers and then address details for each category. He decided to ask them the question again, but first teach them how to use concept- or mind-mapping to generate and organize ideas for such questions. He would teach the technique using several examples including the canal question. He also decided not to ask more than one question in the next writing session, and to provide a few organizers or subcategories within the question. He would give students 20 to 30 minutes to articulate their answers. By asking a similar kind of essay question, the students would be able to compare the first attempts to the second, and really appreciate the effectiveness of the new techniques.

Bob's second reaction was concern about the problem of evaluating answers that differed in use of grammar, spelling, and sentence complexity. He decided to give several grades as follows:

> Spelling: E (excellent), N (needs more care), H (get help)
> Grammar: E, N, H
> Articulation of ideas: E (excellent), G (good), P (practice
>   for next time)
> Content: 5 points for each relevant idea expressed.

Bob felt that using a point system would reward detail and encourage writing more lengthy responses next time. Anticipating that students might adopt a strategy of listing many facts in short sentences, he was careful to point out that two or more credible ideas could be included in one sentence, and that doing so well contributed to the articulation grade. He gave the following grades to the answers above:

A. Alan E, E, E, 25
B. Bobbie H, N, P, 35
C. Carl E, E, P, 10

He used the same system for subsequent written assessments so that both he and the students could track and appreciate individual progress.

Bob's experience illustrates that student responses can be awarded multiple grades in order to address several facets of an answer and that individual answers and patterns of answers often indicate needed attention in specific knowledge or skill areas. In addition, this example illustrates the kind of feedback that helps students grow through an awareness of self-generated success.

"I'm here for my social studies test. How 'bout you?"

The teacher time involved in establishing such a system is worthwhile in terms of the resulting quality of assessment information.

THE EFFECTS OF ASSESSMENT

On Students

Assessment affects students in a number of ways and depends on elements in the assessment environment such as how students perceive the contexts and purposes for evaluation, the fairness of testing and grading procedures, and the variety of assessment strategies used. Here are some effects of assessment on students:

1. Students want to know when they are right or wrong, and when they have done well. Feedback from tests and other evaluation is important as part of the learning process. It also helps students identify their own achievement in comparison to standards already set or to expectations.
2. Students experience a constant pressure to get good grades and score well on tests and projects. Feedback on individual progress and achievement is important for self-esteem. This emphasis on external evaluation reinforces the student's positive sense of worth or confirms the percep-

tion of self as a failure. It can have a disempowering effect if not tempered with experiences that allow students to develop self-esteem from within themselves, to learn to evaluate their own achievements and accomplishments.

3. Middle level students respond to, and are often overly concerned with, external evaluation and reward systems. This tendency can be a result of conditioning in earlier years, the general materialistic views of our culture, and arrival at the age of wavering self-confidence. At the same time, middle level students are eager to learn about their own abilities and are receptive to strategies that strengthen their sense of self-sufficiency as well as their appreciation of intrinsic rewards.

4. Approaches that emphasize content recall, and narrow questions with predictable answers, serve to reinforce the perception that we live in a dichotomous world. What we know or think is either right or wrong. Students should be instructed on the meaning of test results and on what information the results do or do not provide. Students should experience open, broad questions and problems in which the reasoning processes and diversity of thinking are important.

5. Assessment practices and results can greatly affect interest level in and motivation to pursue a subject or topic. Experiences and associated grades can influence high school electives, academic tracks, and career choices.

6. Many students experience test anxiety and consider a test the low point of any unit of study. This anxiety can be alleviated by scheduling a more positive experience at the end of a unit, administering tests that students feel are fair, providing immediate feedback, and assisting students in learning successful test-taking skills. In addition, assessment strategies other than traditional paper-and-pencil tests should be included. These can contribute to the culminating activities at the end of a unit of study.

7. Evaluation embedded in relevant activities—relevant from students' perspectives—seems to yield more positive information about student knowledge and ability than tests or assessment tasks carried out simply for evaluation purposes. Students make a greater effort and produce better results when they are interested in the task. For example, students note that it makes a difference when you're writing to an audience rather than to the teacher.[1] Projects involving penpals, videotape exchanges, or telecommunicating, as in the National Geographic KidNet Program, in which students are communicating with other students, are real experiences. Observing student behavior and inspecting products during project activity provide opportunities to evaluate at the same time that learning is being facilitated. Separate grades can, and should, be awarded for achievement and for more subjective measures such as work habits.

TALKING WITH TEACHERS: ABOUT REWARD SYSTEMS I used to give my students prizes like stickers, name on the homeroom hero roll, gum, candy, buttons, and other trinkets—things I now look upon as pretty trivial motivators. Then I decided to reward students with experiences, such as time to play with an intriguing mechanical toy from the toy cupboard, extra time on the computer, a chance to have the class rat at their desk, a library adventure, a photography mission, a chance to perform in front of the class, and other activities or challenges, all concrete and fun and educational. These new enticements became much more popular and had great return value. That is, students wanted to repeat many of the experiences over and over. And although the rewards were managed externally, the enjoyment seems to be more intrinsic—something I definitely wanted to help develop.

—Eighth grade teacher

On Schools and Teaching

The intent of assessment is to gauge the extent to which objectives have been met and to serve as a basis for maintenance or change in instructional methods. Results of schoolwide assessment, as through standardized testing, can have, in addition, implications for positive or negative comparisons to other schools, future enrollment, and local real estate values. There is pressure on teachers to raise test scores. In response, teachers succumb to the common practice of teaching to the test. When standardized tests place a heavy emphasis on factual content, mastery of factual content is stressed in teaching. Reform efforts in testing are adopting process-oriented testing items,[2] open-ended questions that require students to organize written responses, performance-based tasks, and other alternative assessment practices. Some experts have predicted that even if using innovative evaluation strategies does not relieve the pressure to teach to the test, at least the new tests will stimulate new kinds of teaching with more emphasis on thinking processes, performance with manipulatives, and communication skills.

Parallel efforts must be made to design report documents that accommodate a variety of assessment data. Computer-based record keeping and report generation can be restrictive unless responsive to individual teacher and school assessment strategies.

INSTRUCTIONAL STRATEGIES
AND EVALUATION PRACTICES

In Chapter 9, five contrasting instructional strategies or lesson types were described. Each lesson type suggests corresponding and appropriate evaluation approaches, which are reviewed as follows:

1. Information acquisition is commonly evaluated by instruments that involve fact and concept identification, or recall, and transfer of relevant information to selected situations.
2. Skills attainment can be assessed by requiring direct demonstration of skills and observing for transfer of skills in appropriate situations.
3. Concept attainment is effectively evaluated by requiring students to transfer concepts to new settings, situations different from those in which learning takes place.
4. Inquiry is process oriented and lends itself to assessment by observing nonverbal behaviors as well as reviewing individual reports, explanations, and products.
5. Values clarification must be judged solely on processes employed and not on the values chosen by individual students.

Matching an assessment approach to an instructional strategy is important in maintaining the overall intent of that strategy. Not all lesson objectives are monitored using skill/content mastery checklists nor can all learning be demonstrated through written tests.

ASSESSMENT DESIGN

Assessment can be conducted formally and informally through a variety of devices including traditional question sets; teacher logs, anecdotal records, and observations; student products such as projects, reports, displays, and investigation results; and performance tasks.

It is important to match assessment items to learning objectives, that is, to measure whether what you intended students to learn was indeed learned, or to what extent it was learned. In addition, it is important to distinguish between affective and cognitive domains. Certain forms of assessment allow the teacher to notice attitudes, feelings, and other affective feedback. Behaviors such as joy and enthusiasm, although significant in themselves, and often correlated with success in learning a body of knowledge, are not reliable indicators of concept understanding and skill mastery. It is also important to consider the match between teaching/learning modes and the testing modes. If students learn about a topic through hands-on activities that do not include verbal articulation and discussion, they will be at a disadvantage if they are evaluated by a test requiring them to organize written responses to essay questions. Similarly, students who have read about simple machines without constructing any, would not feel fairly treated, nor be fairly evaluated, if provided a variety of apparatus and asked to demonstrate the ability to assemble a working system of simple machines.

**TALKING WITH TEACHERS: MATCHING INSTRUCTION MODE TO
EVALUATION MODE** Anything I use for instructing can be used for
evaluating and vice versa. The difference is whether or not I help them
arrive at their answers. I usually have three or four activities to teach an
important concept in science. I can just put one aside until the others
have been used and the instruction phase is over, and then bring out the
reserved activity for evaluation purposes. What's really great is that what
they learned through activities is tested through an activity and not in
some out-of-context mode such as a paper-and-pencil, reading-
dependent, multiple-choice test.

—Sixth grade teacher

Different teacher skills are required for (1) recognizing test items that have
already been designed, (2) adapting or customizing test items, and (3) generating or creating tests. Teachers are professionally best prepared to recognize good
from bad, or appropriate from inappropriate test items or tasks. A teacher's time
can be spent very efficiently selecting items from existing pools, particularly if
suggested tests are included in teachers' manuals or if a computer data base
makes it easy to retrieve items and incorporate them into a word-processed test
or set of instructions.

Experienced teachers often prefer to adapt testing items to meet their own
specific topic, include vocabulary familiar to their own students, use local
examples, or make a shift in format. This ability is particularly important for
providing a much-needed supply of tests or tasks that involve higher level
thinking and practical demonstration. Good tests measure student knowledge
accurately and by fair means, address learning objectives and involve students in
a variety of thinking processes including higher level thinking. Creating good
tests "from scratch" is complex and involves trial and revision. Elements included in the design and creation of quizzes, observations, or other kinds of
evaluation are listed in Figure 10.1. These elements can be considered when
formulating a balanced program of assessment, one that provides a variety of
ways for students to demonstrate what they know, how they think, and what
they have achieved. Add your own ideas to the categories listed in the figure.

EXPANDING THE EVALUATION REPERTOIRE

Just as you, as a teacher, build expertise in the use of a variety of instructional
strategies, you need to have the ability to use a variety of evaluation strategies.
This is necessary in order to (1) match evaluation mode to instruction mode, (2)
allow students to demonstrate their learning in several different ways, (3) gain
information relevant to curriculum building efforts when recycling or adjusting
units of instruction, and (4) gain different kinds of insights about one's own
teaching.

FORMATS
True-false, matching, fill in the blank, multiple choice, short answer
Diagram, essay, performance of task
Oral interview, feedback during group discussion
Products: report, project display, model, mural, presentation

THINKING INVOLVED
Recall of facts, identify details, organize
Compare, classify, interpret, relate
Transfer information to new context
Analyze, apply, invent

COMMUNICATION INVOLVED
Speaking
Writing
Demonstrating, including nonverbal means
Drawing
Displaying

STUDENT PARTICIPATION
Paper-and-pencil, bubble sheet, open-ended writing
Problem solving, practical application, manipulative
Performance while carrying out a task or demonstration
Product-based such as project, report, model, display
Collection of product examples in portfolio

TEACHER ADMINISTRATION
Proctor, manage paper distribution and collection
Observe behavior of individuals, groups
Interview individuals, groups
Pretest, posttest

SCORING AND RECORDKEEPING
Numerical rating, letter grade, $\sqrt{}$ + −, criterion check
Individual or group scores
Ouantitative, qualitative, descriptive comments, anecdotal
Portfolio

OTHER FACTORS
Objective, subjective
Efficiency, effectiveness
Validity, reliability
Helpful for advising and for making decisions about instruction

Figure 10.1. Evaluator's Toolbox and Construction Kit.

Traditional Means of Evaluating Progress

Most evaluation for which results are recorded in class grade books occurs through written and oral teacher-generated tests. Paper-and-pencil tests are popular for their efficiency—they can be administered to large groups of individuals at once and can be checked or graded during nonclass time. Efficiency is increased when the test items have short or coded answers that can be checked through quick visual scans or by electronic marking devices. High efficiency usually correlates with low demand on thinking processes. Paper-and-pencil tests, even standardized tests prepared by professional test writers, have featured isolated skills in mathematics and language arts and recall items in social studies and science. Recently, standardized tests at the state and national levels have been designed to measure abilities to communicate by writing to open-ended questions, solve problems, and use higher level thinking processes to observe, organize, and relate information, at considerable cost in terms of design of test items, administration, and evaluation of results.

Traditional testing practices, although valuable for the information they do provide, have limitations. And results should be interpreted with their limitations in mind. They also have strengths that should be appreciated and that are often underrated. In particular, there is a tendency to equate format with thinking level. It is true that most multiple-choice, fill-in-the-blank, short-answer, true-false tests require low-level thinking skills. Such tests are easy to construct. This correlation, however, does not represent a cause-effect relationship. Tests using these formats can be designed to require very complex thinking. Such tests, however, are correspondingly more difficult to design. Each test item should be inspected separately.

Alternatives to Traditional Evaluation Regimes

Informal assessment and evaluation of student progress is carried out constantly in parallel with instruction. Teachers often have a sense of a student's achievement level that differs from what is recorded in the grade book. Recording these informal assessments becomes important, however, when a student's record from other methods is skewed, or when teachers are attempting to use evaluations to plan subsequent instruction or refine the curriculum. In addition, dependence on traditional testing strategies can also bias the evaluation picture. Alternative methods serve to provide a variety of opportunities to demonstrate knowledge among diverse learners, allow a closer match between instructional strategies and assessment strategies, address facets of understanding not otherwise accessible, and serve to check the validity of the traditional methods.

Product-based Assessment. Assignments that require students to utilize acquired knowledge and showcase interests and talents can involve products such as published reports and booklets, displays of projects, murals, working models, inventions, videotapes, and computer data bases or programs. Products can be awarded to several grades, each representing an aspect of the assignment expectations. Or, alternatively, holistic procedures can be applied, matching the product to graded prototypes or sets of standards. Observing students carrying our procedures involved in producing the products can be addressed using process-based assessment strategies.

Process-based Assessment. Careful attention to how students arrive at solutions and to behaviors that reflect understanding can be credited to student achievement through systematic observation and interviews, and recorded in the form of checklists and descriptive comments. This category of assessment involves noting how students perform during activities such as acting in plays, giving oral reports, carrying out group decision making, experimenting. Multiple grades can be given reflecting specific affective and cognitive processes, or a holistic evaluation approach can be used. The products resulting from these activities can be judged using product-based assessment strategies.

Nonverbal Evaluation. Most evaluation or assessment, even in nontraditional settings, centers around communication through writing or speaking. Evaluation incorporating observation of specific nonverbal behaviors can yield valuable information about student learning. Of the nonverbal behaviors considered for assessment purposes, affective behavior is most often observed, and usually it is affective behavior that is recorded in anecdotal records. Second is observable skills such as the use of references, map reading, safe operation of apparatus, and other performances that students are "trained" to carry out. More difficult, but very important, are those nonverbal behaviors that indicate understanding of concepts learned.

Megan, for example, wanted to empty the large classroom fish tank before lunch. She selected materials from a variety of possibilities and deliberately set up a siphon system that would yield maximum flow of water out of the tank. (She used a siphon to avoid damage to the frame that would result from lifting or moving the tank.) In so doing, Megan demonstrated a knowledge of the effects of tube diameter and of difference in water levels on the rate of water flow. In another example, Thom, during a recess break, made up a dance to a popular tune that used semaphore movements he'd learned about in a recent social studies unit on communications. These behaviors are often noted and appreciated by teachers in passing but never recorded on behalf of the individual students.

Picture-based Assessment. Just as the use of pictorial learning strategies needs to be included in instruction, the use of pictorial evaluation strategies should be included in measuring student achievement and progress. Pictorial approaches can include, but are not limited to, posters, photos, diagrams, drawings, movies, videotaped sequences, videodisc images, and computer screen displays. The use of pictures for presenting problems, as a substrate for explanations and for communicating explanations through drawings or organizational schemes, provide many students otherwise unavailable opportunities to succeed in evaluative settings. Including pictorial approaches is especially important for at-risk students who do not speak fluent English, who lack motivation to complete a task, who read below grade level, or whose learning styles are predominantly visual.

Checklists

Student behaviors observed during activity periods provide valuable data for assessment purposes. Following is an example and discussion of the strategy of using a checklist to record such information.[3]

Consider an activity that involves an investigation of the decomposition of plant materials. An initial class discussion considers what is meant by decomposition and what factors might be involved. Students then work in groups to investigate variables that affect decomposition in a garden compost pile. Open-ended questions incorporated in a starter lab exercise lead students to other ideas. Personal observation of student behavior and participation gives the teacher a sense of how things are going and whether or not students seem "with it." However, a teacher's intuition or feelings for success or failure do not provide the concrete data expected of today's records of student achievement. The checklist can provide this record of student behavior and can support evaluations of individual knowledge, abilities, and progress.

Checklists have several advantages:

- They take less time, or no longer, to process than evaluating student papers.
- When they are designed as a customized computer database, they can automate pre- or post-comparisons of skill levels or progress over time.
- They can emphasize specific skills, thinking processes, and/or affective attributes.
- They can serve as a catalyst for the teacher to reflect on the beyond-the-content value of an activity, and
- They need not be extensive for any one lesson. To be meaningful, information added regularly to students' records from checklists, over time, should reflect attention to a broad range of expectations for science learning and skill development. Table 1 [see checklist categories below] provides some generic categories for constructing a customized checklist.

Using the Checklist

Checklists can be challenging to use: It is not always easy to articulate behaviors that reflect learning, particularly nonverbal behaviors. As an assessment strategy, the checklist of student behaviors complements other more commonly employed methods of measuring learning and helps us, as teachers, give credit for progress that before could only be ascribed to "gut-level feelings." Concrete information from the checklist provides leverage for making changes in teaching habits, instructional plans, and guidance standards.

Some Checklist Categories

Observations of skills

- *How well does the student carry out procedures?*
  Follow directions?
  Record data accurately?
  Use appropriate techniques?

- *How well does the student make organizational decisions?*
  Get information from reference books and other sources?
  Organize materials for efficiency?
  Budget time appropriately?

Evidence of thinking processes

- *How well does the student define investigative procedures?*
  Decide on appropriate materials?
  Set up relevant data sheets?
  Schedule investigative steps and budget time?
- *How well does the student demonstrate information processing and critical thinking?*
  Able to debate and look at different sides of ideas?
  Repeat trials to compare or confirm their current beliefs, distinguishing between observations and opinions?
  Draw logical conclusions and weigh the validity of alternative explanations?

Observations in the affective domain

- *How well does the student demonstrate ability to work with others?*
  Adhere to safety rules and show concern for the safety of others?
  Cooperate with peers and recognize when to compromise?
- *What positive personal attributes are evident?*
  Enjoy work activities and their outcomes?
  Demonstrate patience?
  Show respect for materials?
  Follow through to the end of each task?
  Avoid waste?
  Practice good work habits?

Individual, Group, and Program Assessment

Each level of assessment, individual, group, or program, involves specific assessment opportunities with their inherent strengths and weaknesses. Individual progress can be measured by comparing achievement or performance to personal baseline data and using customized or individualized assessment strategies. When measuring achievement resulting from common instruction, everyone in the class takes the same test. Only a certain number of items and topics can be checked for understanding, but individual results can be compared to standard expectations. Often, appropriately or not, such results are compared to those of peers.

Group assessment involves determining achievement through group efforts and products or by sampling the knowledge of individuals within a group. Group assessment methods are used often in cooperative learning environments in which students are made responsible for each other's learning and mastery of information. When the peformance of each member of a group is considered to represent the achievement level of every member of the group, there is pressure to take shared responsibility for the success of everyone. During testing sessions, group members can be asked different questions or to carry out different tasks; a total score for the group is then credited to each individual. Claims that weaker students drag down the potential grade of stronger students and that stronger students represent the weaker students unrealistically are not without certain merit, but are overshadowed by the benefits resulting in the development of teamwork and other than egocentric attitudes. A balance of many methods of evaluation, including nongroup strategies, usually allays fears by individuals of not being given due credit.

Program assessment is particularly valuable for making curriculum and instruction decisions and refining other parts of the student learning environment. Every characteristic in the curriculum design can be assessed for effectiveness, informally or formally. Concerned school faculty and staff include such assessment in their planning. External assessment is available through reviews by visiting district, state, or national committees of professionals and representatives of the community. Measuring student achievement through matrix testing also provides a measure of curriculum program effectiveness. In matrix testing each student takes a different test with different sets of questions, thereby sampling a broad spectrum of knowledge. Thirty students answering ten different science questions each can provide feedback on 300 science concepts, while the same students in an individual testing situation would be compared to each other in science on the results of only ten concepts tested. Matrix testing has great value to schools that want to identify specific curricular areas that teams of teachers need to maintain or work to revise, and to compare their program with those of schools comparable in socioeconomic and demographic background. Matrix testing is not designed to provide individual student results.

Test Administration

Test taking and evaluative sessions need to be planned with the same care that instruction is planned. Evaluation is, in fact, part of the instruction process and learning cycle. Situations that tempt dishonesty can be problematic. Management strategies, based on jointly developed and agreed-upon rules of ethical behavior, serve to regulate student cooperation in most assessment situations. Students who feel prepared, who understand the reasons assessment is taking place, who consider the evaluation practices fair, and who experience success in taking tests are not students who cause management and behavior problems. In fact, these students help mold positive attitudes among their peers. Exceptional problems should be discussed with experienced teachers or administrators. Resource books on management and discipline can provide helpful and constructive strategies. Problems in managing evaluation are not usually isolated phenomena. Student views and solutions can be addressed during advisory sessions with very positive results.

TALKING WITH TEACHERS: TRICKS TO REDUCE DISHONESTY DURING TESTS This is what I do when my students have a tendency to want to "help" each other or "get help" by looking at someone else's answers. I use a word processor which makes it easy to make several forms of a test with variations in questions. To keep track of the different forms, I copy them on different colors of paper. The first time, students let me know right away that their test is different from someone next to them and I reassure them that I made different tests intentionally, so they wouldn't need to help each other. After a few tests have been given, I just make one test and copy it onto different colors of paper and they just think they are different. Sometimes I just rearrange the questions so that the tests look different from a distance.

—Seventh grade teacher

Utilizing High Technology

Computers can be used for word processing, graphics, data bases, and for interfacing with other forms of technology. Efficiency and effectiveness is increased when computers are used for generating tests, redesigning tests, making various forms of a test, and incorporating charts, diagrams, graphs, and pictures. The directions and visual props for innovative assessment strategies can be produced using computers alone or interfaced with videodiscs and/or video cameras. Tests can be printed on paper or presented in multimedia format. Finally, computer software is available for analyzing test items, test trends, and performing other functions that provide detailed information useful in improving instruction, tracking individual student progress, communicating results to parents, and making curriculum decisions. Telecommunications allows the exchange of ideas with distant colleagues or accessing larger data bases established for education and containing question banks, performance task banks, research reports, and other information.

Student Involvement

Students should be included in assessment decisions. They can help in determining what is fair, in establishing standards for themselves or each other when a constructive atmosphere is established, and in developing techniques for self-evaluation. Students who have input in the evaluation process assume more responsibility for positive evaluative results.

Long-Term Evaluations

Although many evaluations address short-term assignments or progress gained during a unit of instruction, certain evaluation covers longer periods: a grading period of several weeks, a semester, a year, or even several years during the whole middle school program. Some evaluation procedures follow students throughout their schooling. A few are described here.

1. Cum folders (aCUMmulated records) are established for each individual student and include grades, school photos, and notations by teachers from kindergarten through high school. Not everyone agrees on their value. Some believe a cum folder prejudices a new teacher who could easily assume defeatist or overcompensating attitudes toward certain students, and some are grateful that certain facts are available at the beginning of their interaction with their students. The value of these long-term records depends on the objectivity of both the recorders and readers. If you are to benefit from and contribute constructively to cum folders, you must as a reader sort out traits that are likely to change—for example, behavior problems—from traits that won't—for instance, allergy to bee stings. You must adopt the practice of verifying information before acting on what you learn from this source. In addition, you must use care and objectivity in making contributions to the folder.

2. Portfolios are maintained by teachers or by guidance counselors. A portfolio is a collection of a student's work over a long period of time, ranging from a year to many years. Portfolios are distinct from cum folders because students decide what goes into them. The practice of maintaining portfolios on a large-scale basis is not common at this time but has great potential as an alternative representation of individual accomplishment. Portfolios are typically maintained by teachers or advisors with contents representing work in all subject areas and selected by students, often after discussion with subject area teachers. Portfolios are reviewed regularly to update the contents and reduce the volume but to ensure inclusion of benchmark work.

Following are some general suggestions for using portfolios:

a. Begin at the beginning of the school year. Plan to collect a variety of products that represent student accomplishment. By the end of the year a typical science portfolio might contain three scientific illustrations, two written papers, one audiotape or videotape, four photographs of displays and 3D models, two lab reports, two graphs and their interpretations, one computer data disk, and one or two special items such as a science cartoon, invention, poem, song, or other creative effort.

b. Store the selected work in individual folders or large envelopes in a secure but readily accessible place. Adding and replacing items can be an ongoing process or take place at specific intervals during the year.

c. Decide jointly with the student which pieces should go into the collection. Keep some benchmark work for comparison to show progress, but allow certain work to be replaced from time to time during the year.

d. Use an end-of-year or periodic critique, jointly written by you and the student, to identify individual strengths and progress.

The portfolio involves a genuinely individualized assessment process and fosters a sense of control in that process by the student. Students may keep their science portfolios at the end of each year, although some work might be kept by a school or district over a longer period of time. Students are often allowed to keep the portfolio at the end of the school year. However, some plans call for adding to it annually through high school. High school graduates could then make use of the portfolio when seeking employment or entrance into college. Some school districts that have adopted portfolios as part of the school assessment plan, add to the portfolios each year until the student leaves the school and then forward it to the student's high school with the idea of allowing the student to keep it after graduation.[4]

3. Pretests and Posttests. Comparisons of performance or of products with similar guidelines are often used to measure the effect of a unit of instruction. Similarly, students can carry out specific activities at the beginning of the year and again at the end of the year to demonstrate growth. Examples of eligible activities are listed here:.

a. Write an essay about an issue in current events. Describe the issue, its roots or causes, why people are concerned about it, and how you think it will be resolved.
b. Draw and label a map of the world.
c. Draw the study environment of your dreams.
d. Describe your career goals and how you plan to meet them.
e. Videotape a presentation of yourself in performance or featuring a special interest or hobby.

Notice that any of these products could, in addition, be included in a student's portfolio.

Activity 10.1: Analyzing Assessment Strategies

Look at the strategies described in Expanding Evaluation Repertoire. Which have you experienced as a student being evaluated or as a teacher carrying out the evaluation? Using the headings given below, expand the ideas into a chart that will allow you to make comments on the strengths and limitations of each strategy and to record a specific example from one subject area among your core areas of expertise.

Strategy	Strengths	Limitations	Example

REPORTING EVALUATION RESULTS

How are results recorded and interpreted? How are they reported? Reading newspaper summaries of local school performance on state or national standardized tests often reinforces the idea that student progress can be represented easily and by selected numbers, and that comparing student achievement between individuals or between school populations is simply a matter of putting the numbers side by side to see who wins. Recording results involves accurate entering of data. Interpreting or giving meaning to the results requires consideration of the contexts surrounding the evaluation. Reporting evaluation results carries with it the responsibility of describing the criteria for interpretations and projecting constructive and objective implications. The rules that apply to widely disseminated public reports also apply to reports of individual marks on student assignments, and to progress and grade reports given to parents at the end of regular marking periods. Here are some questions to ask when reporting evaluation results for any level:

1. What do the scores, letters, checks, or other symbols represent? On what criteria were averages based? On ratings such as good, excellent, outstanding?
2. What is the purpose of the evaluation or assessment? To measure achievement? To establish a base for instructional planning? For tracking individual progress?
3. What were expected results? How were they determined?
4. Did students understand the reason for the evaluation? Did they understand the guidelines for the grading or scoring? Did they think the assignment or examination was fair? Were they motivated to do their best?
5. Did expectations for success include considerations of experience and cognitive levels of development? What were demands on thinking processes and skills?
6. How is any given score balanced against results from other methods of evaluation? Did the method of processing student responses affect the kind of information gathered: for example, reading essays, inspecting models, or using an optical scanner with mark-the-bubble answer sheets.

This list is intentionally short, but does address main concerns related to reporting practices. You should discuss specific practices with colleagues and experienced teachers and/or examine several examples from actual classroom settings, attempting to answer the questions above. You may add to the list in order to make it your own.

EVALUATING YOUR TEACHING

Should teachers consider their teaching successful if their students score well when student progress is evaluated? Although an important indicator of good or not-so-good teaching, this reciprocal approach avoids looking at specific techniques of teaching. When teachers carry out assessments of their own teaching techniques or carry out classroom-based research, they can ask interesting and relevant questions about teaching and learning that takes place with their classes. These questions can be addressed through formal or informal, qualitative or quantitative, descriptive and anecdotal, or experimental research techniques. Here are some examples of questions that could be investigated by teachers:

1. Does an interactive bulletin board precipitate learning independent of class presentations?
2. What is the effect of a three-minute review at the end of the day?
3. What are the effects of assigning problems involving manipulatives for homework?
4. What kinds of test questions do students think are "fair" and what are their reasons?
5. How do editorial partners affect the quality and length of student writing?
6. Does spelling improve at a greater rate when words are based on student reading and student-generated lists, compared to using lessons found in standard spelling books?
7. How successful do students feel before and after taking a written test? How do they rate their own self-confidence and level of knowledge before, during, or after engaging in other types of evaluation, such as projects demonstration, oral examinations, and performance-based tasks?

CONCLUSIONS

Evaluation of learning is important for student self-esteem as well as for making instructional decisions. Many evaluation strategies are available for use at the middle level, each with it own strengths and limitations. A variety of evaluation strategies should be employed in order to measure appropriately the different ways that learning takes place and to give students divergent opportunities to demonstrate achievement. Recording the results of evaluation is challenging for nontraditional assessment but is critical for substantiating curriculum development or proposing reform.

EXTENSIONS

1. Interview experienced teachers to find out more about ways they carry out evaluation and what kinds of records they keep. In what situations do teachers evaluate subjectively, or by "gut feeling," and how do they record or account for this type of evaluation?
2. Choose a specific topic in your favorite subject area. Design three contrasting ways for evaluating student learning in that topic. Indicate the strengths and weaknesses you see in each evaluation method or strategy. Check for a

balance in addressing the content or concept, thinking process, and affective objectives you might set for that topic.

3. Carry out informal classroom teacher research addressing any of the questions suggested previously in this chapter in the section, "Evaluating Your Teaching."

4. Collect examples of tests and other evaluation instruments. Sort them according to formats and thinking processes involved.

NOTES AND REFERENCES

1. Sarah Freedman in *The Educator,* 3 (Fall 1989). University of California, Berkeley.
2. Recent test development by National Assessment of Educational Progress (NAEP) and California Assessment Program (CAP) has included an emphasis on the evaluation of thinking processes and on test items that use diagrams, drawing, and writing in response to open-ended questions.
3. Excerpted and adapted from "Reynolds' Rap," by Karen Reynolds. *Science Scope.* National Science Teachers Association, vol. 13, no. 3. Reprinted with permission from *Science Scope,* a publication of the National Science Teachers Association, Washington, DC (1989).
4. Excerpted from "Reynolds' Rap," by Karen Reynolds. *Science Scope.* National Science Teachers Association, vol. 14, no. 5. Reprinted with permission from Science Scope, a publication of the National Science Teachers Association, Washington, DC (1991).

FOR FURTHER READING

California State Department of Education, *Caught in the Middle: Educational Reform for Young Adolescents in California Public Schools.* Sacramento, CA: CSDE, 1989.

Carnegie Council on Adolescent Development, *Turning Points: Preparing American Youth for the 21st Century.* New York: Carnegie Corporation, 1989.

National Assessment of Educational Progress, *The Nation's Report Card.* Annual publication of the NAEP to report achievement trends in the major subject areas.

Rutherford, F. James, and Ahlgren, Andrew, for American Association for the Advancement of Science, *Project 2061: Science for All Americans.* New York: Oxford University Press, 1990.

CHAPTER 11

Interdisciplinary Units
of Instruction

In the preceding chapters we have outlined challenges for middle level teachers, historical contexts of the middle level movement, characteristics of the middle level student, elements of curriculum design, strategies for curriculum implementation, and approaches to instruction and evaluation. We have been able to explore and discuss the components separately and can appreciate the role each plays in the total middle level curriculum picture. In practice, however, all the components interact. Middle level curriculum in action is a dynamic composite of all the topics we have examined separately. Several scenarios featuring the design and delivery of selected thematic units will serve to illustrate how the components are synthesized.

In this chapter we:

- Outline guidelines and planning strategies for thematic units of instruction, and
- Describe several thematic units that reflect contrasting levels of organization and illustrate, by example, interaction between curriculum design and implementation.

ORGANIZING THEMATIC UNITS

National, state, and local middle level curriculum expectations are met through instructional units, or clusters of related lessons, that not only are carried out by teachers but very often have been originally crafted or adapted by these teachers. When instructional units are organized under a theme that crosses the

"Perhaps we could choose another thematic strand for integrating science and P.E."

traditional boundaries of subject areas or disciplines within a subject area, students are exposed to concepts from several perspectives, yet each exposure can be in a legitimate, or realistic, context. Here are some guidelines that thematic units attempt to follow:

1. Involve topics and themes of interest to the students in the specific school and community.
2. Involve topics and themes of interest within the expertise of the teachers who carry them out.
3. Incorporate a variety of teaching/learning and evaluation strategies.
4. Require skills in an appropriate range of cognitive demand.
5. Contribute to social and psychological as well as relevant physical development.
6. Be feasible within the limitations of the school program, resources, and schedule.

7. Allow interdisciplinary implementation, not only for economy in topical coverage but with emphasis on facilitating the construction of mental connections across disciplines in the learning process.

In a *topic-based* theme, motivation is the primary organizer. Typically, the theme itself and its components can be classified by a descriptive topic, as one would use in a library data base. The common thread that links the components is motivational in nature, is often trivial in its relation to the components, and does not represent the opportunity to practice or gain experience with a transferrable concept or process. For example, the theme entitled "Airway Across the United States" is planned around a balloon trip across America, with touchdowns at a sampling of cities and towns along its route. The fact that the balloon is being carried by air currents has no relation to the politics or cultural history of the locations on the ground. The trip merely provides a motivational transition from place to place.

If, at each stop, certain activities were deliberately included in order to develop specific skills or thinking techniques as a strand throughout the unit, this unit could be considered a *skill-based* theme. For example, for each town students might graph and interpret data about the population, jobs, industry, and weather. The skills of graphing and interpreting graphs serve as an instructional strand throughout the unit, and there is a building of understanding of process or improvement of skills. A major goal in such a unit is to provide extended experience and thus improve the ability to transfer skills or thinking strategies to new situations.

In *concept-based* themes, concepts that are part of more than one discipline are considered from a variety of perspectives with the intention of developing the ability to recognize them in novel situations. For example, when studying each town on the balloon's route, students find that industry and productivity is related to the ability to use local resources. They might conclude that resource limitations result in change in economic conditions or change in resource-dependence patterns. The relationship between resources and the economy of a town or city involves concepts that transfer to many areas of study or help to understand related social complexities now and throughout history.

To see how such units might be developed, let us imagine the following scenario.

Thematic Unit Development
THE "WHAT SHALL I WEAR?" SCENARIO

Phil, Gretchen, Katharine, and Jeff were gathered in the faculty lounge regaling each other with tales of their own teenaged children at home and their behaviors related to personal appearance. These eighth grade teachers were parents who definitely understood the changes their children were going through, who exercised patience, and found that the tense moments often were amusing in retrospect. Jeff gave a perfect imitation of his daughter going through the agony of finding nothing to wear in a closet full of clothes. Gretchen noted that what they considered exaggerated concern about clothes was often expressed in her class by both boys and girls. The idea that clothes might make a motivating theme for integrating subject areas came to the group almost like a professional reflex action. The rationale was there: the theme would be motivational, was real-life-related, had potential for treatment in several subject areas, and could be made to have long-term value.

There were only ten minutes left in their break, but Phil tore four sheets of paper from his notebook and said, "Map time! Ready, set, go!" Each of them rapidly sketched mindmaps of concepts and ideas, as many and as fast as they could for three minutes. They'd done this before and treated the challenge almost as a game. When they finished they had the beginnings of a team effort. During the next three weeks they refined their ideas, checked on resources, recruited some parents and some additional teachers, and produced the following plan to be carried out during the month after the winter holiday. The outline this teacher team developed is as follows:

Main Subject Areas: Social studies, physical and life sciences, mathematics, language arts.

Additional Subject Areas: Art (drawing), technological arts (the name given to the drastically revised industrial arts program).

Time Frame: One month.

Goals and Student Learning Objectives
1. Consider clothing from historical and cultural perspectives.
2. Investigate heat regulation properties of clothing.
3. Describe examples of specialized clothing for specific jobs.
4. Analyze influence of advertising and peer pressure on clothes selection.
5. Consider essential in contrast to ideal wardrobes.
6. Itemize clothing costs in a budget for personal expenses.

Organization: Instructional block and teacher team.

Introductory Activity
1. Have a "favorite clothes" day for which each person wears his or her favorite clothing, including the teachers.

Subtopics and Activities by Subject Area

PHYSICAL SCIENCE (Gretchen's responsibility)

1. Using temperature sensors interfaced with a computer, test and compare the heat insulation and heat reflection properties of a variety of fabrics with different compositions, thicknesses, and colors.
2. Describe and illustrate specialized clothing for specific jobs or tasks, such as beekeeping, fire fighting, space walking, SCUBA diving, mountain climbing, swimming, logging. Have each student research at least one item of clothing, draw and label a diagram of it, and report on the scientific aspects of the design. If possible, students might interview men and women who use such specialized clothing.

SOCIAL STUDIES (shared by Katharine and Phil, who were both language arts/social studies core teachers)

1. In student groups, each with a separate assignment that adds to a total and broad spectrum picture, trace clothing styles through history and across cultures. Note which features are functional in nature or were derived from a functional design component, and which features are primarily decorative or artistic in nature. Identify aspects of clothing that are considered traditional and those that are fads or temporary styles.
2. Survey the clothes you own. Describe three favorite pieces and explain why they are so. Carry out a survey of what students think an essential wardrobe should include. Find out how much such a wardrobe would cost. Carry out the same survey to find out what adults think an essential wardrobe for students should include. Find out the cost and compare to the first survey.
3. Describe or draw a personal view of an ideal wardrobe. Contrast that to a personal essential wardrobe.
4. List the priorities if an emergency required each family member to pack a single suitcase from all personal belongings. Find out about historical events in which that has happened.

LANGUAGE ARTS (shared by Katharine and Phil)

1. In support of other activities, review processes for making lists and placing items in a list in order of priority.
2. In support of other activities, review features of a labeled diagram that improve the power of communication.

MATHEMATICS (responsibility of Paul, who was recruited with a little resistance)

1. Record, graph, and interpret data from science investigations.
2. Use a spreadsheet program on a computer to enter and manipulate data for the personal clothing budget. Consider how to arrive at priorities and budget-making decisions. Avoid invading rights of privacy of other students.

ART (responsibility of Jeff)

1. Review techniques of sketching human figures.

2. Carry out group projects producing "mail-order catalogs" reflecting clothing fashions and work clothes from contrasting historical and future eras—1600s, 1800s, early 1900s, 1950s, and 2050.

TECHNOLOGY ARTS (responsibility of Arloa, volunteer)

1. Field trips to clothing design business and manufacturing plant. Observe computer use in design and pattern making. Observe robotics and skilled labor used in production.
2. Research and develop effective dyeing techniques for selected fabrics using natural dyes.

Culminating Group Activities

1. Display diagrams and/or real examples of specialized clothing.
2. Display and/or report to entire class results from tests of heat regulation properties of clothing fabrics.

Evaluation

1. Completion of individual and group assignments.
2. Participation in reports and displays.

Kinds of Resources and Materials

References on clothing, customs, costumes, work-related attire. Specialty stores in the community, mail order catalogs. Spreadsheet software. People who wear specialized clothing. Variety of fabrics and clothing materials for testing.

From this scenario we can see the interplay between skills and concepts typical in thematic units as well as the spontaneous and opportunistic nature of the planning process that such units often entail. However, there are identifiable sequential steps involved in the planning. They include.:

- Brainstorming opportunities
- Identifying topics of interest and expertise
- Specifying thinking processes, skills, and other learning objectives
- Determining evaluation strategies
- Agreeing on a time frame
- Assigning responsibilities for collecting materials, making arrangements, instructing, and evaluating.

Our scenario stops short of the final steps, but they are obviously crucial for the successful implementation of this unit.

ADDITIONAL EXAMPLES OF INTERDISCIPLINARY THEMES

Not all thematic unit development is as serendipitous as "What Shall I Wear?" Many are deliberately derived from district curricula. It is true, however, that opportunity precipitates theme ideas in the same way that it is often the first step in *planning*. The important point is that the resulting *plan* of the lesson, or thematic unit, matches objectives and goals appropriate for the students, school, and curriculum.

The remaining outlines in this chapter of instructional units include opportunities for using multisubject involvement, themes, and topics of interest to early adolescents, community extensions, mini-experiences, short-term and long-term projects, integration of technology, local and world view issues, and a variety of instructional, organizational, and assessment strategies. The descriptions are necessarily brief but embedded in plausible scenarios. As you review each unit, you might want to use the checklist below to focus on design aspects and to evaluate how they feel to you as a "personal fit."

A Checklist for Reviewing Thematic Interdisciplinary Units

1. For what parts would you like to assume responsibility?
2. How would you team with others?
3. Specifically how do the units address middle level student needs and characteristics in terms of cognitive, social/emotional, and physical growth and development?
4. What opportunities are embedded that incorporate high technology in instruction and in real-life contexts?
5. What examples do you find of two or more subject areas combined in the following ways: fused with no distinction made between them, integrated but with components linked to specific subject areas, and addressed simultaneously but with distinctions clearly maintained.
6. In what order would you recommend the activities be carried out to ensure appropriate sequencing of instruction?
7. What changes, additions, or adaptations do you suggest?

Thematic Unit Development
SOLUTIONS AND SUSPENSIONS IN ART AND SCIENCE

There are many opportunities to apply science knowledge in other areas such as art, or to investigate science principles through the use of materials in art. Examples include (1) studying balance, leverage, and center of gravity in conjunction with constructing mobiles; (2) comparing adhesive characteristics of glues when assembling collages, montages, and particle sculptures; (3) investigating mechanical systems and constructing dynamic sculptures; (4) finding out about light absorption, reflection and transmission, and their relation to color palettes, translucent designs, and light and shadows; (5) appreciating knowledge of anatomy in figure drawing, and learning about the properties of clay, metal, leather, wood, fibers, and other materials used in art.

This short unit allows students to investigate the solubility properties of substances and then apply or experience applications in art activities.

Subject Areas: Art, science.

Time Frame: One week with art projects carried out over an extended period of time.

Goals and Student Learning Objectives

1. Determine combinations of common substances that form solutions and those that form suspensions.
2. Identify solubility characteristics of substances used in art for mixing media and cleaning specific materials.
3. Select media with specific solubility properties to produce specific effects in carrying out an art project.
4. Select correct substances for cleaning art materials.
5. Distinguish between technical decisions and artistic decisions.

Organization

1. Use of block time within one teacher's schedule or cooperatively between science and art teachers.
2. Experimentation with a variety of materials in a science lab setting. Art activities, including technical applications from science lessons, in an art class setting.
3. Activities to be carried out by student teams and/or individual effort.

Activities

SAFETY PRECAUTION: Use all materials in a well-ventilated location. Handle materials safely, avoiding spillage and contact with flames. Dispose of waste materials properly.

1. Experiment in combining very small amounts of oil, water, crayons, water-based paints, including water colors and acrylics, oil based-paints, an organic cleaning solvent, and soap. Organize data, and report which combinations form solutions and suspensions.

2. Carry out contrasting art projects using watercolors and wax resist process, acrylic paints, and oil paints. Invent special effects based on knowledge of solubility properties. Explain the scientific reasoning behind the choice of cleaning materials used.

3. As an extension, interview artists or visit an art supply store and find out what substances painters use for painting, materials preparation, preservation, and clean-up. Organize your findings in a computer-based data base.

Evaluation

Note systematic procedures used during science experimentation and reference to results when applying knowledge during art activities. Test specific knowledge of solubility and applications of knowledge in both science contexts and art contexts. Have students produce a videotape or poster presenting safe use of cleaning agents, appropriate techniques in use of materials, and/or the "science of solutions" for the informed artist.

Kinds of Resources and Materials

Water, oil, soap, crayons, watercolor paints, oil-based paints, acrylic-based paints. Working artists.

Thematic Unit Development
SHOES AND THE HUMAN SOLE

Early adolescents are interested in how they look and what they wear. Shoes provide an egocentric point of departure for addressing issues related to advertising and social pressures dictating style and to life-long health decisions. In addition, shoes can serve as a vehicle for learning about (1) structure and function, (2) properties of construction materials, (3) variation in form, and (4) change and consistency through history. This mini-unit features a narrow topic that is expanded to address aspects of a variety of different disciplines. It allows specialization by groups so that exposure to a considerable amount of information can be done efficiently through group reports. Certain objectives are met by all students, independent of which specific subtopics the individual groups pursue.

Subject Areas: Life science and health, social studies, physical science, physical education/dance/sports, language arts.

Time Frame: One to two weeks.

Goals and Student Learning Objectives

1. Consider the variety of roles shoes play in our lives.
2. Relate foot care to shoe wear. Investigate decisions we make, related to the shoes we wear, that affect our health, safety, physical performance, and social pressures to conform.
3. Provide opportunities to address or reinforce larger ideas in other units of study.

Organization

1. Teacher teams. Cooperatively within a grade level. Correlated or cooperative activities across grade levels are possible.
2. In student groups, investigate one to several problems or academic questions related to shoes, and communicate the results. As a whole class, become informed about a variety of aspects of shoes through group reports and displays.
3. Address everyday issues centered around a common object of interest from the perspectives of several subject area disciplines.

Subtopics and Activities by Subject Area

LIFE SCIENCE AND HEALTH

1. Research and report on anatomy and physiology of feet in relation to shoe design; care of the feet; causes and corrections of foot problems; common diseases (for example, athlete's foot, planter's wart); effects of foot problems on posture, mobility, and other physical conditions of the body; effects of wearing high heels; formation and function of corns and callouses.
2. Produce informational posters or videos.
3. Invite a guest speaker such as a podiatrist, orthopedist, or knowledgeable specialty shoe salesperson.

SOCIAL STUDIES

1. Find out about traditions and customs around the world including shoes as reflections of cultural lifestyles.
2. Collect pictures or other media and discuss effects of shoe advertising and salesmanship (part of a study on propaganda).
3. Trace on an annotated map the economics of shoe manufacturing and sales.
4. Trace the history of footwear using paintings, photos, drawings, and other illustrative evidence of consistency and change.
5. Find examples of shoes used on other animals—for example, horses, sled dogs.

PHYSICAL SCIENCE

1. Test properties of the materials that are used to construct shoes. Inspect shoes for evidence of wear patterns.

2. Test various shoes for traction ability.

3. Survey shoes for safety features.

LANGUAGE ARTS AND PHYSICAL EDUCATION/DANCE/SPORTS

1. Find out about specialty shoes. Interview experts in various activities that use specialty shoes. Gather data on as many different kinds of specialty shoes as possible, and organize it using a computer-based file program.

2. Display information on posters.

LANGUAGE ARTS

1. Videotape and narrate a visual record of shoes in action.

2. Write creative stories, poems, or songs on life from a shoe's point of view, why high heels should be outlawed, shoes of the future, or other themes.

Culminating Group Activities

1. Multimedia day: presentations of videotapes, information posters, reports, repurposed shoe collages, other student projects.

2. Foot Ball, a class dance featuring decorated (but safe) shoes.

Evaluation

1. Oral reports, displays, and other products communicating results of investigations on specialized topics.

2. Creative writing reflecting factual knowledge.

3. Test on ability to transfer knowledge of foot anatomy and shoe construction to situational problems.

Kinds of Resources and Materials

1. Collection of actual footwear from student or community donations.

2. Guest speakers: podiatrist, orthopedist, shoe store manager or salesperson.

3. Chart/diagrams and brochures on foot care and anatomy.

4. Topical literature, poetry, songs, paintings, other forms of art.

Thematic Unit Development
UP AND OUT: MEN AND WOMEN IN AIR AND SPACE

The developments in the air and space industries represent a keystone of progress in the twentieth century. Becoming a pilot or astronaut is among the popular fantasies held by young people. This topic allows students to consider an expanded view of events, developments, and careers related to aviation and the exploration and utilization of space.

Subject Areas: Physical and life sciences, social studies, language arts, mathematics, computer literacy.

Time Frame: Two months.

Goals and Student Learning Objectives

1. Demonstrate knowledge of the physics of flight at the concrete level of being able to control the action of a model paper airplane.
2. Identify the major parts of an airplane and state their functions.
3. Compare the flight of an airplane to a spacecraft in orbit.
4. Describe or identify ten major events in the history of aviation and space travel. Predict three more for the future.
5. Give examples of the use of technology for remote control in aviation and space exploration.
6. Describe several problems that can be addressed or solved gathering information about the earth using a high-altitude airplane or a space station.
7. Describe several technology spinoffs from the space program.
8. Relate the "conquering of air and space" to our "shrinking world." Describe ways our daily lives are affected.

Organization: This unit can be taught during an instructional block by one teacher, a pair of cooperating teachers, or a team representing all the subject areas. Student activities include opportunities for individual and group effort in whole class, cooperative learning groups, and independent work. A field trip to an airport or space facility is recommended.

Subtopics and Activities by Subject Area

PHYSICAL AND LIFE SCIENCE

1. Make and compare the performance of three different paper airplanes. Identify the major parts of an airplane and describe their functions.
2. Find out about the forces at work when an airplane is in flight and a space vehicle is in orbit. Compare the forces to those in effect in rides at carnivals and theme parks.
3. Research the effects on the human body of prolonged periods of weightlessness and ways to compensate.
4. Design an experiment that could be carried out in an orbiting or stationary space station.

SCIENCE AND LANGUAGE ARTS

1. In student teams write an argument for or against colonizing the moon or other space-related issue involving direct human participation. Hold debates on the chosen issues.
2. Write a science fiction story centered around airplane flight and/or space travel and involving a time warp.

SOCIAL STUDIES AND LANGUAGE ARTS

1. Produce an illustrated time line depicting the history of flight and space travel. Add branches to the time line to show historical connections and technology spinoffs related to aviation and space programs. Produce a video-tape of historical events from archival photographs and movie footage available in collections on videodisc.
2. Compare the autobiographies or biographies of two or more pilots or astronauts.
3. Visit an airport. Videotape or photograph and write about the facility and its activities from one of several points of view, such as a passenger, an employee, an airplane, a piece of baggage. Combine your results with those of others for a cross-sectional presentation of the airport.

COMPUTER LITERACY

1. Find out and report on computer applications in the air and space industries.
2. Organize and communicate through a computer during a space mission simulation.

MATHEMATICS

1. Calculate speeds, velocities, flight paths, changes in weight due to changes in gravitational attraction, and other quantifiable measures.
2. Learn how to navigate by reference points such as ground stations or the stars.

Culminating Group Activities

1. Display of models, photographs, and showing of videotapes.
2. Space flight simulation in which the classroom is partitioned into a space station, ground control, and support services for several days with all students participating as personnel supporting and solving problems during a multifaceted "space mission."

Evaluation

1. Written "pilot's test" and "flight technician's test."
2. Construction and control of paper airplane.
3. Models, videotapes, data base, and other group products.
4. Written reports of individual research from references, experiments, and/or situational problems and challenges.

Kinds of Resources and Materials

1. NASA videotapes, pictures, maps, and other government agency publications. Curriculum materials for instructional units and simulations.
2. High-altitude maps or photos and photos from space.
3. Materials for constructing paper airplanes, model space stations, model airports, and other student projects.

4. Use of a video camera, computer, and other technology.
5. Access to videodiscs on air and space of public domain, archival photographs, and news shorts for reviewing historical events. Many images from videodiscs may be transferred to videotape for classroom use.

Thematic Unit Development
BE PREPARED FOR NATURAL DISASTERS

Emergencies from natural disasters can occur at unforeseen times in all parts of the country. Although not all kinds of disasters will happen at all locations, every location is likely to experience at least one of the following: blizzard, earthquake, tornado, hurricane, tsunami, flood, forest fire. In every case, there are ways to be prepared. Being prepared for one kind of emergency, your local specialty, is similar to being prepared for the others in many respects. Basic preparedness involves (1) knowing the causes of the natural phenomenon to reduce panic and anxiety and to improve decision making, (2) knowing a procedure for action when the event occurs, (3) having adequate supplies, (4) possessing skills in first aid and self-sufficiency, and (5) recognizing and dealing with long-term effects. This unit concentrates on earthquakes as an example and can be adapted for other natural disasters.

Subject Areas: Physical, earth, and life sciences, social studies, language arts, mathematics.

Time Frame: One month.

Goals and Student Objectives
1. Explain, using models, drawings or in writing, how earthquakes occur. Indicate an understanding of the worldwide nature of earthquakes.
2. Demonstrate proper immediate action to be taken in the event of an earthquake and knowledge of actions to be taken after the earthquake is over.
3. Survey school and home for unsafe situations in the event of an earthquake. Take action to alleviate the dangers.
4. Prepare emergency plans, including gathering and storing supplies.
5. Discuss long-term effects in terms of property damage, psychological recovery, change in building codes, and other factors.

Organization: All-school approach is recommended or in teacher teams throughout the school.

Subtopics and Activities by Subject Area

EARTH SCIENCE

1. Find out about causes, monitoring, detection, and prediction of earthquakes. Locate areas of common occurrence and relate to world patterns in plate tectonics.
2. Test models of houses, skyscrapers, water towers, and other structures for stability and resistance to damage during an earthquake. Compare damage to buildings from news coverage of earthquakes around the world.

LIFE SCIENCE

1. Learn first-aid procedures.
2. Find out about the occurrence and treatment of trauma and anxiety resulting from fearful experiences like earthquakes, and the importance of understanding what causes earthquakes in preventing high levels of fear.

SOCIAL STUDIES

1. Maintain an ongoing collection of news articles on earthquakes and other natural phenomena as they occur around the world. Compare damage and disruption of social rhythm as well as community response for assistance.
2. Interview people who have experienced earthquakes.

LANGUAGE ARTS

1. Write the directions for the individual family emergency plan in case of an earthquake at various times of day. Include what to do if members of the family are not together.
2. Write a personal statement on priorities in times of emergency.

MATHEMATICS

1. Compare the various scales of magnitude that have been used to describe and record the intensity of earthquakes. Compare these scales to regular number lines.
2. Discuss in general terms how geologists arrive at probabilities for predicting future earthquakes.

Culminating Group Activities

1. Hold a schoolwide simulation of an earthquake, including duck and cover, carrying out first-aid procedures, tuning in to emergency broadcast systems, inspecting buildings, and adjusting to temporary quarters.
2. Establish a school emergency store of supplies. Establish emergency kits at home (not required but highly recommended).

Evaluation

1. Demonstration of appropriate actions to take in case of an earthquake.
2. Demonstration of knowledge of causes of earthquakes and their potential dangers.

3. Completion but not judgment of assignments related to attitudes about priorities and the value of preparedness.

Kinds of Resources and Materials

Information pamphlets on readiness, emergency procedures from Civil Defense or other agencies. Emergency kit for school use. Sample emergency kit for home use. Curriculum materials from professional organizations or earthquake education projects.[1] Videotapes or videodiscs with pictorial example of earthquakes in action and the results.[2]

Thematic Unit Development
THE EARTH AND US

Some themes lend themselves to all-school and long-term units and projects. The following environmental issues are considered top priority now and in the coming decades: air quality, tropical rain forests, ozone depletion, recycling of resources, population growth, and energy. The study of natural resources and their conservation is increasingly important in any school program and is particularly appropriate for the middle level curriculum. Students are interested in social issues, are beginning to comprehend the impact of personal decision making on people and places beyond their local domains, and are enthusiastic about action-oriented activities that are related to causes. "The Earth and Us" involves a month-long study of specific major resources or environmental problems at each grade level and a related year-long citizen action project at the local level. Students in a three-year middle level school in three consecutive years address, first, air and water quality for man and nature; second, the environmental problems of garbage and waste disposal; and third, the management of renewable and nonrenewable resources with emphasis on energy. One or several related projects are carried out by all students in each grade level on a long-term basis. What results, then, are really three sequential grade-level units in one. Alternatively, this series of units can be carried out in three-year cycles with a different all-school, across-grades unit each year.

Subject Areas: Physical, earth, and life sciences, social studies, langauge arts, mathematics, art, other subjects depending on opportunity and teacher interest.

Time Frame: School year.

Goals and Student Learning Objectives

1. Relate nature-based and human activities to the quality of water and air (first year).
2. Engage in and promote water conservation practices.
3. Consider causes and effects of, and solutions for, waste management in our society (second year).
4. Engage in one or more recycling projects.
5. Identify and describe the management of renewable and nonrenewable resources (third year).
6. Practice and promote the conservation of energy.

Organization: All-school or in teacher teams throughout the school, or by grade level.

Activities for Air and Water Quality (First Year)

1. List roles air and water play in our personal lives and in our society. Identify instances in which the quality of the air and water is important.
2. Find out about how local water is supplied and treated for household and industrial use. Research local laws and regulations related to water use, conservation, and waste disposal.
3. Test water in the school and community for acidity and other pollutants. Test air for particle content. Devise a way to measure "air pollution." Find out about the properties of air and water as fluids and solvents.
4. Contribute local data to a larger data base through telecommunications in a multischool cooperative effort arranged locally or through a project such as National Geographic's Kids Network units, *Water, Weather,* and *Acid Rain.*
5. Visit a garage for a smog test demonstration. Carry out a local traffic survey to find out about commuter habits and personal automobile use. Find out about local ordinances or regulations related to water and air quality and how they are established.
6. Carry out a survey to find out how much people know about the causes and effects of various kinds of air and water pollution.
7. Trace the water usage along a major river. Invent and pursue challenges such as: Through how many kidneys does a drop of water pass from the source of the Missouri River to the mouth of the Mississippi?
8. Find out about air and water quality trends in the nation and the world. On a map show how one area of the country or world can affect another.

Long-Term Projects for Air and Water Quality

1. Gather weather and air quality data throughout the school year. Use information from direct meteorological measurements, incidence of "hay fever"

among students, visibility measures, and other sources. Share results with a local agency for meteorology and/or air quality.

2. Practice water conservation measures at home and at school. Publicize the efforts and results. Promote awareness and conservation practices in the community.

Evaluation Strategies for Air and Water Quality

1. Pass a "city planner's test."
2. Pass an "informed citizen's test."
3. Reflect knowledge of cause-and-effect relationships in individual and group projects.
4. Participation in conservation practices and action awareness efforts at school and/or in the community.

Kinds of Resources for Air and Water Quality

Curriculum materials from appropriate government agencies and professional or private organizations. Chemical testing kits. Computer and software for telecommunications.

Additional Considerations

The outline above for air and water quality contains activities without associating them with specific subject areas. How would you sort them? How many belong in overlapping or interdisciplinary categories? The remaining two components of this theme address issues and concepts related to waste management and to energy. We have provided an example using the air and water quality component and encourage you, with a partner, to expand the following unit on waste management and outline the remaining section on energy.

Thematic Unit Development
TURNING GARBAGE TO GOLD

Waste management is a crucial issue in our country and, in fact, the world today. Recycling is emerging as not only a moral solution but a profitable one. Bags, boxes, tubing, wire, containers, rags—all have potential new functions. Finding creative new uses of common items normally thrown away has practical merit and, when used as the basis of an interdisciplinary unit, involves students in diverse thinking, creativity, problem solving, and research and development techniques.

Subject Areas: Physical and life sciences, social studies, language arts, mathematics.

Time Frame: One month.

Goals and Student Learning Objectives

1. Describe the role of waste management in society and recognize the current and impending waste management crisis.
2. Identify examples of recycling.
3. Select a common item disposed as waste and convert it to one or more new uses.

Organization: Instructional block, teacher team, grade level, or all-school. Whole class presentation and discussion, individual and group projects.

Subtopics and Activities by Subject Area

PHYSICAL SCIENCE

Select one or a cluster of common items thrown away in household garbage. Investigate properties of the items that can utilized in their transformation to one or more new uses. Individually or in student teams, develop the selected items into new products with new uses through processes of adaptation, invention, and testing.

SOCIAL STUDIES

1. Find out about laws related to garbage management in the community and rights of privacy related to contents of garbage cans.
2. Find out about at least one profit-making business that relies on recycled materials for productivity.

LANGUAGE ARTS

1. Research and write a story centered around the concept that "Garbage is the fingerprint of a culture or society." Note: to protect rights of privacy, do not survey the contents of a household or any other garbage can without permission from the owner.
2. Design a brochure and description of the new product as a promotion effort.

MATHEMATICS

1. Maintain quantitative performance records and "specs" of the new inventions or improvisations.
2. Calculate the impact in terms of money, time, energy, or other factor on adopting for common use the product developed from the old garbage.

Culminating Group Activities

1. Display student inventions and improvisations in a "Garbage to Gold Fair" in which student projects are on display for the public. Have individual students give scheduled presentations or be available at the display locations to explain and demonstrate their products. Publicize the event in the local media.
2. Enter the "Invent America" competition in your area.

Evaluation

1. Completion of the project involving inventing new products from recycled materials or adapting old items to new uses.
2. Communication through display, demonstration, and/or explanation of the new product development and function.

Kinds of Resources and Materials

Biographies of inventors, junk, household items commonly thrown away (brought from home).

STARTER IDEAS FOR INTERDISCIPLINARY UNITS OF INSTRUCTION

Opportunities abound for interesting topics of study that allow teachers to facilitate the learning of concepts that transfer across fields within a discipline or across disciplines. You need only to engage your imagination or ability to recognize appropriate ideas, and you can generate an impressive list for your own program.

Activity 11.1: Develop a Theme

Consider "Energy" as a theme. Think how main concepts related to energy sources, energy renewal, and energy transformation can be addressed in various fields of science (within the discipline) as well as in social studies topics related to industry, economics, and natural resources, and in other subject areas (across disciplines). Consider how other subject areas can be integrated. The use of energy and efficiency can incorporate mathematics. Language arts can involve reading, writing, and speaking activities to support projects requiring specific communication and research skills. Physical education can take a personal look at energy and human performance, a look at energy from an egocentric perspective. In addition, this theme can involve solving practical problems of energy conservation at school, at home, and in the community. With a colleague, construct a concept map or chart to expand on the ideas provided for this theme and outline a plan for implementation by a team of middle level teachers.

Include provisions for community involvement, uses of technology, and a variety of instruction and assessment strategies.

Activity 11.2: Compare Topic and Theme Ideas

Figure 11.1 presents a list of potential topics or themes that can be developed into interdisciplinary units of instruction. They are a result of a brainstorming session and not organized in any particular way. As you consider the list of examples, you might want to discuss their possibilities with a colleague. Mark each with one or more letters from the key list on the following page.

_____ The Twentieth Century

_____ The 1950s

_____ Patterns of Change

_____ Science against Crime

_____ Time

_____ Paper or Plastic?

_____ Comic Book Literature

_____ World's Natural Resources

_____ Money

_____ Mathematics and Music

_____ A Study of Time

_____ International News

_____ Every Day Is Earth Day

_____ Community Sketchbook

_____ What's in a Language?

_____ Etiquette

_____ Toys without Batteries

_____ Songs about Work

_____ The Color Green

_____ Fiction for the Future

_____ You Are Not Only What You Eat

_____ Housing: Past, Present, and Future

_____ Our Local Supermarket

_____ Domesticated Living Things

_____ When Things Rot

_____ Poverty

_____ Wonderful World of Wood

_____ Influence of Advertising

_____ The Telephone

_____ Satellites

_____ International Air

_____ First Aid, Second Aid

_____ Dances and Dancing

_____ Sky Watch

_____ Inventors' Workshop

_____ Health and Your Social Life

_____ Apples and Other Myths

_____ One Hundred Ways to Use Rice

_____ Robots, Robots, Robots

_____ The Railroad in Daily Speech

_____ The Hardware Store

_____ Less Is Better

_____ Communications

_____ Families and Friends

_____ The Earth from Orbit

_____ Our Elderly Population

Figure 11.1. Topics and Themes for Interdisciplinary Units.

N for those that are narrow topics and might best be taught in an instructional block involving only two or a few subject areas by one or a pair of teachers.

T to indicate topics that suggest teaming of three or more teachers.

S for those suitable for all-school participation.

M for conversion to a mini-course for an exploratory program.

(*) to select several that you might like to develop or help develop as a member of a teacher team.

Most of the topics or themes could be developed in various ways, taking advantage of available expertise, time, interest, and resources. For one of the topics or themes that you marked with an asterisk (*), consider the best organizational format, time requirements, and benefits for students.

TALKING WITH TEACHERS: ABOUT REDUCING STRESS Do you know what I think the most stressful, energy draining part of teaching is? Not having made a decision about what to teach. Just knowing you have to do something, but not having decided what to do causes more worry and sleepless nights than anything. Once you decide what you are going to do, planning the instruction and everything around it becomes efficient and even a pleasure. That's why I make decisions before weekends and holidays, even if it's in the form of simple phrases in my plan book or a five-minute concept map, so I can enjoy my days off without the cloud of indecision hovering over me.
—Seventh grade teacher

CONCLUSIONS

Each of the units outlined in this chapter is centered around a topic or theme and features various characteristics related to scope, duration, subjects involved, instructional approach, interdisciplinary involvement, use of technology, evaluation opportunities, and orientation toward student-centered perspectives. An entire district curriculum or school program could be woven from clusters of units like these. We hope you have incorporated the main ideas from previous chapters in your review of the units and that the units serve as models and encouragement for you in your own unit planning and instruction.

EXTENSIONS

1. With a team of four colleagues representing different areas of expertise, brainstorm a topic and plan a unit of instruction following the guidelines in this chapter and consisting of a cluster of at least three related lessons. Use a topic or theme from the list in Table 11.1 or your own idea. Reflect on personal and professional attitudes that come into play during the process.

2. Find out from experienced teachers about the pros and cons of involving other teachers, school staff, and parents in carrying out instructional units. Probe for views on short-term and long-term benefits for students.

3. Share with your colleagues a sample thematic unit found in a professional periodical. Compile a personal list of professional periodicals that regularly publish instructional plans for teachers.

4. Compile a list of organizations, and their addresses, that develop instructional units and/or resources for middle level use. Find out how you can be added to their mailing lists.

NOTES AND REFERENCES

1. Organizations such as the National Science Teachers Association and the National Earth Science Teachers Association, or earthquake projects such as CALEEP (California Earthquake Education Project, Lawrence Hall of Science, University of California, Berkeley, 95720), produce curriculum materials.
2. ABC produced *Earthquake*, a videodisc on the Loma Prieta earthquake of 1989. Optical Data Corporation also has pictures and movies on videodisc of earthquakes, tornadoes, and other phenomena.

FOR FURTHER READING

Lewbel, Samuel R. *Interdisciplinary Units in New England's Middle Schools, A How-to Guide.* Rowley, MA: New England League of Middle Schools, 1988.
Vars, Gordon F. *Interdisciplinary Teaching in the Middle Grades.* Columbus, OH: National Middle School Association, 1987.

Index